PRIMER

Whether you need a crash-course in staple controls and features of the
Assassin's Creed series, or simply to reacquaint yourself after time spent away
from the Animus, this opening chapter is designed to help you to ease into the
opening hours of Revelations with confidence. Our focus here is purely on features
established in previous episodes: to avoid spoilers, new gameplay elements (and
notable revisions) are covered in our extensive Walkthrough chapter.

BUTTON DEFINITIONS

Initializing ...
Populating...
source\S17.anima.0608200J.SVJ/WXrYmVy...
source\S17.anima.21032002.QmxhY2fiaWxscw==

As Xbox 360, PS3 and PC players own different control devices, we use the standardized terms presented in the table below to refer to each button or key command in most areas of the guide. These should be easy to recognize, but you can refer back here if you need to refresh your memory at any point.

Note that this is not an exhaustive list of controls and commands for Assassin's Creed Revelations, but simply a spoiler-free recap of all functions available during the early stages of the game. You will find all additional features introduced during the Walkthrough chapter, and an exhaustive moves overview in the Reference & Analysis chapter.

XBOX 360	PS3	BUTTON DEFINITION	SUMMARY
Ⓛ	Ⓛ	Ⓛ	Used for basic movement; also employed for directing attacks and blocking during combat.
Ⓡ	Ⓡ	Ⓡ	Used to control the game camera.
✛	✛	Quick Inventory Buttons	Used to instantly equip weapons and items. You can customize the four available slots via the Weapon Selector menu.
Ⓐ	ⓧ	Legs Button	Appears in the Puppeteer Interface (see page 11); used to perform context-specific actions, but principally used in conjunction with the High Profile button to sprint, initiate a climb and perform free running techniques.
Ⓑ	Ⓞ	Empty Hand Button	Appears in the Puppeteer Interface; used for releasing or grasping a hand-hold while climbing, as well as for a wide variety of context-specific actions.
Ⓨ	△	Secondary Attack Button	Appears in the Puppeteer Interface; used for secondary weapons.
ⓧ	▢	Primary Attack Button	Appears in the Puppeteer Interface; chiefly used for melee attacks.
RT	R1	High Profile Button	Switches to High Profile mode, which enables activities such as faster movement, combat, free running and climbing. Also used to block/deflect incoming attacks.
RB	R2	Weapon Selector Button	Opens the Weapon Selector; used to pick weapons or equipment. Use Ⓛ to select slots on the Primary Weapons radial menu, and Ⓡ to interact with the Secondary Weapons menu. With an object highlighted, press a Quick Inventory button to assign it to one of the four available shortcuts.
LT	L1	Target Lock Button	Activates Combat mode when aggressors are nearby, causing Ezio to orient his body and "lock on" to targets; otherwise fixes the game camera to the nearest highlighted individual in the direction Ezio is facing.
LB	L2	Assassin Signal Button	Calls Assassins into the fray; not used until Sequence 03.
Ⓛ	L3	Eagle Sense Button	Activates Eagle Sense.
Ⓡ	R3	Center Camera Button	Forces the game camera to face directly ahead.
START	START	Pause Button	Enter the Animus Desktop – the pause menu.
BACK	SELECT	Map Button	Enter the Map screen; can also be used to access Database entries when an onscreen prompt appears.

| XBOX 360 | PLAYSTATION 3 |

8

▶ GAME OBJECTIVES

MEMORIES

As with previous episodes in the series, Assassin's Creed Revelations begins with a linear collection of missions that gradually introduce gameplay concepts, abilities and different styles of challenges. For newcomers, the low difficulty of these opening tutorials offers a great opportunity to experiment and get a good feel for the game. More experienced players can treat these sections as a quick refresher course, and speed through them with commensurate haste and confidence.

Once you complete the first Sequence (story chapter), the Revelations sandbox begins to open up. In addition to main story missions ("Core Memories"), you will encounter a vast wealth of side quests, minigames and incidental challenges. The majority of these are purely optional, and are not necessary to complete the central storyline. However, these "Secondary Memories" can enable you to make Ezio wealthier – and, as a consequence, stronger and better equipped.

As with Assassin's Creed Brotherhood, progress in the main story eventually unlocks a management metagame where you can invest Ezio's money in restoring aspects of Constantinople's business infrastructure, for which he receives a dividend at regular intervals. Though the initial costs may seem high, the ultimate rewards are far greater. Completing side quests and pouring the profits from Ezio's labors back into Constantinople is the only realistic way to afford all equipment and items. What's more, there are also a number of noteworthy completion bonuses to obtain.

There is no right or wrong way to approach optional objectives in Assassin's Creed Revelations, but there's certainly an ideal path. Throughout the interlinked Walkthrough and Side Quests chapters we present a considered route to full game completion, with an emphasis on minimizing unnecessary effort and maximizing potential profit.

FULL SYNCHRONIZATION & MEMORY REPLAY

All Core and Secondary Memories in Assassin's Creed Revelations have Full Synchronization conditions. These optional objectives are specified once you accept a Memory, and can be checked by visiting the pause menu once they are underway. Completing a Memory and its Full Synch objective leads to 100% Synchronization, increasing the Total Synch level at the DNA Menu by the maximum amount. Fail a Full Synchronization objective, however, and the mission only counts as 50% complete.

While some Full Synch conditions can be completed on first attempt, others are more challenging; it may be that you must entirely familiarize yourself with the demands of a task before you can reasonably expect to satisfy the requirements. In these instances, you can return via the Replay Memory function (again, found at the DNA menu) to try again at a later date.

After a short load break, the Replay Memory option transports Ezio back in time and places him next to the appropriate Memory Start marker. Interestingly, though, he generally retains all weapons, armor and equipment acquired in the intervening period, which can make previously demanding tasks much easier. You can leave Replay Mode at any moment by selecting Exit Replay at the pause menu, and jump through cutscenes with the Skip Cinematic option.

PRIMER

WALKTHROUGH

SIDE QUESTS

REFERENCE & ANALYSIS

MULTIPLAYER

EXTRAS

INDEX

BUTTON DEFINITIONS

GAME OBJECTIVES

LIFE & DEATH

ONSCREEN DISPLAY

MAPS

MOVEMENT & ABILITIES

COMBAT

USEFUL ABILITIES

THREATS & DETECTION

HEALTH

01

The horizontal gauge in the left-hand corner of the screen indicates Ezio's maximum health level, with blocks of pure white used to represent his current state of fitness. The only means of increasing his overall endurance is to purchase and equip armor.

Each block in the Health Meter represents four "hit points" in the underlying combat system. Whenever an attack leaves one of these partially depleted, avoiding further damage for a few seconds will enable it to regenerate completely. Empty blocks, by contrast, are only replenished if automatically refilled at the start or end of a Memory, if Ezio is healed with a dose of Medicine, or after seeking the attentions of a Doctor.

Health Block Status

SYMPTOM	REMEDY
Health Block: full	-
Health Block: half-empty	Avoid taking further damage for a few seconds.
Health Block: empty	Have a Doctor heal you, or use Medicine.
Health Block: damaged armor	Have the corresponding piece of armor repaired by a Blacksmith.

Ezio can also be injured by falling too far. His natural agility enables him to fall distances of eight meters in a straight drop, or twelve meters if he rolls on making contact with a surface to dissipate the full force of the impact. The degree of damage sustained after uncontrolled descents is as follows:

- 30% of total health lost when falling over 8 meters.

- 50% of total health lost when falling over 12 meters.

- 75% of total health lost when falling over 16 meters.

- Death (Desynchronization) occurs if he falls 20 meters or more onto a solid surface.

When Ezio's Health Meter is reduced to zero blocks, he enters a critical state, indicated by a visual disturbances as the display flashes angrily (📷 01). A further injury in this condition will lead to instant Desynchronization. However, if you can avoid further damage for a few seconds, his final health block will always regenerate.

DESYNCRONIZATION

Though the Assassin's Creed Revelations story focuses primarily on Ezio, players are – strictly speaking – playing the role of Desmond Miles who, in turn, is experiencing his ancestor's life as a genetic memory accessed via a high-tech device known as the Animus. Success or failure rests on your ability to maintain Desmond's "Synchronization" with Ezio. Diverging too radically from the true course of events in Ezio's history causes Synchronization to be lost – which, in pure gaming terms, sends you back to a previous checkpoint or nearby landmark.

The following conditions all lead to a loss of Synchronization:

- **Death:** This occurs whenever all blocks of Ezio's Health Meter have been depleted.

- **Failed objectives:** Desmond (and, therefore, you the player) must experience Ezio's life with a degree of precision. Failing to comply with mission parameters may lead to a return to a previous checkpoint.

- **Moving out of bounds:** Attempting to visit a specific locale before the appropriate time (or moving outside the confines of a current mission area) can cause a loss of Synchronization. There is a clear visual cue that warns whenever you approach such boundaries (📷 02). Take heed, and move away swiftly.

- **Anomalous behavior:** If you attack allies or civilians indiscriminately, Desynchronization can be swift. There is, of course, a little leeway – accidentally striking the wrong individual during a pitched street brawl won't lead to serious repercussions.

02

anima.30082003.UGFpbkfpbGxlcnM=
anima.23082003.RmFjZXNNJblN0s25l
anima.16082003.RXNjYXBl
anima.23082003.V2hhdElzVGhpc13sYWNl

PRIMER

WALKTHROUGH

SIDE QUESTS

REFERENCE & ANALYSIS

MULTIPLAYER

EXTRAS

INDEX

BUTTON DEFINITIONS

GAME OBJECTIVES

LIFE & DEATH

ONSCREEN DISPLAY

MAPS

MOVEMENT & ABILITIES

COMBAT

USEFUL ABILITIES

THREATS & DETECTION

1 **Templar Awareness Gauge:** This feature is inactive for the opening hours of the adventure, so you can find a full explanation of its function in the Walkthrough chapter.

2 **Health Meter:** This represents Ezio's current state of health.

3 **Puppeteer Interface:** This controls HUD offers a contextual display of actions that can be performed with your controller's face buttons (or equivalent keystrokes in the PC version, if applicable), based on Ezio's current stance and proximity to points of interactivity.

4 **Equipment:** The item or weapon currently set for use.

5 **Currency:** The sum of money in Ezio's possession. The icon stands for "Akçe", the currency of the Ottoman empire.

6 **Mini-Map:** See overleaf.

7 **Compass:** This pointer always faces north.

8 **Risk Indicator:** The frame of the mini-map offers a simple indication of Ezio's current combat status: red when opponents are actively seeking to engage him in battle, yellow when he is out of sight but still sought by pursuing aggressors, and blue when he is safely concealed in a suitable hiding place. There is no specific frame when Ezio is incognito.

9 **Distance Meter:** Provides a numerical indication of the distance to the next active waypoint.

USING THE MAP & MINI-MAP

199

01

■ All places of interest, points of interactivity and active waypoints are marked by icons on the main Map screen and mini-map (📷 01). If you are unsure of what a particular symbol represents, visit the main Map screen – press the Map button (◄/**SELECT**) or select the equivalent pause menu option – and move the cursor over the icon in question. You can view a complete legend by pressing **LB**/**L2**.

■ When you arrive in Constantinople, details on both the main Map screen and mini-map are obscured until you reach and Synchronize with local Viewpoints. This feature is introduced at a very specific point in the story, so we'll return to this subject in the Walkthrough chapter.

■ Many icons on the mini-map only appear when relevant. For example, hiding places are not shown unless Ezio is in active combat. Others, such as those representing shops, shrink and disappear from view as Ezio moves away from them. Active waypoints or Memory Start locations are always clearly displayed.

■ The main Map screen enables you to place a Custom Marker with the Legs button (**A**/**X**). This is an incredibly useful tool for navigating the circuitous streets and alleyways of Constantinople, and is often an efficient way to plot an escape route if you need to make a swift departure.

■ Later in the story, the Map screen can be overwhelmed by a huge number of symbols. Press the Primary Attack button and use the pop-up menu that appears to activate and disable individual categories of icons.

Key Map Icons

❗	Memory Start
◎	Objective
◎	Target
◎	Destination
⬤ ⬤	Guard/Potential Enemy (Red = Byzantine, Orange = Ottoman)
⬤	Hiding Spot
▼	Viewpoint

■ As a general rule, main streets and alleys appear as a dark gray; surrounding buildings are a lighter gray.

■ Icons situated at a different elevation to Ezio (such as rooftop sentries stationed above a street as he runs beneath) appear slightly faded on the mini-map.

2003.UGFpbktpbGxlcnM+
2003.RmFjZXNJblNOb25?
2003.RXNjYXBI
2003.V2hhdElzVGhpc18sYWNs

02

As much of your time in Assassin's Creed Revelations is spent bounding from pillar to post, performing daring leaps with scant regard for the dizzying drops below, mastering the art of free running is a vital step in your journey through the story. For those new to the series, it's important to understand that the lack of a traditional "jump" button makes your role something more akin to a navigator. Cast aside any expectations or preconceptions fostered by traditional platform games: the Assassin's Creed adventures have a very different approach.

As there is generally no need to manually instruct Ezio to jump or catch a particular hand-hold, the trick to achieving consistently fluid, decisive movement isn't to focus on where you are, but where you are going to be. You will gradually learn to "read" the distinct visual language of each environment, instinctively recognizing each point of interactivity as you swing, scale, vault and leap with increasingly effortlessly flair. Ultimately, once you completely familiarize yourself with Ezio's remarkable athletic prowess – and, of course, his limitations – you will acquire the ability to plan discrete steps in a journey several seconds in advance (📷 02).

FREE RUNNING & CLIMBING

Hold the High Profile button (RT/R1) in conjunction with 🕹 to break into a **run**. With this movement style, Ezio will vault low obstructions or drop safe distances to a surface below, but will not attempt to climb or leap.

While running, press and hold the Legs button (Ⓐ/Ⓧ) to break into a **sprint**.

- When Ezio makes contact with a surface, this button combination will always initiate an attempt to climb. If there is no handhold within range, he will wall run briefly before dropping back to the ground. Once Ezio begins scaling a wall, you can release the Legs button until you have a specific need to use it.

- If Ezio reaches the end of a surface while sprinting (such as the edge of a rooftop), he will leap in the direction of movement. Ezio will automatically regulate the length and height of his jumps to land on the next solid surface in range, or to grab ledges within reach.

- To drop to a lower level without jumping while free running, hold the High Profile button only. You can also momentarily release and press the Legs

button during a sprint to perform a brief "hop". If speed is of the essence, this slightly more advanced technique can be used *just* before you reach a drop to maintain momentum while transitioning from one elevation to another on an otherwise uninterrupted surface.

- With the High Profile and Legs buttons held, Ezio will automatically swing on poles and hanging fixtures (such as lamps or baskets) when he encounters them.

Learn to regulate your use of the Legs button. Don't feel the need to sprint everywhere: this is a high-risk movement mode that should only be employed when you have clear ground ahead, or when specifically required to begin a climb or leap over a gap. Another big step in becoming an accomplished climber is to use 🅡 to plan the route ahead, enabling you to identify the best path to your destination as you move. Poor camera control is often the cause of Ezio's most ruinous free run mishaps.

Falling great heights can injure or even kill Ezio outright. To increase his ability to survive long falls, hold 🕹 in the direction of movement to roll on landing.

As scaling the tallest buildings and towers can be a protracted process, a traditional descent would be extremely time-consuming. Fortunately, Ezio – as the foremost Assassin of his era – is the master of a miraculous technique known as the **Leap of Faith**. This enables him to dive from a great height into a suitable "soft" landing spot far below (such as a pile of straw or leaves) and emerge without a scratch (📷). Positions where Ezio can perform a Leap of Faith include Viewpoint perches marked by an eagle flying overhead (introduced in the Walkthrough chapter), or ledges or beams covered in droppings, frequented by birds who disperse as he approaches. To perform the jump, move 🕹 in the direction of the landing position below, then press the High Profile button (RT/R1) and Legs button (Ⓐ/Ⓧ).

If Ezio must reach a ledge below his position but there are no available hand-holds for a measured climb, tap the Empty Hand button (Ⓑ/Ⓞ) to make him **release** his grasp. As he falls, press and hold the same button to **grab** the next ledge below as he approaches it (📷). When there is no Leap of Faith to be found on a tall building, this skill can be employed to make moderately swift descents to lower elevations. Similarly, if you misjudge a leap and find Ezio plummeting to the ground with ledges within reach, hold the Empty Hand button and press 🕹 in the direction of the surface to perform a **Catch Back**. This can also be used to curtail a fall if Ezio loses his grasp when attacked while climbing.

Lifts enable Ezio to improvise a rapid ascent to higher elevations simply by running into them (📷). Not merely a convenient shortcut, they also offer a novel and effective way to escape pursuing guards – who may be killed as the counterweight crashes to the ground.

While climbing, release 🕹, hold the High Profile button and tap the Legs button to perform a **Back Eject**. This is used to reach surfaces behind Ezio's current position (📷).

The **Side Eject** enables Ezio to leap to either side of a surface while climbing. Hold the High Profile button, then tap the Legs button and press left or right on 🕹 simultaneously (📷). If you are attempting to reach a ledge on a flat surface parallel to the direction of the jump, you will need to perform a Catch Back (Empty Hand button + 🕹 towards ledge) to take hold of it.

The **Wall Eject** move, though rarely called for in main story Memories, makes it possible for Ezio to reach positions that would otherwise be just beyond his reach. Sprint into a solid "blank" surface and, at the height of his brief vertical wall run, tap the Legs button and hold 🕹 left or right to jump to either side (📷). To spring backwards, press the Legs button only.

Use **L** to **move in water**. Hold the High Profile button to swim at an increased pace, and add the Legs button to move at maximum speed (⊡) or climb out of water in close proximity to a suitable surface.

When you leap into water from above, tap the Legs button to transform the jump into a purposeful **dive** (⊡).

Press and hold the Legs button alone to **dive** beneath the surface for a limited period of time; you also can move slowly with **L** while underwater. This can be employed to avoid detection, or pass beneath obstructions (⊡).

To pilot small **boats**, approach the pole at the rear of the vessel and press the Empty Hand button (**B**/○) to enter the rowing position. Tap the button at regular intervals to gain speed, and use **L** to steer (⊡). Press the Legs button to stop rowing.

Ezio rarely fights a single adversary at a time, with the vast majority of confrontations pitting him against several opponents who may possess varied weapons and tactical inclinations. A successful confrontation is almost always one that ends swiftly – and so introducing new ways to beat opponents decisively is a major feature of the Walkthrough chapter.

BASIC COMBAT TECHNIQUES

You can enter **Combat mode** by attacking an opponent, or by pressing the Target Lock button (🔘/🔘) while facing an appropriate adversary. Ezio's stance is adjusted whenever he enters Combat mode, with all movements made in relation to the assailants that surround him. 🔘 is used to both move and direct attacks towards targets (📷). As Ezio usually faces several opponents at once, try to keep him in motion constantly to isolate individuals from the surrounding crowd for easy kills, or maneuver him to occupy a more defensible location. Both during and outside combat, and whether you activate the Lock function or not, you can switch targets by tilting 🔘 in the direction of your chosen victim.

To **"Deflect"** (for which, read: "block") enemy attacks in Combat mode, hold the High Profile button (🔘/🔘) and press 🔘 in the direction of an incoming blow. Though Ezio will automatically block attacks made by opponents directly ahead or just off to one side of him when the High Profile button is held, it's absolutely essential to master the art of using 🔘 to make him turn and meet strikes from behind. Pay close attention to the health meters that appear above the heads of all opponents. These always flash to signal which aggressor is next in line to attack (📷).

Press the Primary Attack button (❌/🔲) and a direction on 🔘 to **attack** an opponent in the specified direction (📷). With weaker opponents, an uninterrupted sequence of blows to a single adversary will wound and disorient the target during the first few strikes of the **combo**, with the final attack resulting in an instant finishing move. The Secondary Attack button (🔘/🔺) is used principally to perform **ranged attacks**.

Hold the High Profile button (🔘/🔘), press 🔘 in the required direction and tap the Legs button (🔘/❌) to **dodge** just before an opponent launches an attack (📷). In addition to evading an incoming blow, this can also set up a combo opportunity against assailants who might usually block Ezio's default attack.

Hold the Weapon Selector button (🔘/🔘) to bring up the **Weapon Selector** screen. This features two radial menus (📷). Use 🔘 to select items on the left-hand menu (assigned to the Primary Attack button), and 🔘 for the right-hand side (for the Secondary Attack button). When you return to the action, Ezio will equip the highlighted weapon or item. You can also assign equipment to one of four Quick Inventory buttons (✛). Select an item at the Weapon Selector screen, then tap the required direction to specify a slot.

COUNTER KILLS

To perform a Counter Kill, hold the High Profile button and tap the Primary Attack button (**RT**+**✕**/**R1**+**□**) and press **L** in the direction of an enemy as they launch an attack on Ezio.

- Counter Kills performed with swords and daggers offer a very generous timing window. They are consistently successful against low-rank opponents, but may fail when employed against stronger adversaries.

- Those who mastered Assassin's Creed II and Brotherhood will doubtlessly have a penchant for the technically demanding yet peerlessly efficient art of Hidden Blade combat (📷 01). Counter Kills executed with the Hidden Blade are lethal when employed against most opponents that Ezio encounters, but this versatility and power comes at a price: the timing window for a successful kill is comparatively tiny. As a rule, the trick is to press the required buttons *just* before a blow lands. This definitely takes time to master, but it's worth the effort.

DISARM

To perform the Disarm technique, Ezio must either be unarmed, or have a ranged weapon equipped. The button commands for a successful Disarm are the same as the Counter Kill move.

- When Ezio successfully performs the Disarm move, he will wrestle an opponent's weapon from their grasp (📷 02). Attack the unarmed assailant again to kill them. Ezio will now wield his opponent's weapon as if it were his own.

- You can drop an acquired weapon by pressing the Empty Hand button, or return to the unarmed fighting style via the Weapon Selector menu, or a Quick Inventory button: by default, Ezio's fists are set to **♢**.

- As with Counter Kills, some enemies can resist the Disarm move.

TACKLE & SHOVE

There are instances where Ezio must accost but not kill a particular target. The Puppeteer Interface in the right-hand corner of the screen will notify you when the Tackle move can be performed.

- To leap and grab an opponent within range with the Tackle move while running, tap the Empty Hand button when Ezio draws sufficiently close to his target (📷 03).

- Tackles can also be performed from above a target. Ensure that the individual in question is highlighted, then use the same button commands to leap down and knock them from their feet.

- In some instances, using the Target Lock button to fix Ezio's attention (and the game camera) during a pursuit can make it easier to perform this move.

Hold the Empty Hand button while running to perform the Shove move. This can also be employed to knock a target from their feet, though only if you can manually engineer a direct collision. It can also prove useful if Ezio has a need to barge civilians aside while escaping aggressors, or if chasing a target.

PRIMER

WALKTHROUGH

SIDE QUESTS

REFERENCE & ANALYSIS

MULTIPLAYER

EXTRAS

INDEX

BUTTON DEFINITIONS

GAME OBJECTIVES

LIFE & DEATH

ONSCREEN DISPLAY

MAPS

MOVEMENT & ABILITIES

COMBAT

USEFUL ABILITIES

THREATS & DETECTION

KILL STREAKS

04   05   06

To begin a Kill Streak, Ezio must defeat an adversary with a combo attack, a Disarm and finishing move, or a Counter Kill (📷 04). During the killing animation, press 🔘 to highlight another opponent (the closer the better), then press the Primary Attack button to "stack" a subsequent assault. If successful, Ezio will lash out and dispatch this second target instantly (📷 05). This can, theoretically, be repeated until all combatants lie beaten on the ground (📷 06).

Kill Streaks end instantly if Ezio is hit, or should he fail to make contact with an opponent. In pitched battles featuring several antagonists, employ Counter Kills to maintain a Kill Streak whenever you do not have sufficient time to dispatch an adversary before they strike Ezio.

KICK

When opponents block Ezio's attempts to perform combo attacks, the Kick move acts as a "guard breaker". To perform it, press the Legs button alone while in Combat mode.

- The Kick move has a very short range. Move in close to your opponent before you attempt it (📷 07).

- After a Kick lands, the target will become vulnerable as they react. This is your opportunity to launch a combo attack while their guard is down.

- Not every opponent can be incapacitated with the Kick move. If they leap back or sidestep each attempt, switch to a different technique to disable them.

07

GRAB

Press the Empty Hand button to Grab an opponent. Grabbing an enemy opens up a range of contextual attacks.

08

- Once Ezio takes hold of an adversary, the Throw move (Empty Hand button and a direction on 🕹) can be tactically advantageous in certain situations – especially when used to hurl an aggressor over a ledge (📷 08) or into water. You can also direct an opponent into a solid surface (or other combatants) to knock them from their feet, then finish them with an instant-death kill before they clamber to their feet.

- With a weapon drawn, release all buttons and 🕹 and tap the Primary Attack button (❌/▢) to instantly kill an opponent held in a Grab.

- If an opponent resists a Grab attempt, you can perform the Kick move to break their guard and try again.

- If an enemy attempts to grab Ezio, press the High Profile and Empty Hand buttons simultaneously to perform a Counter Grab; hold them to throw the assailant to the ground. If he is held in a grapple, press these buttons rapidly to wrestle free.

ASSASSINATIONS

09

Ezio can perform a diverse range of assassination techniques with his Hidden Blades (📷 09). As a general rule these can only be performed when he is not actively engaged in combat, though it is sometimes possible to perform these instant-kill assaults on opponents who are facing away from him. Study the accompanying table to learn more about how assassinations can be put to use.

PRIMER

WALKTHROUGH

SIDE QUESTS

REFERENCE & ANALYSIS

MULTIPLAYER

EXTRAS

INDEX

BUTTON DEFINITIONS

GAME OBJECTIVES

LIFE & DEATH

ONSCREEN DISPLAY

MAPS

MOVEMENT & ABILITIES

COMBAT

USEFUL ABILITIES

THREATS & DETECTION

Main Assassination Types

EZIO'S POSITION	ASSASSINATION TYPE	PRIMARY ATTACK BUTTON	PRIMARY ATTACK + HIGH PROFILE BUTTONS
Level with target	**Standard Assassination**	Ezio will stab his target discretely at close range.	Ezio is more likely to perform a showy kill, leaping the intervening ground. This will attract attention.
Surface above target	**Air Assassination**	Ezio will jump down and assassinate the victim instantly.	
Ledge beneath target	**Assassinate from Ledge**	Ezio will reach up and hurl a target's body over the edge. He remains on the ledge throughout this process.	Ezio will jump onto the surface above and stab his target. Useful if you would prefer to avoid creating a stir on the street below.
Hiding spot (pile of hay or leaves, well, et al.)	**Stealth Assassination**	Ezio will reach out and stab the victim as he passes, then conceal him in the hiding spot.	Ezio will leap out from his hiding spot to kill the target in public.

76 Initializing...
77 Populating...
78 source\S17.anima.06j92001.SVJbWVrYrEmVy...
79 source\S17.anima.21032002.QmxhYZtlaWxscw...

EAGLE SENSE

01

Press the Eagle Sense button (▲/L3) to activate Ezio's uncanny ability to discern and interpret details that are otherwise invisible (📷 01).

■ Eagle Sense is occasionally employed to find secret entrances or locate specific individuals during Core Memories and Secondary Memories. In these instances, a prompt will always appear to notify you to use it.

■ There is a distinctive color scheme in Eagle Sense: objective-specific targets are gold; enemies are red; allies are blue; innocent citizens are white. Points of interest (including treasure chests and areas of special interactivity) are also highlighted.

■ For those who prefer a silent and discrete approach to objectives whenever possible, Eagle Sense also reveals information on enemy movements. Look carefully, and you will see faint red lines that mark the routes of active patrols in the current area.

■ Looking at treasure chests or collectibles through Eagle Sense will permanently mark their position on the main map and mini-map. If you do not have time to pick a collectible up or loot a container, this enables you to mark them for later attention.

PICKPOCKETING & FAST WALK

02

Ezio can steal money from civilians by Pickpocketing. To achieve this, hold the Legs button to activate the Fast Walk movement speed and steer him into a collision with a suitable target with 🕹 (📷 02).

■ Pickpocketing is an illegal action, so any guards that witness it may automatically attack Ezio. Unless you make a swift departure from the scene of the crime, you may find that certain bold civilians will put up their fists and seek to remonstrate with the Assassin.

■ The funds acquired through individual acts of Pickpocketing are rather low. This can be a moderately effective way to accumulate extra currency when you first reach Constantinople, but a new feature introduction renders the talent prohibitively inefficient later in the story.

While Pickpocketing is an ability that (certain objective-based applications aside) is ushered into early obsolescence, the Fast Walk ability used to initiate it can be astonishingly useful. If you need to evade suspicious guards, holding the Legs button makes Ezio move at a more purposeful stride than the basic walk, but does not attract any greater degree of attention. If you are creeping up to assassinate an oblivious target, it also enables you to close any intervening gap at a greater pace, but without creating any noise.

Naturally, it should go without saying that Fast Walk is only effective as a stealth technique if you can avoid inadvertently colliding with civilians…

LOOTING

03

To loot a corpse or rifle through a treasure chest, stand above it and hold the Empty Hand button (**B**/**◎**) until the meter that appears is completely filled (📷 03). Looting vanquished foes and containers can provide Ezio with a variety of useful items and rewards.

- Most adversaries tend to relinquish practical items, such as ammunition and Medicine. They may on occasion hold small sums of currency, though these sums become trivial very early in the adventure. The principle reason to loot most enemies is to replenish Ezio's stocks of consumable items and ammo.

- High-rank opponents (particularly senior Templars) may carry unusually large sums of money. If you kill an individual who seems in some sense noteworthy, be sure to rifle through their pockets in anticipation of such windfalls.

- Treasure Chests can contain variable sums of money, special crafting ingredients (which we cover in the Walkthrough chapter), or both bounties at once.

MOVING BODIES

04

Briefly tap the Empty Hand button (**B**/**◎**) to pick up a corpse. If discretion is important, this can enable you to remove an incriminating cadaver from a potential guard patrol route. Press the button again to throw the corpse to the ground. You can also drop bodies into hiding spots (📷 04) or deep water to permanently hide them. Alternatively, you can dump a corpse in plain sight with the specific intention of creating a distraction or general commotion…

THROWING MONEY

05

The Throw Money ability can be used to lure low-rank guards from their posts or patrols (📷 05) and generally reduce their vigilance, or to create walls of avaricious civilians who may block the path of aggressors in pursuit of Ezio. Hold the Weapon Selector button and select the money pouch in the right-hand radial menu, then press the Secondary Attack Button (**Y**/**△**) to scatter coins.

PRIMER

WALKTHROUGH

SIDE QUESTS

REFERENCE & ANALYSIS

MULTIPLAYER

EXTRAS

INDEX

BUTTON DEFINITIONS

GAME OBJECTIVES

LIFE & DEATH

ONSCREEN DISPLAY

MAPS

MOVEMENT & ABILITIES

COMBAT

USEFUL ABILITIES

THREATS & DETECTION

ma.23082003.V2hhdEIzVGhpc1BsYWNl
ma.16052003.Q2hpY2Fnb0dpcmxz
ma.27082003.Tm90RmFyRW5vdWdo
ma.14082004.MTUUUY
ma.11032004.VGhloVdchGuG=WEVTWU

Though the core story of Assassin's Creed Revelations begins with Ezio visiting the fortress and small town at Masyaf, much of your time will be spent exploring the magnificent city of Constantinople. In this section, we look at the inhabitants you will meet, and ways in which you can avoid (or escape) unwanted attention.

GUARDS

During the first two main story Sequences, Ezio will generally encounter only two different types of assailant: hostile Byzantine Militia and Gunmen in Masyaf and, on arrival in Constantinople, the Ottoman Elites and Gunmen who maintain law and order in the city. Though they have different uniforms and allegiances, both factions are functionally analogous in combat.

There is, however, one key difference. Though the Templar-controlled Byzantines are naturally suspicious of Ezio, and will draw their weapons with murderous intent if they identify him, Ottoman guardsmen are usually indifferent to his presence unless he does something to arouse their anger. Even so, it's sensible to keep a low profile whenever an Ottoman city patrol passes by. They will react to inadvertent collisions or minor infractions within their field of vision by scolding or pushing Ezio. In these instances, it's prudent to stand still and accept the rebuke and minor assault to avoid open conflict.

These opponents are vulnerable to most of Ezio's abilities and are inclined to flee if the tide of a battle turns against them. Though less athletic than Ezio, they will attempt to pursue him through streets and over rooftops if he withdraws from battle. They will also throw rocks in an attempt to knock him down if he attempts to climb or free run during an active combat situation.

Ottoman Elite

Byzantine Militia

Byzantine Gunman

Ottoman Gunman

Generally stationed on rooftops, and quick to attack those who trespass in their lofty domains, Gunmen fire from a distance during open combat, and will back away as Ezio approaches them. They are always priority targets in battles with multiple opponents, as their guns will disrupt Kill Streaks. They can be disabled with short combo attacks, felled with projectiles (once you obtain them), or thrown to the streets below with the Grab move or a well-placed blow.

PRIMER

WALKTHROUGH

SIDE QUESTS

REFERENCE &
ANALYSIS

MULTIPLAYER

EXTRAS

INDEX

THE DETECTION LOOP

01

Down-facing arrows appear above guards or potential hostiles whenever Ezio's presence is arousing their suspicion (📷 01). These visual indicators are also accompanied by distinctive audio prompts, and appear under the following basic conditions:

- If Ezio performs antisocial or extravagant actions – such as free running over rooftops, jostling civilians (or, worse, guards), or acts of violence or theft.

- Whenever Ezio is seen trespassing in a Restricted Area, marked in red on the mini-map, or if his current objective leads him to a place where his presence is not welcome.

- If Ezio is known to potential assailants: the Byzantine Templars, for example, recognize him with relative ease.

- Special conditions that determine that certain individuals are set at a high state of anxiety or alertness – for example, a target tailed by Ezio as an objective during a Memory.

The Detection Loop has three distinct stages.

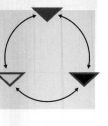

- During the first phase, Detection Meters gradually fill with a yellow hue while Ezio remains in range. Moving closer or performing certain actions (such as breaking into a run or climbing) will cause the gauge to fill at an increased rate. Retreating calmly to a safe distance, Blending with a group of civilians (see the page to your right) or breaking the direct line of sight between Ezio and his potential assailants will clear the gauge.

- Once the gauge is completely yellow, the second stage begins. As it fills with a red hue, guards and other hostiles will actively pay attention to Ezio, and will often approach him to investigate – thus accelerating the fill rate. You can still escape by Blending, though the most surefire way to evade this heightened scrutiny is to move out of sight and put at least one additional corner between you and the investigating party or group.

- When a Detection Meter is completely red, Ezio is identified, which will cause all nearby antagonists to attack. If your current Memory objectives specify that the Assassin must remain unseen, this will cause immediate Desynchronization – and a return to the last saved checkpoint. Once hostilities commence, all potential adversaries in the vicinity will seek to engage Ezio in combat, or give chase if he attempts to flee the scene. You can end a battle by killing all hostiles in the immediate area, or escaping.

- If you manage to escape out of sight, a circle on the mini-map represents the area where Ezio's opponents will actively search for him, with the very center representing his last known position. If you can move out of this zone without attracting further attention, or seek refuge in a hiding spot without being found, the Detection Meter will turn gray and hostiles will soon give up the chase. If Ezio is spotted by an alert opponent while attempting to flee the area, the circle will be reset to his current location and the chase will resume.

CITIZENS

02

BLENDING

03

From a pure gameplay perspective, the presence of citizens adds moving bodies that Ezio must weave between as he runs through the city streets. While walking through crowds, hold the Empty Hand button to utilize the Gentle Push ability. This allows Ezio to glide through heavily populated roads or squares with relative ease. Collisions at Ezio's basic running pace will cause him to stagger; at a full sprint, he will be bowled from his feet. The Gentle Push ability is essential for navigating crowded areas when discretion is important.

Performing reprehensible acts (such as pickpocketing or committing an assault) will cause all citizens in the immediate vicinity to back away from Ezio (📷 02).

Indiscriminate killing of civilians will cause Desynchronization, sending Ezio back to a previous checkpoint (or, while not actively engaged in a Memory, a nearby location). While you will not be penalized for accidental blows, mindless brutality will be punished swiftly after an initial warning.

Whenever stealth or subtlety are called for, Ezio's ability to disappear among crowds is a talent that you will employ regularly. Ezio will automatically "Blend" whenever he mingles with a group of at least three civilians (📷 03).

- Though you can maintain full control whenever Ezio Blends with a group of moving citizens, releasing 🕹 will cause him to automatically stroll in formation with them until you intervene.

- While Blending, Ezio is effectively invisible to most potential enemies, individuals that he must follow or avoid, and troublesome "harassers" – a special type of civilian who we will introduce in the Walkthrough chapter.

- When Ezio leaves a group, there is a short period of grace where he remains invisible. You can exploit this to transfer seamlessly between different collections of citizens.

- Illegal or reprehensible actions can immediately break a Blend. In open combat, citizens will often back away or flee from Ezio as he approaches them, which makes Blending impossible.

- Finally, pay close attention to individuals carrying items (usually boxes) as you walk among civilians. Colliding with one of these will cause a commotion as the box smashes, dispersing nearby citizens as they turn to regard the spectacle – thus ending a Blend instantly.

HIDING SPOTS

Diving into one of these hiding spots (marked by blue dots on the mini-map during open conflict) after breaking a clear line of sight between Ezio and his pursuers will enable you to end a combat encounter. They can also be used as refuges where Ezio can survey the surrounding area without fear of detection.

Wells

Bushes and piles of hay

Benches

Filled carts

Covered terraces and rooftop shelters

PRIMER

WALKTHROUGH

SIDE QUESTS

REFERENCE &
ANALYSIS

MULTIPLAYER

EXTRAS

INDEX

BUTTON
DEFINITIONS

GAME
OBJECTIVES

LIFE & DEATH

ONSCREEN
DISPLAY

MAPS

MOVEMENT &
ABILITIES

COMBAT

USEFUL
ABILITIES

THREATS &
DETECTION

WALKTHROUGH

This chapter has been designed to guide readers through all Core Memories in Assassin's Creed Revelations and, in conjunction with the companion Side Quests chapter, plot a course to a perfect 100% Total Synch rating – and, therefore, full game completion.

PRIMER

WALKTHROUGH

SIDE QUESTS

REFERENCE &
ANALYSIS

MULTIPLAYER

EXTRAS

INDEX

Before you continue, take a few moments to familiarize yourself with the structure and systems used in the Walkthrough chapter.

A **Left-hand pages: main walkthrough** – These sections have been written to provide a balanced range of prompts, suggestions and tips to complete each Core Memory in the main storyline. By avoiding extraneous or unnecessary details, we aim to offer players concise guidance that won't spoil set-pieces or gameplay surprises.

B **Right-hand pages:**
new features, tactics and points of interest – The right-hand page of each walkthrough spread is dedicated to subjects pertinent to your current position in the storyline. These can include:

- **Feature introductions:** Whenever Ezio acquires an ability or encounters something new within the game world, we offer an appropriate selection of insights, advice and trivia to help you master or understand it, or provide a page reference to a complete overview elsewhere in the guide.

- **Expanded strategies:** For the most challenging Core Memories and Full Synch requirements, we offer extended walkthrough guidance and annotated screenshots to help you conquer them with greater ease.

- **Analysis:** As Ezio faces ever-escalating adversity throughout his adventure, we'll keep you up to date with all the most effective techniques and tactics.

- **Additional Memories:** Whenever optional objectives, minigames and metagames are unlocked, we provide page references to guidance in the comprehensive Side Quests chapter.

C **Side Quests** – The Side Quests chapter can be used in conjunction with the walkthrough to reach 100% completion, or as a stand-alone source of reference if you would prefer to complete optional tasks in your own preferred order.

D **Primer** – All game features that are available from the start of the adventure are introduced in the Primer chapter (see page 6). If you're unfamiliar with the Assassin's Creed series, you may want to make this your first port of call.

SEQUENCE 02: THE CROSSROADS OF

MEMORY 01

A WARM WELCOME: Once the opening cinematics end, follow Yusuf through the streets of Constantinople until Byzantine aggressors attack, then dispatch them without ceremony (🎬 01). Be careful not to stray too far from your companion during the brief fracas in order to complete the Full Synch requirement. This short but informative Memory ends on arrival at the Assassin's HQ. Interact with the marked door to enter.

MEMORY 02

UPGRADE AND EXPLORE: Leave t If you have been diligently looting co should have no need to collect additi you can earn it easily by pickpocketi You could also take a stroll around assignments where Ezio provides as see page 98 for details. When you a the Blacksmith at the waypoint marke

A

01

34

PRIMER

WALKTHROUGH

SIDE QUESTS

REFERENCE & ANALYSIS

MULTIPLAYER

EXTRAS

INDEX

USER INSTRUCTIONS

SEQUENCE 01

SEQUENCE 02

SEQUENCE 03

SEQUENCE 04

SEQUENCE 05

SEQUENCE 06

SEQUENCE 07

SEQUENCE 08

SEQUENCE 09

E WORLD

s HQ via the door at the waypoint.
he start of the story in Masyaf, you
f you are short of the total required,
until you have the required 343 **A**,
n search of City Events, optional
vilians in need for a small reward:
w the Azap Leather Spaulders from
hen return to the Assassin's HQ.

COLLECTIBLES

There are three types of "collectibles" in Assassin's Creed Revelations: Animus Data Fragments, Memoir Pages and Treasure Chests. You can find comprehensive area maps that reveal the locations of all of these – and a variety of useful hunting tips – in a dedicated section of the Side Quests chapter that begins on page 109.

There are 100 **Animus Data Fragments** to find in total. Reaching five set collection milestones unlocks special portals on Animus Island that Desmond can enter: see page 109 of the Side Quests chapter for details. There is an Achievement and Trophy for collecting them all.

There are ten **Memoir Pages** in total. Collecting all of these unlocks a special Secondary Memory (see page 102) and an accompanying Achievement or Trophy.

Treasure Chests can contain Bomb Crafting ingredients – more on which on page 45 – and variable sums of currency. Though you can acquire both by other means, looting all Treasure Chests in Constantinople also contributes to the Total Synch percentage – which makes it a must for those aspiring to 100% game completion. Note that Treasure Chests are distinct from Bomb Stashes, which are humble wooden boxes or slightly more ornate chests with rounded edges that only contain crafting ingredients. Bomb Stashes do not count towards the Total Synch percentage.

PRIMER

WALKTHROUGH

SIDE QUESTS

REFERENCE & ANALYSIS

MULTIPLAYER

EXTRAS

INDEX

USER INSTRUCTIONS

SEQUENCE 01

SEQUENCE 02

SEQUENCE 03

SEQUENCE 04

SEQUENCE 05

SEQUENCE 06

SEQUENCE 07

SEQUENCE 08

SEQUENCE 29

EQUIPMENT

Though Ezio's arsenal of weapons and choice of armor is limited at this early stage in the story, the beginning of Sequence 02 (and its opening Memories) introduces a few new pieces of equipment.

Ezio now carries a supply of **Throwing Knives**. After selecting them, tap the Secondary Attack button to throw a blade at a highlighted or locked target. Hold the Secondary Attack button down for a brief period to hurl up to three knives simultaneously; when the "power up" is complete, the potential targets will be highlighted with a red outline. You can then use 🕹 to adjust the selection before you release the button to hurl the blades.

Ezio's **Pistol** can also be used to kill opponents from afar, but is extremely noisy: avoid using it when subtlety is required. Hold the Secondary Attack button to aim at an individual highlighted or acquired with the Target Lock function, then release it to fire once Ezio's aim has steadied.

Memory 02 sees Ezio make his first **Armor** purchase. Each piece of protective garb worn (with a full set consisting of spaulders, bracers, greaves and chest guard) increases his total Health Meter blocks. Armor is susceptible to gradual wear and tear as Ezio sustains damage, and will eventually break; this removes the health bonus. To repair armor, or to perform preventative maintenance, visit a Blacksmith.

The **Crossbow**, a powerful tool in Memories where stealth is mandatory or simply beneficial, is available for purchase from the very start of Sequence 02. Unfortunately, its base price is prohibitively expensive at this stage of the story. Though it can be useful for meeting certain Full Synch requirements, we suggest that you invest your money in buying properties and businesses (see "Rebuilding Constantinople") and save this investment for Sequence 04 at the earliest, when it becomes easier to accumulate large sums of finance in a relatively short space of time.

✛ REBUILDING CONSTANTINOPLE

As in Assassin's Creed Brotherhood, Ezio can use his income to purchase stakes or controlling interests in business premises, organizations and landmarks throughout Constantinople. A complete step-by-step guide to this process, with advice on each investment type and what you can reasonably hope to accomplish in each Sequence, can be found on page 86 of the Side Quests chapter.

D

C

B

35

SEQUENCE 01: A SORT OF HOMECOMING

MEMORIES 01 & 02

THE HANGMAN & A NARROW ESCAPE: Run along the shore when play begins, then follow Subject 16 for a short stroll on the mysterious Animus Island; when he disappears, walk into the portal to begin Sequence 01. Once Ezio lands in the spectacular introductory cutscene (completing the gameplay-free The Hangman Memory), A Narrow Escape begins automatically. The first part is a relatively uncomplicated introduction to free running and climbing. Follow the ghostly apparition of Altaïr to reach the roof of Masyaf's central keep, paying attention to pop-up prompts and tips as they appear.

01

There are two points during the climb where you must fight Byzantine Templars directly: the first a brief fistfight, and the second a weapons-based confrontation after Ezio has retrieved his equipment. In the second of these, employ a Counter Kill (Primary Attack button + High Profile button just before an opponent attacks; see page 17) to kill one guard and fulfil the Full Synch requirement (📷 01). You will need to perform two ledge assassinations on oblivious guards before you reach the top (see page 19). Approach the statue at the waypoint marker and press the Empty Hand button to interact with it.

MEMORY 03

A JOURNAL OF SOME KIND: After Ezio lands in the pool of water, kill the guard, then follow the corridor to reach a chamber where the next Memory Start position awaits. Kill the four marked targets (the first with an air assassination, as directed), then approach the highlighted individual and press the Empty Hand button.

You must now follow the waypoint markers to reach a guard captain carrying an item of interest to Ezio. Fight or attempt to avoid the guard patrol after returning outdoors as you travel to the waypoint marker, then climb the ladder. On the wall above, dispatch the next group of Templars before you continue your climb (📷 02). At the final waypoint, follow the onscreen prompts to parachute from the wall, steering to land a safe distance behind the marked Templar and his bodyguards.

02

Stay out of sight and follow from a safe distance as you follow your target down the slope. You can satisfy the Full Synch requirement by successfully tailing this first individual without attracting attention. If you are discovered, you will need to activate Eagle Sense (press ⬆/L3) to locate a new Templar to follow.

PRIMER

WALKTHROUGH

SIDE QUESTS

REFERENCE &
ANALYSIS

MULTIPLAYER

EXTRAS

INDEX

USER
INSTRUCTIONS

SEQUENCE 01

SEQUENCE 02

SEQUENCE 03

SEQUENCE 04

SEQUENCE 05

SEQUENCE 06

SEQUENCE 07

SEQUENCE 08

SEQUENCE 09

GENERAL TIPS

- On Animus Island at the very start of the game, don't walk straight into the portal. If you wait for a moment, you will hear a dialogue between Shaun Hastings and another individual filtering into Desmond's consciousness from outside the Animus.

- In addition to its default function, the Map button (◀/ SELECT) can also be used to view Database entries and play tutorials that cover both fundamental and advanced playing techniques. Whenever an onscreen prompt appears, tap the button to be taken to the information or lesson described in the accompanying text.

- After killing each Templar in this opening Sequence, take the time to loot their corpses to gain small amounts of currency and other objects. Everything you accumulate during these early Memories is carried forward into Sequence 02, which will give you a head start when you leave Masyaf. The exotic-sounding items that Ezio collects are special ingredients used to craft bombs later in the story.

- Players who enjoyed the original Assassin's Creed may wish to head up the staircase before leaving the building at the start of the A Journal of Some Kind Memory. Though it may take a moment to recognize it, this is Al Mualim's study (📷 03). Take a moment to interact with objects shimmering with classic Animus effect to see hidden sights, and reminisce as you peer into the garden where the climatic confrontation between Altaïr and his former mentor took place.

- Parachutes were a special reward in Assassin's Creed Brotherhood, given to players who completed each of Leonardo's War Machine missions, but they are rather easier to come by in Revelations. You can purchase additional Parachutes from Tailor stores from the start of Sequence 02.

 ## POISON BLADE & POISON DARTS

Available from the beginning of the story, these weapons enable Ezio to create distractions and perform unique delayed assassinations.

- Whether delivered up close by blade, or from range with a dart, Poison has a unique effect: it does not kill the target immediately. Instead, they will begin to stagger drunkenly as its deadly toxin courses through their veins, lashing out at imaginary assailants as they begin to experience hallucinations. This will cause all guards and citizens in the vicinity to turn and regard the ghastly commotion. After a variable delay (but usually no more than twenty seconds), the victim will collapse and die.

- The Poison Blade (🗡️) is used in the same way as the Hidden Blade. To avoid detection, move out of sight quickly after injecting your victim.

- To fire Poison Darts (🗡️), target an individual and hold the Secondary Attack button until Ezio's aim steadies; release the button to fire. The benefits of being able to deliver the toxin from a discrete distance make this a powerful tool in later Sequences.

- Ezio can carry five doses of poison, with one unit consumed per dart or blade attack. You can replenish his stocks by looting bodies, or by purchasing supplies from a doctor.

MEMORY 04

A HARD RIDE: Commencing immediately on completion of Memory 03, this dramatic episode begins with Ezio dragged along the ground at the back of a fast-moving carriage. Use to steer him left and right to avoid obstacles (including bushes and rough terrain). When the rope frays, you can begin to hold up to move Ezio closer to the carriage. However, doing so prevents you from adjusting his position to avoid hazards. The required technique, then, is to move him forward in bursts, steering him away from dangers as they appear.

04

In the second part of this Memory, Ezio must ram opposing carriages from the track. Use to move away slightly, then hold it towards your target to slam them with sufficient force. At the same time, do your utmost to avoid patches of rough terrain (📷 04). These damage the carriages at a phenomenal rate (far more so than ramming), so the best strategy is to push your opponent into these hazards whenever you see them on the road ahead. The second carriage is driven by Ezio's quarry, the Templar captain Leandros. In this final section, ram your adversary to the right to skirt around otherwise unavoidable rough terrain; certain patches can be safely bypassed by moving to the far left side of the track. The damage that you inflict is an irrelevance: the priority here is to survive for a set period of time.

05

MEMORY 05

THE WOUNDED EAGLE: The final Memory of Sequence 01 begins with a short fight, but is perhaps best approached as an exercise in discretion. Use your sword to employ safe Counter Kills to kill the initial trio, then run towards the waypoint. When you reach the wooden bridge, wait for the guard to walk to the left, then slip past to the right to reach and climb the steps to reach the waypoint; Ezio will automatically step onto the water wheel to reach the upper level.

Equip the Hidden Blade and assassinate the guard standing directly ahead, then observe the area below; activate Eagle Sense (🔼/L3) to observe the route taken by the Templar captain. The injured Ezio cannot climb, so successfully infiltrating the castle without incident is a question of staying out of sight, using Blend opportunities and picking an optimal route. If you are keen to avoid conflict and complete the Full Synch requirement, refer to the annotated route map and advice on the page to your right.

Once inside the castle, kill the guards with safe, sword-based Counter Kills, then loot the fallen bodies to obtain Medicine; use this as prompted to heal Ezio and regain access to his full repertoire of athletic abilities. With Ezio's back to the portcullis, turn to the right and follow the path behind the first building, where you can safely assassinate a guard from a hay pile. From here, you can slip by the guards on the rooftops and to your left by following the path alongside the rock wall on your right – use the Fast Walk ability to move with the necessary purpose and avoid detection. Walk into the waypoint and begin your ascent of the tower (📷 05). Byzantine Gunmen will shoot at Ezio during his climb, so don't linger in one position for too long.

At the top, execute Leandros with a Hidden Blade assassination. Back at Animus Island with Desmond, walk into the waypoint to begin Sequence 02.

THE WOUNDED EAGLE: FULL SYNCH

The Full Synch requirement for Memory 05 challenges you to assassinate five guards while concealed inside haystacks. To perform assassinations from these hiding spots, first move into one, then release ❷ to lie in wait. When your victim approaches, tap the Primary Attack button to perform a swift kill and conceal the body in one fluid movement.

There are actually only three locations in this Memory where Templars will automatically stand close to or move past a haystack, so you will need to employ both stealth and a little creativity to fulfill this secondary objective.

As Ezio cannot hide in a haystack while in view of hostiles in open conflict, you must lure guards to their doom by standing in their field of vision until their Detection Meter turns red. At this point, discretely move into the hiding spot and wait for them to walk over to investigate.

In this annotated map, we mark the locations of all haystacks and offer advice on how to avoid detection and obtain the necessary kills as you travel to confront Leandros. Blue arrows represent the path you need to follow, and red arrows the patrol routes of guards.

I Wait until the guard moves to the right, then take up position in this haystack while his back is turned. After checking that there are no potential witnesses, assassinate him when he moves within range. You can now attempt to lure nearby guards to the hiding spot to obtain additional kills.

II Take a left here to run along a back alley, out of sight.

III At the end of the deserted path, wait at the opening and watch the path to your left for a guard to arrive. When he walks into the market area, follow him at slow pace.

IV The guard walks in a rectangular patrol route around the market area, with a second alternating between two positions at the back of the area. Blend with a group of civilians until the second guard moves to the left, then run forward and take the path to the right. Jump into the haystack immediately, and wait for another guard to approach for a simple assassination. If you have fewer than four of the five required stealth kills, you should again attempt to draw guards to this position.

V There is another guard here who can be enticed to the nearby haystack. If you already have four kills, you can just bypass him and head straight for the gate.

VI After the battle inside the portcullis, sneak around the back of this building and enter the haystack to kill the stationary guard. If you still have not accrued the necessary five kills, you will need to draw guards to this haystack (or one of the two closer to the waypoint marker) to complete the objective.

MEMORY 01

A WARM WELCOME: Once the opening cinematics end, follow Yusuf through the streets of Constantinople until Byzantine aggressors attack, then dispatch them without ceremony (🎦 01). Be careful not to stray too far from your companion during the brief fracas in order to complete the Full Synch requirement. This short but informative Memory ends on arrival at the Assassin's HQ. Interact with the marked door to enter.

MEMORY 02

UPGRADE AND EXPLORE: Leave the Assassin's HQ via the door at the waypoint. If you have been diligently looting corpses since the start of the story in Masyaf, you should have no need to collect additional money. If you are short of the total required, you can earn it easily by pickpocketing civilians until you have the required 343Å. You could also take a stroll around the streets in search of City Events, optional assignments where Ezio provides assistance to civilians in need for a small reward: see page 98 for details. When you are ready, buy the Azap Leather Spaulders from the Blacksmith at the waypoint marker (🎦 02), then return to the Assassin's HQ.

01

02

COLLECTIBLES

PRIMER

WALKTHROUGH

SIDE QUESTS

REFERENCE &
ANALYSIS

MULTIPLAYER

EXTRAS

INDEX

USER
INSTRUCTIONS

SEQUENCE 01

SEQUENCE 02

SEQUENCE 03

SEQUENCE 04

SEQUENCE 05

SEQUENCE 06

SEQUENCE 07

SEQUENCE 08

SEQUENCE 09

There are three types of "collectibles" in Assassin's Creed Revelations: Animus Data Fragments, Memoir Pages and Treasure Chests. You can find comprehensive area maps that reveal the locations of all of these – and a variety of useful hunting tips – in a dedicated section of the Side Quests chapter that begins on page 109.

 There are 100 **Animus Data Fragments** to find in total. Reaching five set collection milestones unlocks special portals on Animus Island that Desmond can enter: see page 109 of the Side Quests chapter for details. There is an Achievement and Trophy for collecting them all.

There are ten **Memoir Pages** in total. Collecting all of these unlocks a special Secondary Memory (see page 102) and an accompanying Achievement or Trophy.

Treasure Chests can contain Bomb Crafting ingredients – more on which on page 45 – and variable sums of currency. Though you can acquire both by other means, looting all Treasure Chests in Constantinople also contributes to the Total Synch percentage – which makes it a must for those aspiring to 100% game completion. Note that Treasure Chests are distinct from Bomb Stashes, which are humble wooden boxes or slightly more ornate chests with rounded edges that only contain crafting ingredients. Bomb Stashes do not count towards the Total Synch percentage.

EQUIPMENT

Though Ezio's arsenal of weapons and choice of armor is limited at this early stage in the story, the beginning of Sequence 02 (and its opening Memories) introduces a few new pieces of equipment.

 Ezio now carries a supply of **Throwing Knives**. After selecting them, tap the Secondary Attack button to throw a blade at a highlighted or locked target. Hold the Secondary Attack button down for a brief period to hurl up to three knives simultaneously; when the "power up" is complete, the potential targets will be highlighted with a red outline. You can then use 🕹 to adjust the selection before you release the button to hurl the blades.

 Ezio's **Pistol** can also be used to kill opponents from afar, but is extremely noisy: avoid using it when subtlety is required. Hold the Secondary Attack button to aim at an individual highlighted or acquired with the Target Lock function, then release it to fire once Ezio's aim has steadied.

 Memory 02 sees Ezio make his first **Armor** purchase. Each piece of protective garb worn (with a full set consisting of spaulders, bracers, greaves and chest guard) increases his total Health Meter blocks. Armor is susceptible to gradual wear and tear as Ezio sustains damage, and will eventually break; this removes the health bonus. To repair armor, or to perform preventative maintenance, visit a Blacksmith.

 The **Crossbow**, a powerful tool in Memories where stealth is mandatory or simply beneficial, is available for purchase from the very start of Sequence 02. Unfortunately, its base price is prohibitively expensive at this stage of the story. Though it can be useful for meeting certain Full Synch requirements, we suggest that you invest your money in buying properties and businesses (see "Rebuilding Constantinople") and save this investment for Sequence 04 at the earliest, when it becomes easier to accumulate large sums of finance in a relatively short space of time.

REBUILDING CONSTANTINOPLE

As in Assassin's Creed Brotherhood, Ezio can use his income to purchase stakes or controlling interests in business premises, organizations and landmarks throughout Constantinople. A complete step-by-step guide to this process, with advice on each investment type and what you can reasonably hope to accomplish in each Sequence, can be found on page 86 of the Side Quests chapter.

MEMORY 03

THE HOOKBLADE: Approach the Memory Start marker outside the Assassin's HQ to receive a new piece of equipment. Follow Yusuf and onscreen directions to put this device through its paces; see the page to your right for a summary of the techniques used (and all other Hookblade-based abilities). Sections of the free run course that Yusuf leads you on may be a little demanding for players new to the Assassin's Creed series. If so, you may find it useful to stop periodically to watch Yusuf's movements and identify the correct route before you attempt to follow his example (📷 03).

You have three opportunities to perform each of the techniques he imparts, so the Full Synch requirement shouldn't be difficult to complete. In the final challenge, note that you must *hold* the Empty Hand button to perform a Hook and Run on the marked sparring partner. Merely tapping the button will cause Ezio to perform a Hook and Throw, which won't count.

MEMORY 05

ADVANCED TACTICS: This Memory begins automatically once Ezio reconvenes with Yusuf at the bottom of the tower, and introduces the use of ziplines. After performing your first zipline assassination to successfully achieve Full Synch, you must travel to Galata Den and enter the waypoint marker on the rooftop. The zipline directly ahead once Yusuf departs presents another opportunity for an assassination on a rooftop sentry if you failed the first attempt (📷 05).

As you near the waypoint, you may wish to first climb the adjacent tower to Synchronize with its Viewpoint before you continue. Interact with the Assassin on the rooftop to end the Memory.

03

04

MEMORY 04

THE VIEW FROM GALATA: Speak to Yusuf at the Memory Start marker, and he will challenge Ezio to follow him in scaling Galata Tower. This acts as a tutorial on the Hookblade's applications while climbing. As long as you keep up with the Assassin, you should comfortably satisfy the Full Synch requirement. Whenever the next ledge in line appears out of reach, perform the Hook Leap technique to continue your ascent.

Once you reach the top, stand on the perch (📷 04) and press **⬆**/**L3** to Synchronize: refer to the "Viewpoints" entry on the page to your right for further details. Before you perform a Leap of Faith from the perch back to the ground, loot the chest on the opposite side of the spire and then climb to the top to find the first Memoir Page: see "Collectibles" on the previous double-page spread for details.

05

- Press and hold the Empty Hand button in midair to perform the **Extended Reach** technique. This enables Ezio to grab ledges that might otherwise fall just outside his grasp, or to grip hand-holds as he falls past them. (This essentially replaces the traditional Catch Back move.)

- Press the Empty Hand button in midair before performing a "lamp turn" (or, indeed, any 90-degree swing on any suitable object hanging from a corner) to perform a **Long Jump**. Instead of swinging around, Ezio will be propelled forwards.

- Run at an opponent and hold the Empty Hand button as you approach them to perform a **Hook and Run** on contact. This non-lethal ability is particularly effective when you need to bypass an opponent while fleeing combat, especially guards standing with weapons drawn in anticipation of Ezio's arrival.

- Run at a potential opponent and tap the Empty Hand button briefly to perform the **Hook and Throw** maneuver. This automatically puts Ezio into Combat mode on completion. As it leaves the target prone on the ground, you can follow it up with an instant Hidden Blade kill.

- With civilians and other non-hostiles, the contextual Hook and Run and Hook and Throw moves are replaced with the **Leg Sweep** technique (📷 06), which bowls a target from their feet but inflicts no lasting damage. This act will attract a stern rebuke from any Ottoman guards who witness it.

06

- While climbing, hold 🕹 forward and the High Profile button, then tap the Legs button to perform a **Hook Leap**. This enables Ezio to reach ledges outside his usual range with the Hookblade. If an arrangement of continuous surface features allows it, hold the Legs button while climbing to ascend at a slightly accelerated speed.

- Hold the High Profile and Legs buttons to jump over to and **ride a zipline**: Ezio will automatically extend his Hookblade to grab it and begin sliding. While in motion, you can release the High Profile button to descend at a reduced pace; this can be useful if there is a need to avoid the attention of nearby guards. Press the Empty Hand button to release the zipline at any time.

- To perform a **zipline assassination**, press the Primary Attack button as Ezio approaches a victim situated below.

- Acquiring the Hookblade unlocks the **double assassination** techniques, enabling Ezio to kill two targets in close proximity simultaneously.

- Last, but by no means least, the Hookblade enables you to perform several types of **Counters** unique to combat situations. The (non-lethal) Counter Hook-and-Throw move (📷 07) is functionally identical to a Hidden Blade Counter Kill in terms of the tight timing window and end result, but requires that you press the High Profile button and Empty Hand button instead. The Counter Grab requires the same input on the controller but can only be performed as an enemy attempts to grab you. The Counter Hook-and-Run also uses the same buttons (though you need to hold the Empty Hand button once you press it) and enables you to exit Combat Mode on completion for a fast escape. Finally, the Counter Steal – hold the High Profile button and Secondary Weapon button – enables you to pickpocket an assailant as he attacks you. This can cut down on time spent looting after battles.

07

VIEWPOINTS

Synchronizing at Viewpoints with the Eagle Sense button uncovers the surrounding map area, revealing both topography and otherwise invisible points of interest such as shops and Secondary Memory markers. There are 22 Viewpoints in Constantinople, and we strongly advise that you Synchronize with all sites (marked by the 🦅 icon) when they become available. They can be visited during Memories unless your objectives dictate otherwise, so feel free to make detours when you pass close by.

Certain Viewpoints are located in Restricted Areas with a heavy Templar presence, and should generally be left until you are ready to evict Ezio's enemies from these militarized zones.

MEMORY 06

ON THE DEFENSE: This Memory begins immediately when you reach the final waypoint of Advanced Tactics, and acts as an introduction to a major new feature in Revelations: the Den Defense minigame. See "On the Defense: Step by Step" for useful advice (including a trick that enables you to unlock an Achievement/Trophy). You can find a comprehensive guide to Den Defense controls, features and tactics on page 90 of the Side Quests chapter.

08

MEMORY 07

ON THE ATTACK: Before you begin this last Memory of Sequence 02, you may wish to unlock any remaining Viewpoints and expand your property portfolio by reopening shops in the Galata District. See page 86 of the Side Quests chapter for details on the Rebuilding Constantinople metagame.

When you are ready, head to the Memory Start marker and interact with the highlighted individual to take a boat to the Imperial District. On arrival, lend assistance to Yusuf, then follow him through the streets. After his demonstration of Cherry Bombs, use one to distract the guards when prompted to do so. Hold the Secondary Attack button and use 🕹 to manually aim the bomb at the marked location, then release the button to throw it. You can then safely run through the archway once the guards move to investigate.

When you reach the rooftops, watch the brief cutscene, then quickly perform a zipline assassination on the Templar Gunman ahead of your position when play resumes. The Den Attack formally begins when you speak to Yusuf at the waypoint. To complete the Full Synch objective, you must avoid open conflict

as you liberate the Templar Den – but this is actually easier than you might suspect.

Use Eagle Sense to identify the Templar Captain in the streets below your position. When he walks away, follow the route specified here (📷 08). Approach the first guard when his back is turned and kill him with a Throwing Knife. Slay the next Gunman with another hurled blade when he walks to the right-hand side of his rooftop. Jump over to this next building and select the Poison Darts. Hit the Templar Captain with a single projectile, then immediately move out of sight. After checking the street below for patrols, leap over to the tower and ascend to the walkway quickly to avoid detection. You can then watch the Captain's final death throes from above, then press the Empty Hand button when prompted to light the Retreat Signal – and end both the Memory and the Sequence.

Our complete guide to conquering all Templar Dens in Constantinople begins on page 88 of the Side Quests chapter.

ON THE DEFENSE: STEP BY STEP

Interestingly, the On the Defense Memory provides an opportunity to unlock an Achievement/Trophy that will be rather more challenging during subsequent visits to this minigame. As initial waves of Templars are thoughtfully paused to enable players to familiarize themselves with controls and concepts, you can sit and wait for the Morale level – the "currency" used to purchase all features during Den Defense – to gradually rise while the action is on hold. If you are patient enough to allow it to reach at least 50 each time, you can have an overwhelmingly powerful force in place for the final section of the Memory.

When the minigame begins, use 🅡 to direct Ezio's gaze, and 🅛 to move the cursor. Follow the directions to place a Leader to unlock the rooftop to the left of the arch on the opposite side of the street, and two Crossbowmen for the first wave; we suggest the sloped section as a prime position for these. When prompted to place a Barricade, build one just to the left of the arch. Add at least three further Crossbowmen during this assault.

When directed to add another Leader, place him on the rooftop to the left of Ezio, then place at least three Gunmen at the most distant position. For those seeking to unlock the Iron Curtain Achievement/Trophy, this is the vital point: ignore the prompt to use the Cannon attack, and leave the killing of Templars to your Crossbowmen and Gunmen.

With this wave complete, move the cursor over the Barricade and upgrade it to the maximum level, then place an even mixture of both attacking unit types to fill all available rooftop slots (📷 09). When the siege engine arrives, you can optionally place an additional Barricade in order to slow its advance. As long as you steer clear of using the Cannon, Iron Curtain will be awarded once this final Templar attack has been repelled.

09

TEMPLAR AWARENESS

The conclusion of the Den Defense introduction in Memory 06 activates a major new feature: Templar Awareness. Though similar to Assassin's Creed Brotherhood's Notoriety concept, this new system has some significant differences.

The Templar Awareness meter (🔳) increases when Ezio performs very specific activities, with the gains reflecting how troubling his actions are to his Byzantine opponents. Until the meter is 100% full, Ezio's status is "Secret". Killing adversaries in combat leads to nominal raises; buying property will fill the gauge by almost a quarter; conquering a Templar Den (with the exception of the one captured in Memory 07) will instantly move it to the maximum level. Once the gauge is filled, the Templars become "Aware". When this occurs, there is a high probability that they will launch a retaliatory strike on an Assassin Den, heightened if Ezio performs a reprehensible act (such as entering open conflict). This must be repelled by visiting the location to fight off the aggressors via the Den Defense minigame.

There are two ways to reduce the Templar Awareness meter. The first is to bribe Heralds (marked by the 👤 icon on the main map and mini-map), which offers a 25% decrease for a mere 100 🅰. The second, available once when the gauge reaches the halfway mark, is to kill a Corrupt Official (marked by the 👁 icon) for a 50% decrease. These individuals are accompanied by bodyguards. Whether you execute them discretely or initiate an open brawl is entirely at your discretion (📷 10).

Careful management of the Templar Awareness meter is important if you do not wish to spend too much time travelling back and forth between frequent sieges. You can find a complete overview and analysis of the Templar Awareness system on page 157. We strongly suggest that you at least study it briefly before you continue.

10

SEQUENCE 03: LOST AND FOUND

Initializing ...
Populating ... · · · · · ·
source\S17.anima.06102001.SVJbVkY/YmVy
source\S17.anima.21032002.QmxhY2llWxscw==

MEMORY 01

THE PRISONER: After a brief return to Animus Island, Ezio's story resumes in the Imperial District. Approach the cage at the Memory Start marker and speak to the captive to hear about his plight – and, more pertinently, his proposal.

The guard carrying the key to the prisoner's cell is located a short journey to the east, with conventional avenues of approach to the green "search zone" blocked by stationary guards or patrols. To complete the Full Synch objective of pickpocketing the target, a stealth approach is mandatory. When you near the area, jump into the water and approach the green search zone displayed on the mini-map from the jetty that extends to the north (📷 01). Watch the steps to

your right, and wait for a lone patrolling guard to arrive; his path is marked on the accompanying screenshot. When he departs, climb the wall and, while hanging out of sight on the ledge, activate Eagle Sense to identify your target.

When the marked Templar turns away from Ezio, jump up and hold the Legs button to Fast Walk. Collide with him before he turns to regard the Assassin, and you will obtain the key without conflict. Immediately turn and run back to the jetty, leaping into the ocean to make good your escape; there is no point in raising the Templar Awareness Meter with needless bloodshed at this point. Return to the prisoner to end the Memory.

01

40

TUNNEL ENTRANCES & FERRIES

Constantinople is a huge city, which can make journeys by foot rather time-consuming. To cut down on arduous travel between distant places of interest, Ezio can take ferries and use Tunnel Entrances to move almost instantly between specific locations.

- To cross the Golden Horn – the body of water that separates the Galata district from the rest of Constantinople – you can take a ferry (⛴) between the two docks. Speak to individuals in the positions marked on the accompanying cut-out map to make the short trip. You can also appropriate a boat to row across if you wish, though this takes a little longer.

- There are twelve Tunnel Entrances (⟳) located throughout Constantinople. Interact with one of these, and Ezio can use a network of underground sewers and tunnels to move swiftly to different areas of the city.

ENEMY ARCHETYPES

Though the first two Sequences pit Ezio against Ottoman Elites, Byzantine Militia and Gunmen of both factions (as introduced in the Primer – see page 22), Sequence 03 marks the point at which he will encounter far more capable foes. For comprehensive analysis of their strengths and weaknesses, refer to the Enemies section of the Reference & Analysis chapter on page 151.

The **Ottoman Agile** is a guardsman of a slender, athletic build, armed with a dagger. These quick and nimble opponents are adept at free running, and will pursue Ezio doggedly if he attempts to flee combat; they can even outpace him in a straight-line sprint, necessitating clever maneuvers or diversionary tactics to shake them off. In combat, they will evade Ezio's attempts to launch a combo, and will deftly leap away from kicks. For this reason, Counter Kills – of any variety – are the best way to dispatch them, though they are also susceptible to grabs and attacks launched after a successful dodge.

The **Byzantine Varangian** is easily identified by the polearm he carries. These vigilant and inquisitive soldiers possess the unique ability to search hiding spots, and can on occasion even detect Ezio when he is Blending. When fought they will block standard attacks, but can be briefly incapacitated with a kick or momentarily disoriented by a dodge – providing a brief window of opportunity to launch a deadly combo. They tend to maintain a greater distance from Ezio in combat, and will periodically seek to incapacitate him by throwing sand in his direction; either dodge or move out of range to avoid this special attack. Performing a Disarm will enable you to take possession of a Varangian's polearm, which can confer a considerable advantage in a melee featuring a mixture of different opponent types. Most (but not all) Varangians are immune to Counter Kills.

The **Byzantine Almogavar** is the slowest of Ezio's opponents, but can inflict huge damage with his heavy weapon. These opponents generally stand on the frontline of any conflict, and possess a special unblockable attack: when you see them slowly draw their weapon back for a giant strike, be ready to dodge or move out of range. Though they can block basic attacks, a simple kick renders them vulnerable to a combo kill.

Ottoman Agile

Byzantine Almogavar

Byzantine Varangian

PRIMER

WALKTHROUGH

SIDE QUESTS

REFERENCE & ANALYSIS

MULTIPLAYER

EXTRAS

INDEX

USER INSTRUCTIONS

SEQUENCE 01

SEQUENCE 02

SEQUENCE 03

SEQUENCE 04

SEQUENCE 05

SEQUENCE 06

SEQUENCE 07

SEQUENCE 08

SEQUENCE 09

Counter Kills: Per Weapon Results vs Archetypes

ARCHETYPE	COUNTER KILL	DISARM	COUNTER STEAL	COUNTER HOOK-AND-THROW
Elite/Militia	Kill	Success	Success	Success
Agile	Kill	Success	Fail	Success
Varangian	Fail*	Success	Success	Success
Almogavar	Kill	Fail*	Success	Fail

In the accompanying table, we provide a brief appraisal of how Ezio's arsenal of counterattacking techniques will perform against Ezio's opponents; we also include details on the efficacy of the Disarm technique.

Gunmen do not launch conventional attacks, and are therefore not susceptible to Counter Kills.

*There are certain exceptions to these two rules: see our analysis of Almogavar and Varangian archetypes on pages 151 and 152 of the Reference & Analysis chapter for details.

MEMORIES 02 & 03

THE SENTINEL, PART 1: Travel to the Assassin Den in northeast Galata via the ferry on the docks in the north of the Imperial District. Once inside, assign your Den Leader as directed, then speak to him to formally begin the Memory. Once Ezio's new apprentice has finished his explanation, you are free to travel solo to the rooftop waypoint.

After the cutscene, assassinate the Templar closest to your position, then use an Assassin Signal to deal with his ally on the next rooftop along, unlocking the Full Synch requirement (📷 02). You can then air assassinate the final Templar below. Approach the next waypoint, then use Eagle Sense to examine the nearby bench. Turn to the right to find a bloodstain, and further ghostly evidence of the murder of Assassin recruits. Chase the Sentinel at street level until he escapes, then fight alongside your apprentice. When the battle is over, walk with Ezio's apprentice until the Memory ends.

GUILD CONTRACTS: Directly after the previous Memory, interact with the highlighted pigeon coop to begin this introduction to the Mediterranean Defense metagame. You can find details on this new feature on the page to your right. To complete this short objective, you must send Ezio's senior apprentice on a mission.

02

 ## RECRUITING ASSASSINS

Once you have completed "The Sentinel, Part 1", liberating each Templar Den (see page 88) will enable you to enlist a further two Assassin Recruits, up to a maximum of twelve. Whenever there is a free berth, special icons (▣) will appear on the main map and mini-map. When you visit these locations, you will either find a citizen in a stand-off with the local soldiery, or a Memory Start marker. In the first instance, defeating the guards and saving the prospective Recruit's life will lead him or her to pledge their support to Ezio's cause; in the second, you must complete a Secondary Memory to achieve the same result. See page 92 of the Side Quests chapter for further details.

ASSASSIN SIGNALS

Once Ezio obtains his first Recruit at the conclusion of The Prisoner, a new icon (➤➤➤) appears in the upper-left corner of the screen. This is the Assassin Signal Meter.

Assassin Signals can be used in three ways. The first is an assassination order issued outside of open conflict. Highlight or Target Lock an assailant, then tap the Assassin Signal button (**LB**/**L2**) to instruct Ezio's subordinates to slay the highlighted individual (📷 03). If necessary, they will engage other active hostiles before making their escape. In open conflict, press the Assassin Signal button to summon assistance. Guild members will rush to Ezio's aid, departing once the fracas ends. Finally, there is a special Arrow Storm attack (hold the Assassin Signal button) that can be unlocked once Ezio has six active recruits.

03

The ability to summon Assassins is a powerful weapon, but there are rules, features and conditions that you should bear in mind before you begin to employ it regularly.

■ Ezio will not be attacked or sustain Templar Awareness penalties when he orders Assassins to kill targets unless you send him into the fray. You can, if you wish, lend assistance from a safe distance with projectile weapons.

■ Assassins will die in combat if they sustain critical damage. Watch the Health Meters that appear above their heads, and be ready to intervene if a battle is going badly. If an Assassin dies, you must enroll a new replacement. We strongly advise that you avoid calling them while fighting close to deep water – like all non-player characters, submersion leads to instant death.

■ When ordered to perform an assassination, Assassins will tailor their arrival in accordance with the position of their targets. They can jump down from rooftops, leap from hiding spots, or dash from nearby alleyways to strike. If a target is under the cover of a roof, though, Assassins will need to approach by a more conventional route – with obvious tactical repercussions.

■ Assassins usually attack in pairs. A new Assassin Signal is added to the Signal Meter for every two active Assassins, up to a maximum of three (➤➤➤ ➤➤➤ ➤➤➤). Assassin Signals are subtracted when the number of available Assassins falls to five and three, though only one recruit need be available for the first Assassin Signal.

■ Ezio's available Assassins are always summoned in order of seniority. Though Assassins gain experience points (XP) if called into combat, the sums accrued are fairly nominal. The best way to level up recruits is to send them on specific assignments in the Mediterranean Defense metagame.

■ The ability to call Assassins is unavailable during certain memories.

MEDITERRANEAN DEFENSE

The Mediterranean Defense metagame enables you to send recruited Assassins to complete missions in different cities, which can lead to noteworthy rewards. In addition to monetary gains (and, in select instances, feature unlocks), the successful completion of these contracts will lead Assassins to gain XP. As they rise through the ranks of the Brotherhood, you can spend points obtained at each level to upgrade their equipment and armor, making them more effective and durable in combat.

You can access the Mediterranean Defense screens and manage your Recruits via pigeon coops situated throughout the city and maps located inside each Assassin Den (📷 04). The drawback to sending Assassins on contracts is that you cannot call on their services via the Assassin Signal command until they return to Constantinople. This is less of an issue once you capture a few Templar Dens and enlist more than six individuals, but it's something that you must always bear in mind.

For a full guide to completing the Mediterranean Defense metagame, see page 93 of the Side Quests chapter.

04

PRIMER

WALKTHROUGH

SIDE QUESTS

REFERENCE & ANALYSIS

MULTIPLAYER

EXTRAS

INDEX

USER INSTRUCTIONS

SEQUENCE 01

SEQUENCE 02

SEQUENCE 03

SEQUENCE 04

SEQUENCE 05

SEQUENCE 06

SEQUENCE 07

SEQUENCE 08

SEQUENCE 09

MEMORY 04

BOMB CRAFTING: Return to the Imperial District via a Ferry or Tunnel Entrance (The Grand Bazaar is the exit closest to your destination), then enter the Assassin Den to begin this Memory.

After the cutscene, loot the nearby containers to obtain ingredients, then approach the Crafting Table to create your first bomb. In the tutorial that follows, select the highlighted ingredients as directed, then tap the Secondary Attack button to test your bomb. Feel free to experiment in the test chamber for as long as you like, then press ▶/START to continue. Finally, craft the bomb, then add two additional units to your pouch to end the lesson.

Leave the Den, then travel to Piri Reis's shop at the waypoint marker (📷 05).

BOMBS & BOMB CRAFTING

Bombs are a major new feature in Assassin's Creed Revelations, and add an entirely new tactical dimension to its stealth and combat mechanics.

- Highlight or Target Lock an opponent, then press the Secondary Attack button to throw a bomb at the highlighted individual (📷 06).

- To perform a manual throw to a specific location, hold the Secondary Attack button to bring up a target, then use 🕹 to fine tune your aim. Release the button to perform the throw, or press the Empty Hand button to cancel and return the bomb to its pouch.

- Tap the Secondary Attack button to drop a bomb while running.

- Be wary of collateral damage! If you are using harmful explosives, killing civilians will lead to Desynchronization.

06

Though you can acquire bombs ready-made from Black Market Dealers and, very occasionally, by looting corpses or chests, the most cost-effective way to obtain them is to make them yourself with the ingredients you find.

Bomb Crafting tables are represented by the 🛎 icon. These are located throughout Constantinople, and can also be found inside Assassin Dens and Piri Reis's shop. Ezio can carry three types of bomb at once in his Lethal Pouch, Tactical Pouch and Diversion Pouch, with each pouch having a default capacity of three. If you craft or attempt to purchase a different type of bomb in a particular category, you will need to dismantle any existing bombs of that type, though individual components will be returned to Ezio's inventory.

You can find a guide to bomb crafting on page 140 of the Reference & Analysis chapter.

PIRI REIS

Introduced during Memory 03, Piri Reis is an individual who offers a number of unique services and opportunities.

- Reis can always be found at his premises in the Grand Bazaar (▣). His store features a Crafting Table and the Bombs Challenge Board. Reading the book to the left of these two amenities leads you directly to Database entries on bomb crafting.

- Interact with the shimmering paintings on the wall to the right of Reis to begin Secondary Memories: see page 99 of the Side Quests chapter for details.

- You can shop with the master bomb maker for Casing, Gunpowder and Effect ingredients, though his inventory is limited until you finish his Secondary Memories and complete certain Mediterranean Defense objectives.

- Reis's most unique service is his willingness to buy crafting ingredients from Ezio, which can be a profitable sideline – especially if you would like to bankroll an aggressive acquisition strategy in the Rebuilding Constantinople metagame at this early stage. If you rarely use bombs, or find that you have a surplus of ingredients, visit his store to offload Casings, Gunpowder and Effects whenever you reach or near the carrying capacity for individual items.

MEMORY 05

A FAMILIAR FACE: This Memory will take you away from the streets of Constantinople for a time, so it's a good idea to withdraw your current balance from a Bank if it is nearing capacity, and send any available Assassins away on reasonably lengthy contracts before you enter the door at the Memory Start marker.

After conversing with Sofia, use Eagle Sense to locate a hidden entrance (📷 07). Once Ezio identifies it, Memory 06 begins automatically.

07

🔴 BLACK MARKET VENDORS

If you are short on crafting ingredients, or need tactical explosives as a matter of grave urgency, these common merchants (📷 08) sell bombs – though naturally, at a premium. They are marked on the main map and mini-map by the 🔴 icon. You can learn more about these individuals – and their range of wares – on page 150 of the Reference & Analysis chapter.

08

Stalkers (🎞 09) are Templar agents sent to locate and eliminate Ezio, and are quite unlike other opponents.

- Stalkers (marked on the mini-map by the ⚔ icon) run behind Ezio and attempt to stab him. You have a brief moment to press the Primary Attack button to foil their attack, which leads to the immediate death of the Templar agent. If you fail to react in time, the Stalker will inflict a grievous injury on Ezio before attempting to escape.

- You should always chase and kill fleeing Stalkers. If one can successfully disappear from sight, it leads to a massive +25% increase in Templar Awareness. If your quarry has a head start, you should employ projectiles (or even an Assassin Signal) to dispatch them with relative ease. After killing them, always take the time to loot their corpses: they generally carry something in the region of 1,000 **A**.

- There is a brief flash of ominous music before a Stalker strikes. If you hear this and turn Ezio to face his assailant before he can move into position, the hired killer will abort his attack. Once again, it's vital that you give chase immediately.

09

Templar Couriers (🎞 10) do not attack Ezio, and will flee if they see him.

- Whenever you see the 🛡 icon appear on the mini-map, you can chase him down and perform a non-lethal Tackle or Leg Sweep to relieve him of Templar taxes.

- The sums you can obtain are not inconsiderable during early Sequences, but become less attractive (given the potential effort involved) once Ezio begins to accumulate revenue from the Mediterranean Defense and Rebuilding Constantinople metagames.

- Under no circumstances should you kill Templar Couriers, as doing so will fill the Templar Awareness meter instantly.

10

Marksmen are Gunmen stationed inside sealed booths (usually encountered in Templar Dens) who will shoot at Ezio during combat situations. They can only be killed with projectiles or bombs. If conflict breaks out in an area overlooked by one of these booths, it's wise to break off hostilities and move to a position out of their firing range. They are represented by the 📷 icon on the mini-map.

Templar Captains are a rare opponent type mostly encountered in the Templar Dens they control. Some are cowards, and will flee from battle; others will stand and fight with great bravery and no small degree of prowess. See page 88 of the Side Quests chapter to learn more about these foes.

Marksman

Templar Captain

MEMORY 06

THE YEREBATAN CISTERN: This Memory takes place in an area populated by numerous Templars searching for a Masyaf Key. On a first visit, we would suggest that you ignore the Full Synch objective and instead return here at a later date to complete it.

There are two reasons for this. Full Synch is rather easier to accomplish once you are familiar with the environment. Secondly, there are numerous chests containing crafting ingredients that you can loot, so it's actually a great opportunity to try different varieties of bombs. You will encounter Crafting Tables

at regular intervals, with many opportunities to loot additional ingredients from corpses if you systematically exterminate all Templars in each area. Even if you don't intend to use the ingredients, you can turn a fine profit by selling them to Piri Reis. Best of all, your actions in this area do not contribute to your Templar Awareness level when you return to Constantinople.

Our walkthrough here focuses on the challenging Full Synch requirement. If you are opting for rewards over 100% completion, you can safely ignore the stealth-oriented guidance in favor of raw aggression when you encounter guards.

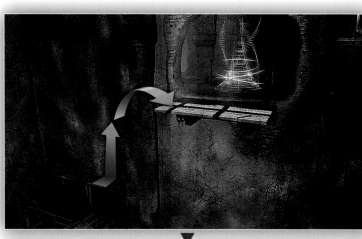

I: The first room has no hostiles, so just drop down to the lower level and loot the chests at the south end for ingredients. When you are ready to leave, the easiest way to reach the waypoint marker is to perform a Side Eject. Climb the pile of crates to the left of the opening above, run up the wall, then tap the Legs button and press ❸ to the right simultaneously.

II: When you reach the Crafting Table, create at least one Cherry Bomb. Select the Diversion Pouch, then choose the Impact Shell, any Gunpowder ingredient you please (though the British variety works best, if you have it), and Sulfur as the payload. In the next chamber, you must kill a Templar Captain to obtain the key to the exit. Kill the guard directly ahead after the cutscene ends, then climb to the platform above him. From here, ready the Poison Dart weapon – an essential tool for Full Synch in this Memory, as it enables Ezio to kill rather openly without raising the alarm – and watch the Captain's patrol route. When he reaches the position marked on the accompanying screenshot, shoot him. Now use the beams, suspended platforms and Long Jumps via the hanging lanterns to reach the suspended platform directly above his position. Equip a Cherry Bomb. When the Captain finally expires, throw your diversionary bomb to lure the crowd of guards away from the gate. Once they have moved, jump straight down and sprint for the exit; press the Empty Hand button to open it.

III: After passing through the room with a Crafting Table, you will enter a large chamber. From your position on the beams, wait until the guard to the right moves to inspect the containers on the east end of his patrol, then kill him with a Throwing Knife. Dispatch the Templar smashing rocks to your left, then drop to the ground. The Templar Captain in this area can be found on an elevated walkway opposite the position where Ezio enters. To reach him, look for the stairs on the left-hand side of the room. The guards patrolling on the boardwalks here are not particularly vigilant, so just walk calmly for the opening when they turn away. Carefully proceed up the stairs, then look to your left when you reach the opening to see the Captain. He is more suspicious than most other Templars here, so don't linger in the open while he is facing you; when he walks to the east, run over to the sentry on your right and eliminate him. Now watch the Captain from cover, and emerge to strike him with a Poison Dart while his back is turned. Head back down the stairs and, timing your movements to avoid the two patrols, move calmly to the exit.

IV: In the next room, kill the lone guard when he arrives with a Throwing Knife from afar. Loot the chests, then follow the route in the accompanying screenshot to reach the next waypoint.

V: There is one last Templar Captain to kill to obtain a final gate key. After the cutscene, employ Long Jumps on the two lamps and use the wooden beams to reach an optimal elevated vantage point on the south side of the chamber, as illustrated in the accompanying screenshot. Use Eagle Sense to identify the Captain on the central island, then hit him with a Poison Dart. If the Varangian patrolling the boardwalk in front of the exit moves to investigate, especially when the Captain succumbs to the toxin, jump to ground level and run to the gate immediately; if not, pick an optimum moment to eliminate him with another Poison Dart. Do not use Throwing Knives: Varangians must be struck with two blades for a kill, which leads to a risk of detection.

VI: Once through the final gate, loot the three high-yield Treasure Chests, then use Eagle Sense to scan the walls for an entrance to a hidden chamber. Once you have identified it, head through and collect the Masyaf Seal from the statue. When play resumes in Sofia's shop, exit via the highlighted door.

MEMORIES 07 & 08

QUID PRO QUO: This Memory begins on Ezio's return from the Yerabatan Cistern, and ends on completion of the cutscene with Sofia. After leaving the building, you can either return to the Assassin's HQ to begin Memory 08, or travel to the southwest of the city to begin Memory 09. We follow the order set out by the in-game DNA menu.

THE MENTOR'S KEEPER: Return to the Assassin's HQ in Galata. Send your recruits on missions before you enter the Memory Start marker: you won't be needing them for the immediate future.

Altaïr is armed with a sword, a Hidden Blade, Throwing Knives and has five doses of Medicine. If you wish to complete the Full Synch requirement, you need to dispatch all Templar aggressors at the locations in Masyaf village marked by black circles on the mini-map. These only appear when you are not openly engaged in combat; you will be notified once all sites have been cleared.

Most Templars are easy fodder for Altaïr's whirling onslaught, irrespective of the weapon you choose, but there are two varieties of Templars that can be more difficult to beat unless you favor Hidden Blade combo kills. Those with polearms are functionally identical to the Varangian archetype, and must generally have their guard broken with a kick or dodge to begin a combo. A few other Templars can resist combos; once again, use kicks and dodges (or, better still, Counter Kills or Kill Streaks) to dispatch them. Use Throwing Knives to kill Templar crossbowmen stationed on rooftops.

You should have a fair sense of Masyaf's layout from your earlier visit in Sequence 01; here, you must travel up the slopes from the village to reach the fortress above, engaging (or avoiding) battles as you see fit. After the cutscene at the waypoint, you have a limited period of time to climb the exterior wall to the right of the portcullis, stealth assassinate the four Templar guards – detection will lead to immediate Desynchronization – and then air assassinate the target from the position marked in the accompanying screenshot (11). Completing this final objective ends the Memory.

source\S17.anima.16082003.RXNjYXBI
source\S17.anima.23082003.V2hhdElzVGhpc1BsYWNI
source\S17.anima.16052003.Q2hpY2Fnb0dpcmxxz
source\S17.anima.27082003.Tm90RmFyRW5vdWdo

HIRING FACTIONS

There are numerous groups of Thieves, Mercenaries and Romanies dotted around Constantinople who will gladly lend assistance to Ezio – for a price. Each faction has its own individual set of talents, and can be extremely useful in a wide variety of situations.

■ To hire a group, approach the quartet and press the Empty Hand button (🎮 12). They will then follow Ezio automatically until ordered to stop or if abandoned (for example, if you travel to a different area of the city via a Tunnel Entrance). Hiring another faction or a different party affiliated to the same faction will immediate dismiss a group currently in Ezio's employ.

■ Tap the Empty Hand button to order a group to stop. This can be useful if you would like to scout ahead, or specifically need to keep them out of harm's way.

■ Each faction has a unique proficiency. To use these, Target Lock or highlight an adversary with 🕹, then press the Empty Hand button.

PRIMER

WALKTHROUGH

SIDE QUESTS

REFERENCE & ANALYSIS

MULTIPLAYER

EXTRAS

INDEX

USER INSTRUCTIONS

SEQUENCE 01

SEQUENCE 02

SEQUENCE 03

SEQUENCE 04

SEQUENCE 05

SEQUENCE 06

SEQUENCE 07

SEQUENCE 08

SEQUENCE 09

Faction Traits & Abilities

FACTION	UNIQUE SKILL	STRENGTHS	WEAKNESSES
Romanies	**Distract:** The Romanies will leave Ezio and draw the attention of all nearby guards and civilians. The group is lost permanently when this ability is used.	▪ Groups of Romanies move in formation around Ezio while he moves at walking pace, providing a Blend opportunity that is not subject to the whims of milling civilians.	▪ Two Romanies will automatically peel away to distract suspicious guards who pass within a certain distance. ▪ Unsuited to combat encounters; they will fall swiftly to enemy blades. ▪ Cannot climb or free run.
Mercenaries	**Fight:** The Mercenaries will attack the highlighted individual and their allies in the area. Ezio accrues no Templar Awareness penalties if you refrain from entering the battle.	▪ Hired Mercenaries will automatically rush to Ezio's aid in combat. ▪ Using their special ability does not cause them to leave Ezio's employ. ▪ Peerless combat abilities.	▪ Incapable of climbing or free running. ▪ Cannot be recalled while still engaged in combat: you must wait for the battle to end. ▪ Torturously slow movement speed; Ezio outpaces them at a basic run.
Thieves	**Lure:** The Thieves will leave Ezio and provoke guards to give chase; those who do will not return to their posts or patrols for (generally) in the region of thirty seconds. Group is lost permanently after using this skill.	▪ Extremely fast; excellent free running and climbing abilities. ▪ Will fight alongside Ezio if he is attacked or enters combat.	▪ Thieves will fall quickly to the blades of stronger opponents unless Ezio intervenes.

MEMORY 09

CURSE OF THE ROMANI: Before you begin this Memory, ensure that you have a full supply of five doses of Poison. You can replenish your stocks by visiting a Doctor or by looting slain adversaries.

As the approach to the Romani faction headquarters leads through unrevealed territory and two Templar Dens (unless you have already taken the time to liberate them), we strongly recommend that you use a Tunnel Entrance to simplify the journey. Select the Arcadius exit and, on arrival, travel west to avoid the outskirts of the Templar Den, then head north to reach the Memory Start marker.

After accepting the commission, travel to the south to avoid the Templar Den, then head east to reach the waypoint; you will need to avoid Byzantine patrols during the journey. Hire the group of Romanies when prompted to do so, then walk among them to Blend and evade the attention of the hostiles that line the path.

On arrival at the first waypoint, the Romani group will revert to their standard behavior: they will surround Ezio as he moves. Select the Poison Darts, line up a clear shot from range (hold the Secondary Weapon button until the targeting line solidifies), then shoot the highlighted Templar (📷 13). When his companion picks up the chest, tail him from a discrete distance. A countdown timer will appear whenever your target passes out of sight, but don't run: you can easily catch up at walking pace before it expires. When prompted, poison the second Templar in the same manner as before; after a further short walk, execute a final target with a dart to complete the Full Synchronization objective and the last real challenge of this Memory. Pick up the chest, then enjoy the sights during the return to the Romani HQ.

13

MEMORY 10

THE SENTINEL, PART 2: Travel to the Memory Start marker in the south of Galata, close to the ferry. Speak with Ezio's apprentice, then travel to the northeast of the district. The two Assassin hostages are held captive in two areas with guards stationed at all available entrances at street level. To complete the Full Synch requirement you must free both without being detected (see the page to your right for guidance), though you can fight your way in if you prefer.

After both captives have been freed, travel to the waypoint close to the Assassin's HQ. You will see Templars and Assassins fighting in the streets as you approach, but there's no need to involve yourself. In the final action of this Sequence, chase the Sentinel around Galata Tower until Ezio's apprentice makes a timely intervention.

PRIMER

WALKTHROUGH

SIDE QUESTS

REFERENCE & ANALYSIS

MULTIPLAYER

EXTRAS

INDEX

USER INSTRUCTIONS

SEQUENCE 01

SEQUENCE 02

SEQUENCE 03

SEQUENCE 04

SEQUENCE 05

SEQUENCE 06

SEQUENCE 07

SEQUENCE 08

SEQUENCE 09

CHALLENGES

With so many activities to get involved in, Challenges are a feature that many players may fail to notice – which would be a shame. Challenges are arranged in five different categories (Assassins Guild, Mercenaries Guild, Romanies Guild, Thieves Guild and Bomb), with each one divided into three sets of objectives. Completing each set of tasks leads to a variety of rewards, some of which are really quite noteworthy. See page 100 of the Side Quests chapter for more information.

You can study your current progress in all Challenges at the Secondary Memories section of the DNA menu, or via glowing boards located at faction HQs.

THE SENTINEL, PART 2: FULL SYNCH

Reconnoiter the first waypoint (the one to the east) from the rooftops south of the waypoint marker (📷 14).Two guards are stationed outside, with a patrol passing their position approximately once per minute. Hire the nearby Thieves, then wait for the patrol to walk by. Highlight or Target Lock one of the stationary guards, then press the Empty Hand button to order the cutpurses to lure them away. You should then have thirty seconds to drop to the streets below, free the Assassin – and, if you're especially bold, loot the Treasure Chest – then return to the rooftops via the conveniently placed ladder situated just outside.

14

Travel over rooftops to approach the second waypoint from the east until you see a second group of Thieves. Once again, two guards stand watch outside the Assassin's prison, while a patrol arrives at regular intervals (📷 15). This includes a Varangian who examines a nearby hay cart before the patrol retraces its steps. When they depart, order the Thieves to lure away the stationary guards and then drop down to free the captive. The Full Synch objective is fulfilled immediately, so you're free to engage in open conflict as you depart.

15

SEQUENCE 04: THE UNCIVIL WAR

Note: Both Memory 01 and Memory 03 are available to play from the start of this Sequence. The order that we present here follows the progression in the DNA menu.

MEMORY 01

THE PRINCE'S BANQUET: Speak to Yusuf at the Memory Start marker at the Hippodrome; the Memory Start marker to the southwest is Memory 03, which can be ignored for now.

After speaking with Yusuf, travel to the waypoint on the outer wall of Topkapi Palace; see the page to your right for advice on beating the Full Synch objective. On arrival, your second objective is to knock out the marked Italian minstrels (a task that experienced Assassin's Creed players will embrace with relish) and then transport the unconscious troubadours to a waypoint. You have two Assassins to help you in this task, and need only carry one body at a time. The first trio are easy enough, but the three that follow are in close proximity to a group of Janissaries. As detection leads to instant Desynchronization, run alongside the outer wall, then climb up to engage the minstrels before they can move from their starting position. You must then sneak on the path behind the guards to deposit the body at the waypoint at the far side of the building.

The third and final group of minstrels are located much further away, with the intervening grounds populated by too many guards for Ezio to avoid. Climb to the palace's outer wall via the building then, after waiting for the Janissary patrol to move away, drop to ground level. Quickly climb onto the rooftop above the musicians. You can now jump down and incapacitate them with a flurry of fists (📷 01).

After hiding the minstrels, proceed to the marked waypoint and follow the onscreen prompts to play the lute. Inside the party, move to the marked position and activate Eagle Sense. Study each of the highlighted civilians in turn to identify the target, then stand at the waypoint and play tunes to mask the assassination. Repeat this process with the second target, then reconvene with Yusuf at the waypoint marker.

In the next section of this large Memory, you must identify four killers concealed in crowds of civilians as Suleiman moves to stand among them. Once again, use Eagle Sense to scan each individual in turn, then stand and play in a position that causes the crowd to face away from the subsequent killing. Each waypoint marks the approximate location of a single target.

After the cutscene, race to intercept and kill Suleiman's assailant with an improvised assassination to conclude the Memory.

01

MEMORY 02

AN UNEASY MEETING: Travel to the Memory Start marker in the northeast corner of Topkapi Palace and speak with Suleiman. This is a Restricted Area, so avoid all guards on your journey there.

Ezio is tasked to climb Topkapi's Tower of Justice. The intervening courtyard area is packed with vigilant Janissaries, so it's much better to turn around at your start position, head through the archway, then climb to the rooftops to reach the waypoint without incident (and therefore complete the Full Synch objective). Before you enter the hatch, take a moment to Synchronize with the Viewpoint above if you have yet to do so.

02

To complete the Full Synch requirement for this Memory, you must beat Yusuf to the waypoint on the outer wall of Topkapi Palace after the opening cinematic. Unless you are astonishingly adept at free running, it's a feat that you are unlikely to achieve by free running over the intervening rooftops – at least not without several practice runs. Fortunately, there is a much easier solution.

From the starting point, jump over to the rooftops directly ahead, then drop down to street level and run up the steps to the northeast (📷 02). From here, there is a continuous road that – bar two instances where you must run around architectural features – leads directly to Topkapi Palace. You will need to be reasonably careful in the way that you weave through civilians, but should find that Ezio soon outpaces his rivals on their rooftop assault course. When you reach the main entrance, turn left to find a building that allows easy access to the outer wall where the waypoint lies (📷 03).

03

ENEMY ARCHETYPE

The **Janissaries** are the Sultan's household guard, and are by far the most dangerous of all enemy archetypes to face in combat. Though rarely encountered in city patrols at this stage, they appear with increasing frequency in later Sequences. While single Janissaries mixed with standard guards can be tough to beat, large groups are astonishingly difficult to fight against. Our advice would be to avoid conflict with these foes, and to withdraw from unnecessary confrontations.

- Janissaries carry swords as their primary weapon, employing single fast lunges or multi-hit combos.

- In addition to melee attacks, Janissaries can (and regularly will) draw a firearm. After targeting for a variable period of time, they will shoot Ezio. Difficult to dodge, the only reliable way to avoid injury is to strike them as they take aim – though you can also attempt to take cover behind another combatant.

- Janissaries foil Ezio's attempts to initiate combos, evade the Kick, Grab and Disarm moves, and need to be hit with no less than three successful Counter Kills or Kill Streak attacks before they fall. While a Kill Streak assault will fail to disable a Janissary unless they have been sufficiently weakened, the attempt doesn't end the Streak: you can still move on to hit another target.

You can find a complete breakdown of the Janissary's strengths and weaknesses on page 154 of the Reference & Analysis chapter.

Janissary

55

MEMORY 03

THE FOURTH PART OF THE WORLD: Travel to the Memory Start marker by the docks at the south of the Imperial District. Ezio must reach the waypoint on the impounded boat deep inside a sizable Restricted Area. While it is certainly possible to brazenly fight your way through to the vessel, those who wish to maintain a low profile and complete the Full Synch objective should consult the annotated screenshot on the page to the right.

Once you reach the vessel, use Eagle Sense to identify Sofia's delivery (📷 04) and then collect it. Escape the marked zone (via the water if you wish to avoid conflict), then return to Sofia at her bookshop.

MEMORY 04

SIGNS AND SYMBOLS, PART I: Climb to the very top of the tower to reach the Memory Start position. Activate Eagle Sense, then scan the glowing Polo Symbols to discern the location of a hidden treasure (📷 05). Once you are provided with a new waypoint, perform a Leap of Faith into a hay cart far below (face northwest to find it), then proceed to your next destination. The Memory ends after Ezio retrieves the book.

Memory 05 sees Ezio leave the streets of Constantinople for a time, so take a moment to send Assassins on assignments and withdraw funds from a Bank if you are nearing your account limit.

04

05

THE FOURTH PART OF THE WORLD: FULL SYNCH

PRIMER

WALKTHROUGH

SIDE QUESTS

REFERENCE &
ANALYSIS

MULTIPLAYER

EXTRAS

INDEX

For those seeking Full Synch in Memory 03, the safest and least effortful way to safely board the vessel is to take the small alleyway a short walk to the southwest of the guards in front of your starting position. Dive into the water and swim to the south side of the ship inside the Restricted Area. Move to approximately the middle of the vessel then, being careful to stay out of sight, climb close to the deck (📷 06). Watch the two guards on board; they have short patrol routes, as marked on our annotated screenshot. Wait until the individual closest to you is facing away, with his partner elsewhere, then leap onto the deck and perform an assassination. The second guard can be felled with a single Throwing Knife, though be careful not to attract attention from the soldiers on the dock below.

After you retrieve Sofia's delivery, leap back into the sea and return via the same route. The Full Synch objective will be satisfied once you leave the highlighted area.

06

USER
INSTRUCTIONS

SEQUENCE 01

SEQUENCE 02

SEQUENCE 03

SEQUENCE 04

SEQUENCE 05

SEQUENCE 06

SEQUENCE 07

SEQUENCE 08

SEQUENCE 09

HARASSERS

Harassers are a unique class of citizen who will rush to accost Ezio whenever he encounters them, potentially impeding his movement and drawing attention to him at inopportune moments. Harassers have distinct "zones" where they operate, and will not move beyond these invisible boundaries. When there is no need for subtlety, they can be outpaced at full sprint.

Beggars

Beggars usually move in groups of three, and will loudly implore Ezio for a donation of Akçe. Unless you quickly outrun or otherwise deter them (for example by bumping into them), they will act in tandem to block his path. If a Memory calls for discretion, use the Throw Money ability to divert their attention elsewhere. You can also have Ezio draw his sword to cause them to beat a noisy yet hasty retreat.

Though not technically classed as Harassers, **citizens carrying objects** will drop them if accidentally jostled by Ezio, or if sufficiently startled by his actions. Some will then seek to remonstrate loudly with the Assassin. These events cause a commotion, which may draw unfriendly eyes to regard the scene.

57

MEMORY 05

GALATA TOWER: Scale the tower to find a marked entrance near its summit, then interact with the secret doorway to begin.

The Full Synch objective of completing the Memory within six minutes might – just *might* – be plausible for Assassin's Creed players of experience, confidence and no small measure of luck, but a more realistic goal might be to treat this first visit as an exercise in familiarization. Once you understand the course layout, you can then return to obtain Full Synch via the Replay a Memory feature.

I: Descend the staircase, then leap over to the platform. Use ⓛ to guide Ezio left and right as he careens down the slope. At the end of the ensuing cutscene, climb up and change sides on the ruined mechanism. Continue ascending, then perform a Back Eject to the ledges behind Ezio. From here, traverse to the right, then jump onto the platform. Ride the zipline down, then head through the open doorway.

II: At the end of the tunnel, climb the wooden surface immediately to your left, then perform a Long Jump via the hanging lamp. Jump over the wooden beams, then traverse to the right, around the corner, until Ezio can move no further and the camera angle is automatically adjusted. Back Eject onto the pole, then swing down and hop over the wooden platforms to reach a zipline.

III: In the next cavern, jump onto the water wheel and traverse to the left, then Back Eject onto the hanging platform. Hook Leap to the top of the wooden planks behind it, then traverse right to reach the beam that extends from the wall. Haul Ezio onto this, then swing on the pole to reach solid ground. If you should make a misstep and fall into the water, you can find a ladder near the entrance to the chamber.

IV: Continue forward and climb to reach a zipline, then ride it down. If you are not racing to beat the clock on a first playthrough, there is a Treasure Chest on a ledge below and to your right when Ezio lands. Hop, swing and jump over the free run elements directly ahead to reach another zipline. At the bottom, follow the route on the accompanying annotated screenshot to reach a third zipline.

V: Perform a Leap of Faith at the perch beside the waterfall, then run along the boardwalk and perform a Long Jump via the hook. From the rickety bridge, follow the path illustrated here until you reach an opening. Ride the zipline, then swing on the poles to reach another zipline. After a brush with death on a third zipline, climb the ledges to reach the platform above and head through the tunnel to your right.

VI: At the final waypoint, use Eagle Sense to identify a hidden entrance to Ezio's right as he enters (🔳), then press the Empty Hand button to open it. Loot the high-yield Treasure Chests before you continue. If you are on the brink of achieving Full Synch, you will need approximately twenty seconds to spare to open all three and reach the Masyaf Key.

MEMORY 06

THE MENTOR'S WAKE: This is the final Memory of Sequence 04 and, once again, marks an opportune time to send available Assassins on Mediterranean Defense missions.

Return to the Assassin's HQ and walk into the waypoint. When play resumes, carry Al Mualim's body to the gate; after the cutscene, walk down the slope and convey it to the pyre at the next waypoint marker. In the fracas that ensues, you must disarm seven Assassins. Altaïr will default to his fists throughout this fight, and it's vital that you don't accidentally select a lethal weapon: killing an Assassin will force you to restart the battle.

In the final part of this Memory, Altaïr must reach Abbas before he is killed by the intermittent and violent pulsing of the Apple of Eden. The shockwaves have a secondary effect: if one should hit Altaïr as he is climbing, he will automatically lose his grasp and go limp for a fraction of a second. While you can subsequently grab a ledge with the Catch Back move as he falls, it's better to perform brief bouts of climbing and then take refuge on a solid surface until the subsequent pulse occurs.

To meet the Full Synch requirement, you must simply fight an extremely cautious battle when called to disarm the Assassins, and ensure that Altaïr does not fall as he attempts to reach the Apple of Eden. While the initial climb up the first two wooden scaffolds in the closing set-piece is simple enough, scaling the tower where the Apple of Eden awaits is far more demanding. Use the highlighted route (📷 07), waiting at the marked locations until the next pulse passes.

07

PRIMER

WALKTHROUGH

SIDE QUESTS

REFERENCE &
ANALYSIS

MULTIPLAYER

EXTRAS

INDEX

USER
INSTRUCTIONS

SEQUENCE 01

SEQUENCE 02

SEQUENCE 03

SEQUENCE 04

SEQUENCE 05

SEQUENCE 06

SEQUENCE 07

SEQUENCE 08

SEQUENCE 09

GUARD RANKS & PATROLS

As Ezio challenges Byzantine hegemony in Constantinople, subtle but ultimately meaningful changes can be observed in the composition and, though less obvious, combat prowess of the patrols and sentries encountered throughout the city. By this stage, you will find that you encounter the more powerful enemy archetypes with greater frequency (📷 08).

If you are guilty of economizing on armor purchases so far, this is definitely a good time to begin upgrading Ezio's garb. If you have yet to fully master the art of flowing Kill Streaks, it's also in your best interests to hone your skills immediately. You can learn more on this subject on page 18 of the Primer chapter.

08

OPTIONAL ACTIVITIES

The conclusion of Sequence 04 marks the approximate midpoint of the main story, so this is definitely a good time to refer to the Side Quests chapter to learn about the many Secondary Memories and assorted diversions you can enjoy.

- If you have been remiss in liberating Templar Dens, see page 88 for a full guide.

- You should by now be obtaining a fair amount of income from properties purchased in Constantinople (see page 86) and the Brotherhood's activities in the Mediterranean Defense metagame (see page 93). If you have yet to do so, we suggest that you begin exploiting these profitable sidelines immediately.

- If Ezio's balance of accounts is healthy, begin spending a proportion of his funds on available capacity upgrades, better armor and the Crossbow. As you will be facing Janissaries more frequently, you could also buy the Heavy Sheath and a two-handed axe or long sword to replace your Medium weapon: see page 138.

- Training Recruits to full Assassin status at Level 10 enables you to assign them to an Assassin Den, which unlocks Master Assassin missions. See page 96 for details.

- Finally, refer to our Completion Roadmap (see page 84) to learn about all other Secondary Memories that are available at this stage.

MEMORY 01

THE JANISSARIES: Speak to the man at the waypoint marker inside the Grand Bazaar to begin this Memory. After the opening cutscene, loot the nearby chest to acquire the Cherry Bombs that you need to complete the Full Synch requirement, then walk into the green search zone further south. Head left at the intersection, and you will find Tarik in the next room; if he is not immediately revealed, use Eagle Sense to identify him. Take cover behind a pillar, then follow when he departs. Transfer from stationary to mobile Blends to track him seamlessly until you reach a checkpoint. When the brief cinematic ends, either hide in the nearby hay cart or retreat back along the corridor you arrived by to avoid detection when Tarik reenters the Grand Bazaar.

01

Tail your target until you reach another cutscene. This is your opportunity to use a Cherry Bomb to complete the Full Synch condition. From a Blend position just inside the red Restricted Area, quickly throw a bomb at the entrance to the north corridor, then sneak into the corridor to your left (leading west) when the Janissaries standing guard stroll over to investigate (01). Once again, tail Tarik from a distance. Outside, hire the group of Romani opposite the exit, and follow him to an entrance where two Janissaries stand guard. When he passes through, order the group in your employ to distract these sentries (02). At the next guard position, hire the Thieves to achieve the same result; once you walk through the arch, ascend to the rooftops for the final leg of your pursuit. There is a rooftop sentry in the vicinity, so have Throwing Knives at the ready. Tarik will stroll beneath a covered walkway, but you can simply jump over to this and wait at the end for him to emerge. The Memory ends after the subsequent cutscene.

MEMORY 02

THE ARSENAL GATES: Approach Yusuf at the waypoint marker to begin this Memory; we suggest that you have all three Assassin Signals at your disposal and a full supply of poison (plus, optimally, a supply of Tactical and Diversion bombs) before you travel here. After the opening cinematics, interact with the highlighted orators to incite a disturbance (03). Be careful to avoid the Janissaries at the center of the area – direct conflict will quell the ire of the civilians. When the number of rioters reaches a set total, a cutscene will begin.

03

When play resumes, you must defend the civilians from attack. If their numbers fall below 40, you will fail the Full Synch condition; if the total drops below 25, you will be returned to the previous checkpoint. There are two waves of soldiers to defeat. See the page to your right for tips on winning this battle.

When the final guard falls, the next Memory will begin automatically.

02

THE ARSENAL GATES: FULL SYNCH

Enter open conflict with an Ottoman soldier, then use an Assassin Signal to call for assistance when the battle begins. In the first wave, the generic Ottoman Elites are easy to dispatch; indeed, you can casually stroll behind most of these and slay them with the Hidden Blade as they are restrained by vigilantes in the crowd. However, if you can line up a clear shot with the Crossbow or Throwing Knives (📷 04), this is much faster.

05

04

The second wave features a Janissary, and this individual is your priority: he can kill citizens at a far faster rate than his less powerful allies. Engage another soldier to enter open conflict, and summon any remaining Assassins into the fray. Don't allow yourself to be drawn into a conventional fight with the Janissary: instead, hit him with a Poison Dart, and he will fall quickly to the enraged citizens (📷 05). With your Assassins working their way through the remaining hostiles, you should easily meet the Full Synch requirement. If you still struggle to save a sufficient number of civilians, you can employ bombs with a non-lethal incapacitating payload to further tip the odds in your favor on a second attempt.

06

MEMORY 03

ARSENAL INFILTRATION: Activate Eagle Sense and follow Manuel's trail through the conflict inside the Arsenal district. The Janissaries fighting civilians will not engage Ezio unless you confront them directly. As you move further west, though, you will reach an area with numerous patrols; when the fighting dies down, look for a building with a large archway. At this point, take to the rooftops and follow the route detailed in the accompanying screenshot (📷 06). There are several Gunmen to deal with, but these can be easily dispatched from a safe distance with Throwing Knives or Crossbow bolts. When you pass above the gate with guards stationed below, don't delay for a second: if you bound straight across and disappear from view, they won't engage you. Once you reach the green search zone, return to ground level when the coast is clear and approach the center of the circle to trigger a cutscene.

Your final objective is to reach the waypoint to escape the Arsenal district. See the page to your right for an annotated route map and advice on how to achieve the Full Synch requirement.

MEMORY 04

PORTRAIT OF A LADY: Enter Sofia's bookshop to begin this Memory; ensure that you have at least one Smoke Screen Bomb to complete the Full Synch requirement. You now need to make the short journey to the Grand Bazaar to identify the thief. There is an open window on the rooftop in the southwest corner of the green search zone that places you right beside your target. Use Eagle Sense to identify the culprit in the nearby group of civilians, then engage him in a fistfight.

After Ezio learns the location of the painting, head to the next waypoint. You can acquire Sofia's stolen portrait by any means (even buying it for 950 𝐀, if you so wish), but to complete the Full Synch requirement, you'll need to be more than a little devious. The vigilant merchant will watch Ezio at all times. Throw a Smoke Screen Bomb at his feet and steal the painting while he's blinded by the smoke (📷 07). You could also hire the nearby Romanies and steal the painting while blended among them. Meet Sofia at the waypoint to complete the Memory.

07

MEMORY 05

SIGNS AND SYMBOLS, PART II: Climb to the top of the Column of Marcian to reach the Memory Start position; time your ascent to avoid a sentry on the rooftop to the northwest. As before, use Eagle Sense to identify Polo Symbols in the surrounding area. Return to ground level with a Leap of Faith, then climb the adjacent building to reach the waypoint marker and retrieve the book (📷 08). Send your Assassins on contracts before you travel to the next Memory Start marker: you won't need them for a while.

08

ARSENAL INFILTRATION: ESCAPE ROUTE

Sprint straight ahead after the cutscene ends, hopping over the wooden poles and a boat until you reach a boardwalk and, just beyond it, a small tower (09). If necessary, use the Hook and Run move to bypass guards that stand in your way. Climb to the top of the ladder on the tower, then slide down the zipline (10). Immediately tap the Primary Attack button to perform an assassination on one (or both) of the soldiers below – completing the Full Synch condition – then jump over to the jetty directly ahead and climb the next tower. Free run to the boat under construction, then zipline down to the lower level; this enables you to leave your pursuers far behind. The final dash to the waypoint marker is a now a mere formality.

09

MEMORY 06

THE FORUM OF OX: Your objective in this Memory is to follow the Templars on their boat without falling into the water (📷 11). The route is very straightforward, being more a test of reactions and free running skills than navigational prowess. You will find guidance on the page to your right where we focus purely on points of interest or potential difficulty.

11

MEMORY 07

A NEW REGIME: Return to the Assassin's HQ to begin this final Memory of Sequence 05. If you are heading straight there after retrieving the Masyaf Key, there is a convenient Tunnel Entrance a short walk to the north of the Forum of Ox exit.

When play resumes, walk with Maria to the meeting with Abbas. Once hostilities commence, you are free to fight the assailants or simply escape. All opponents in this area use standard swords, so the battles are not taxing. When you leave the garden, head upstairs and sprint into the window to leap through it, then run down to the upper section of the village.

After the next cutscene, you must use Throwing Knives to foil assassination attempts as you follow Darim (📷 12), then fight groups of aggressors when prompted to do so. You have a limitless supply of blades and so, with no Full Synch requirement to worry about, completing this Memory is a relatively simple process. The only real complication of note is that panicking civilians have a tendency to run into the path of Throwing Knives. Pick your targets carefully to avoid Desynchronization.

12

I: From the start of the Memory, you have one minute to catch up with the Templars. Follow the route pictured here, then climb into the tunnel; you will encounter the boat and hit a checkpoint.

II: Falling into the rapids will lead to Desynchronization, so it's better to slow down for a second and study the course ahead if you are unsure of your next step. There are a handful of opportunities for Long Jumps, so watch out for these. Missing them will put you on an alternative, slightly longer path.

III: In the later stages of the chase, explosions and smoke can obscure the route ahead. Always take a second to identify the path in such situations. When Ezio rides a zipline directly over a boat, press the Primary Attack button when prompted to perform an assassination.

IV: After the cinematic, Ezio must fight the surviving Templars. To easily complete the Full Synch objective, either focus on safe, sword-based Counter Kills, or employ a bomb to incapacitate your assailants. When the battle ends, loot the Treasure Chests, then use Eagle Sense to identify the correct entrance on the nearby wall. Collect the Masyaf Key from the statue to end the Memory.

SEQUENCE 06: FORTUNE'S DISFAVOR

e\S17,anima.04022003.Qm9yZWRPZidhclN0b3JjZXP
e\S17,anima.30082003.UGFpbktpbGxlcnM≈
e\S17,anima.23082003.RmFjZXNJbIN0b25l
e\S17,anima.16082003.RXNjYXB0
e\S17,anima.23082003.V2hvbExmb21eTHv3Y

MEMORY 01

INTO THE SHADOWS: This Memory begins when you draw close to the Memory Start marker in the Constantine district. The Janissary you seek is standing in the south of the search zone, where he can be found remonstrating with a civilian. The area is crisscrossed with Ottoman patrols, but you can learn to predict the motions of these by observing them from a nearby roof.

You must kill the Janissary without being detected, but the Full Synch requirement specifies that you must do so from a hiding spot. To achieve

01

this, loot the chest behind your target to acquire Cherry Bombs, then go stand beside the haystack a short walk southeast of the Janissary (📷 01). Wait until the patrols have passed – there is a lone Elite who you can eliminate from this hiding spot when he walks directly by, should you wish – then throw a Cherry Bomb into the haystack. Immediately jump inside. When the Janissary moves close to investigate, assassinate him to end the Memory.

MEMORY 02

HONOR, LOST AND WON: This Memory begins automatically on completion of the previous objective. Walk with the Janissaries through the streets. When

they are assaulted by a rock-throwing civilian, beat him up with a non-lethal takedown; the rest of the journey will pass without incident.

On arrival at the compound, you face a stealth-oriented puzzle. While the Janissaries are indifferent to Ezio's presence as long as he does not attract their attention through acts of violence, presuming him to be one of their number, the Elites are rather more vigilant. Using hiding spots (including tents) and blend opportunities among groups of Janissaries, you must infiltrate the north section of the camp without being detected. You can find annotated screenshots that show the most convenient route on the page to your right.

After you have assassinated Tarik, you will find yourself surrounded by a decidedly unfavorable arrangement of furious Janissaries. Don't try to fight them: make an immediate escape via the route on the accompanying screenshot (📷 02). Once on the wooden roof, leap onto the wall; from here, Ezio can *just* reach the building below if you hold the Empty Hand button during his descent to extend the Hookblade. The next step is to head for the rooftop shelter hiding spot (as highlighted), then run past it and leap to the street below. Continue east until you reach the waterfront and dive in, then swim away from the shore to end the Memory.

Ottoman patrols will be on high alert until the end of Memory 03, so it's prudent to stick to roads less travelled and avoid starting Secondary Memories for the time being.

02

MEMORY 02: STEALTH ROUTE & FULL SYNCH

I: The first area is easy. Walk into the tent on the left, then emerge on the opposite side. Blend with the group of Janissaries when they arrive, then stroll past the Elites stationed at the gate. Walk into the tent almost directly ahead.

II: The second area features additional Elites on patrol. From the first tent, walk into the one behind it when the coast is clear; from here, wait for the guard to walk to the back entrance and then assassinate him from your place of concealment. You can also simply wait for him to move to the right-hand side of the tent. Once you are ready, climb the wall quickly.

III: On arrival in the third area, watch the guards patrolling below. When the coast is clear, simply drop down from the platform and Fast Walk over to the waypoint. When play resumes, an additional guard will patrol by the well. Watch nearby Elites carefully, then sneak over to and Blend with the group of Janissaries close to the wall. When both patrolling Elites are facing away from Ezio, free run and climb onto the scaffolds. You can now move undetected to a position above Tarik. Press the Target Lock button to select him in the crowd, then perform an air assassination to fulfill the Full Synch condition.

BEAT UP DUCCIO

Sequence 06 begins with Ezio standing at the heart of the Constantine district. If you take a short diversion before attending to other tasks or Memories, you can meet a familiar face. Follow the route pictured here to reach Duccio, once betrothed to Ezio's sister Claudia and, more recently, an aspiring suitor to Sofia Sartor. Switch to Ezio's fists and beat the libertine up to unlock the Bully Achievement or Trophy.

03

MEMORY 03

BEARER OF MIXED TIDINGS: Though the Memory Start marker is situated at the heart of Topkapi Palace, this Memory begins when you enter the Restricted Area that surrounds the entire palace and its grounds. Ezio cannot be detected at any point during the journey, but is allowed to reach Suleiman by any route you choose. We suggest that you attempt to find your own way in to meet the prince on your first try: navigating this huge area unseen is an enjoyable challenge. You can, however, find the easiest way to meet with Suleiman (and effortlessly complete the Full Synch requirement) on the page to your right.

Fortunately, leaving the palace is much easier than making your way in, but you must move purposefully after the cinematic ends. Follow the route in the accompanying screenshot to reach a position shielded from Janissary eyes, then watch the four soldiers patrolling in the grounds below (📷 03). When they walk away from Ezio, drop down and run over to the outer wall; from here, climb to the outside of the palace or dive into the water below to complete the Memory.

MEMORY 04

A LITTLE ERRAND: After speaking with Sofia, travel to the waypoint to meet the florist. Maintain a safe distance when you tail him: the route isn't complicated, and you can easily hide or Blend when he turns to examine the path behind him (📷 04). Pick three white tulips when prompted to do so, then travel to meet Sofia at the final waypoint.

MEMORY 05

SIGNS AND SYMBOLS, PART III: Climb to the perch high on the column to reach the Memory Start position, then – as previously – activate Eagle Sense to scan your surroundings for Polo Symbols. Once you have located the book, ascend to the rooftop to collect it from the waypoint.

The next Memory will take Ezio away from the streets of Constantinople for a time, so send all of your Assassins on contracts and make a withdrawal from a Bank before you continue.

04

BEARER OF MIXED TIDINGS: FULL SYNCH

Though the Full Synch requirement does not allow Ezio to kill any guards, you can sneak up behind lone sentries and perform non-lethal takedowns if he is unarmed. By using the route detailed here, however, you won't need to engage in combat at all.

Scale the outer wall in the far northeast of the Imperial district, close to the lighthouse (📷 05), then traverse to the left on the ledge to reach a tower. Wait until the patrolling sentry looks away, then jump onto the tower; this marks the formal beginning of the Memory.

05

From the tower, watch the patrolling Janissaries from above, then leap down to the lower level when they face away (📷 06). Move to the far side of this wall section. When the Janissaries walk past to the right, run to the east and climb the second set of pillars to reach a ledge beneath the balcony. Wait for the patrolling Janissary to move to your left, then climb up behind the two stationary sentries and run to meet with Suleiman at the waypoint.

06

ENEMY ARCHETYPE

Though encountered far less frequently than other enemy archetypes, and usually stationed on rooftops, **Bombmen** can be awkward opponents unless you neutralize them quickly. They will draw a sword to fight in close proximity, but may sheathe this at any time to begin bombarding Ezio with explosive projectiles. As long as he is equipped with suitable armor, the stun effect of these devices is more dangerous than the damage they inflict. In a pitched brawl, however, having Ezio reeling from the effect of each impact can be ruinous. As with Gunmen, it pays to disable them quickly at the start of any confrontation. If they are attacking from range, a single Throwing Knife will suffice.

PRIMER

WALKTHROUGH

SIDE QUESTS

REFERENCE & ANALYSIS

MULTIPLAYER

EXTRAS

INDEX

USER INSTRUCTIONS

SEQUENCE 01

SEQUENCE 02

SEQUENCE 03

SEQUENCE 04

SEQUENCE 05

SEQUENCE 06

SEQUENCE 07

SEQUENCE 08

SEQUENCE 09

MEMORY 06

THE MAIDEN'S TOWER: Speak to the man at the Memory Start marker in the southeast of the city to begin. This Memory features a number of timer-based "puzzles" that challenge you to move between switches before a countdown expires. The trick to completing each one without incident is to identify the required route beforehand – something that the annotated screenshots in this section should make a great deal easier. If you fail in a timed challenge, you must retrace your steps to the switch and try again.

I: Interact with the highlighted manhole cover, then examine the grate directly ahead. Pull the lever, then follow the route pictured here to reach and interact with a mechanism before the timer expires. After the cutscene, jump over to the ledges on the giant stone block, climb down, then perform a Back Eject to reach the ledges behind Ezio. From here, descend, move around the corner, and perform another Back Eject to reach a small walkway. Use the protruding ledges to reach a large platform in the center of the room, then free run to the east to reach the next waypoint.

II: Pull the lever to begin the countdown, then climb the nearby ledges after the cutscene. Perform a Back Eject at the top to reach a pole, and swing to the next ledge. Jump to the hanging fixture and press the Empty Hand button to perform a Long Jump, then hop over to the ledge directly ahead when you land (🎮). Traverse to the left, then perform a Side Eject to the adjacent ledge. Jump over to the platform, then take a left. You will see the next mechanism in the distance. Free run in a straight line to reach it. Once you have stopped the countdown, travel to the next waypoint to the west.

III: Pull the lever, then jump to the ledges directly ahead after the cutscene ends and climb up. Free run all the way to the north, then turn and head east until you reach an opening to your right. As illustrated on the screenshot, hop over the broken archways to reach a column with three evenly spaced ledges; climb to the top of these, then traverse to the left and Back Eject to the column behind Ezio. Traverse a little to the right, then Back Eject to the protruding ledge. You can now free run to the east to operate the next mechanism.

IV: Pull the next lever, then jump over to the ledge on the stone block suspended to the right of it. Traverse to the left, around the corner, until the camera angle changes, then Back Eject to the narrow metal platform. Free run all the way to the west corner of the room (📷); though it may not be immediately apparent, there is a ledge that Ezio will grab after swinging on the final pole. Traverse to the right, then perform a Side Eject onto the ledge protruding from the wall. Free run to the north over these ledges, then face east at the final one. Jump to the pole and swing through the opening to reach the mechanism.

V: After the cutscene that reveals the location of the Masyaf Key, climb the ledges directly ahead. At the top, turn left and free run over to the ledges to the west, then climb to the top of the stone block. Jump onto the ledges further west, climb to the top, then ascend the wooden ledges to your left (📷).

VI: Climb the wooden frame on the stone block in front of you, then jump over to the next set of ledges and Hook Leap to the top (📷). Turn left and leap over to the central platform to reach the Masyaf Key. Loot the Treasure Chests, then interact with the statue to end the Memory.

MEMORY 07

THE MENTOR'S RETURN: Travel to the Assassin's HQ to begin the next Altaïr Memory. When it starts, follow the Assassin up the slope, then walk between the two captains to perform a double assassination. Trail the next captain until he marshals his troops then, ignoring all other combatants, run straight over to assassinate him (or, should he attack, fell him with a Counter Kill). The final captain at the gates will pledge himself to his former mentor, so simply walk past him into the castle.

After the cutscene, Altaïr has the ability to order Assassins to kill anyone who attempts to engage him (press the Assassin Signal button), but this will cause you to fail the Full Synch condition. Instead, disarm them or just press the Primary Attack button to defeat them with instant non-lethal takedowns (📷 07). After the next cinematic, hold and then release the Secondary Attack button to execute Abbas, and end the Memory.

MEMORY 08

SETTING SAIL: This Memory marks the beginning of an extended stay away from Constantinople: see "Loose Ends" on the page to your right for details. Having a full stock of Smoke Screen bombs and other projectiles before you begin may help if you wish to secure Full Synchronization, but are not mandatory.

After the conversation with Yusuf, head towards the waypoint. Hire the group of Romani to distract the two Janissaries standing guard, then watch the two patrols at the top of the steps. If the patrol that stops at the top is taken in by the Romani show, just stroll straight past them; if not, wait for them to walk away, then run behind them to reach the base of the Great Chain. Interact with it immediately before you are detected (📷 08).

After the spectacular cinematic interlude, disengage Combat Mode and simply run straight past the Ottomans (use the Hook and Run move if necessary) to reach the boat. Climb onto the upper deck to the left and wait for your allies to deal with the aggressors. If any hostiles should follow you,

07

74

you can perform a Grab and hurl them overboard. Approach the Greek Fire Cannon at the waypoint and press the Empty Hand button to use it. Hold the Weapon Hand button to unleash a continuous torrent of fire and, moving from left to right, destroy each ship in turn; the larger vessels must be targeted in a handful of positions.

In the final section of the Memory, free run and climb between the regularly spaced waypoints to reach the departing ship before the timer expires. When Ezio is confronted by a group of Ottomans, just ignore them and sprint for the final waypoint to end the Sequence. Back on Animus Island, listen to the conversation, then enter the portal to begin Sequence 07.

08

LOOSE ENDS

Ezio leaves Constantinople for an entire Sequence after the conclusion of Memory 08, so it's wise to attend to unfinished business in the city before you start it.

■ Without wishing to spoil anything, it would be remiss not to warn you that Ezio's return to the region for Sequence 08 introduces certain complications that will make it more difficult to complete Secondary Memories and other miscellaneous tasks.

■ Ezio cannot call his Assassins into combat or send them on Mediterranean Defense missions during Sequence 07, so try to send all available recruits and apprentices on the most lengthy and lucrative assignments you can find before you begin Memory 08.

■ If you have yet to clear all Templar Dens and purchase all shops in the Rebuilding Constantinople metagame, this is a good time to invest the effort. You will still accrue revenue and be able to withdraw it from a Bank while away from Constantinople, so it's definitely worthwhile.

■ In the event that you have been frugal with capacity upgrades so far, this is an opportune moment to visit a Blacksmith and a Tailor to purchase better armor, weapons and carrying capacity enhancements.

SEQUENCE 07: UNDERWORLD

source\S17.anima.08212002.TW90aGVyU2Fk
source\S17.anima.08212002.RmF0aGVyTWFk
source\S17.anima.22072002.Trh90aGluZ0lzVHJ1ZQ==
source\S17.anima.22072002.RXZicnI0aGluZ0lzUGVybWl0dGVk
source\S17.anima.04022003.Om9uZWRPZndibcINQb3.InZXM=

MEMORY 01

THE HIDDEN CITY: Run to the waypoint to enter the caves of Cappadocia then travel to the imposing column of rock at the center of the cavern. Though the Full Synchronization condition may lead you to believe that the Byzantines in this area are in a stage of high alert, that isn't the case: they will only react if you trespass on rooftops or draw their attention through reprehensible acts.

Follow the climbing course on the rock column to reach a Viewpoint high above (📷 01). Synchronize with it, then perform a Leap of Faith. There may be a Gunman on the roof where you land, so don't emerge from the haystack immediately. You can assassinate him as he walks past if you wish. Drop back to the streets, then run to the Doctor's stall inside the green search zone, west of a Bank. Scan the small crowd beside the physician with Eagle Sense to identify the spy, then chase after her when she flees. Colliding with a Byzantine guard will lead to conflict, so take care as you run through the narrow alleyway.

MEMORY 02

THE SPY WHO SHUNNED ME: Head to the waypoint marker in the south of the cavern to begin this Memory. The steps leading to the prison cells are a Restricted Area, so wait until there are no Byzantine patrols at the bottom before you run up.

After the cinematic, use the free run course on the south wall to leave the Restricted Area without attracting attention. The guard who holds the key can be found in the northwest area of the green search zone among a crowd watching a fight (📷 02). Pickpocket him, then quickly walk away before he can spot Ezio.

Return to the prison. There is now a group of guards at the foot of the steps leading to the Restricted Area, so climb to a rooftop just east of their position and free run above them, retracing your steps earlier. Interact with the cell door to unlock it.

01

02

CAPPADOCIA

The events of Sequence 07 take place entirely in the caverns of Cappadocia. While much smaller than Constantinople, you will find that it has all the amenities you will need for the foreseeable future.

■ The subterranean settlement has a Bank, Blacksmith, Tailor, Book Shop, three Doctors, two Black Market Dealers and a single Crafting Table. Though you cannot access the Mediterranean Defense interface during your stay here, you will find all other requirements are catered for. However, as the area is under Byzantine control, you will pay a 10% premium on base prices from all stores (though Black Market Dealers are exempt from Templar taxation).

■ Though we suggest that you save most major purchases until Sequence 08 due to the Templar tax, there are certain weapons and books that can only be acquired in Cappadocia: see pages 148 and 149 respectively.

■ Cappadocia has twelve hidden Animus Data Fragments and a dozen Treasure Chests to collect and loot respectively. You can find a map revealing the locations of these on page 126 of the Side Quests chapter. However, those seeking full 100% Synchronization should note that it is not essential that you attend to this task before the end of the Sequence. The open-ended start to Memory 01 means that you can use the Replay Memory feature to return here and find collectibles at a later date. The same applies with shop purchases if you cannot afford them on your first visit.

■ Memory 04 marks the start of four consecutive Memories, with no real opportunities to shop or explore. If you have business to attend to in Cappadocia, do by the end of Memory 03 at the latest.

PRIMER

WALKTHROUGH

SIDE QUESTS

REFERENCE & ANALYSIS

MULTIPLAYER

EXTRAS

INDEX

USER INSTRUCTIONS

SEQUENCE 01

SEQUENCE 02

SEQUENCE 03

SEQUENCE 04

SEQUENCE 05

SEQUENCE 06

SEQUENCE 07

SEQUENCE 08

SEQUENCE 09

MEMORY 03

THE RENEGADE: Speak with Dilara at the Memory Start position in the west of the city. The Full Synch objective here is to assassinate Shahkulu before Janos loses half of his total health. First, though, you must dispatch four Gunmen stationed above the arena (📷 03).

Free run to the west after the cinematic; when you reach the broken pillar, traverse to the right-hand side and tap the Primary Attack button to assassinate the first Gunman. Follow the route detailed in the accompanying screenshot to kill the remaining sentries, then run out onto the cross and acquire a Target Lock on Shahkulu before you tap the Primary Attack button to leap down.

In the fight that ensues, perform Counter Kills on guards to set up Kill Streaks, then land blows on Shahkulu. He's very similar to the Janissary archetype in terms of his overall endurance and resistance to certain attacks. When you face him on his own, use dodges to set up combos, or stick to basic counterattacks. When he finally falls, the Memory ends.

03

MEMORY 04

DECOMMISSIONED: The Full Synch condition for this Memory requires that Ezio sustains no damage of any kind, so it's prudent to craft or purchase a full complement of each variety of bomb before you begin. You should also ensure that you have a full supply of Medicine (and, ideally, all related capacity upgrades) for a later Memory.

After the opening cutscene, follow the route you took to reach the Viewpoint earlier, but instead run over the ropes spanning the gap between the rock column and the outer wall when you reach the third waypoint. Now use the free run course to reach a fourth waypoint.

04

This is where the danger begins if you are determined to meet the Full Synch requirement. This area contains several groups of Byzantines consisting of the Militia and Almogavar enemy archetypes. We suggest that you use bombs to wipe out or incapacitate larger groups before they detect Ezio (📷 04), and use projectiles on individuals or pairs. Quick flurries of individual Throwing Knives work rather well.

Loot the chest at the waypoint marker to collect the Incendiary Explosive, then climb the stairs. There are many more Byzantines to fight here, including a large group at the end, so inch forward carefully and try to engage them separately. Take the time to loot all fallen foes to resupply your stock of knives, bullets and Crossbow bolts. When you reach a dead end, interact with the gate to end the Memory.

MEMORY 05

LAST OF THE PALAIOLOGI: This Memory begins automatically on completion of Decommissioned. Once again, Ezio must sustain no damage for you to complete the Full Synch requirement, though it's rather easier to achieve that here.

05

Your priority here is to keep up with Manuel, not fight his henchmen, so we suggest that you stick to the rooftops and evade the Byzantines. Follow the route specified in the accompanying screenshot to reach a zipline (📷 05), then ride it down. Drop carefully to ground level close to Manuel to trigger a cinematic. When it ends, sprint straight for the gate and climb over it; if you are seeking to achieve Full Synch, you will find it beneficial to drop a bomb of some description immediately once play resumes.

When you catch up with Manual, he can be dispatched with a simple Counter Kill – though you can also run away and employ projectiles from a safe distance if you are feeling especially cautious.

MEMORY 06

ESCAPE: Fight the initial group of guards when the Memory begins, then loot their corpses to resupply (with Medicine a priority). Now run to the waypoint. After the cutscene, you will find the cavern filled with smoke from the fires Ezio started earlier. This becomes a thick fog as you run to the exit, requiring that you activate Eagle Sense to navigate (📷 06). A further complication is that Ezio will periodically lose health as he suffers the effects of smoke inhalation; this also momentarily disables Eagle Sense. The Full Synch condition for this Memory specifies that Ezio's Health Meter should not fall below 50%, but you can regularly top it up with Medicine to prevent that.

See the page to your right for a guide to the quickest route to the cavern exit. Byzantine guards will attack when you emerge into the sunlight, but there is no need to fight these: just sprint to the final waypoint to end the Memory.

06

MEMORY 07

PASSING THE TORCH: After the opening cinematic, walk through the gate and head down the slopes to reach the village. Whenever assailants attempt to engage Altaïr, hold the Primary Attack button to unleash the awesome power of the Apple of Eden. When you reach a tower, climb to the top of the ladder and use the Apple to wipe out all hostiles on the battlefield, then descend to rejoin the Polo brothers below. The Memory ends when you reach the next waypoint.

PRIMER

WALKTHROUGH

SIDE QUESTS

REFERENCE & ANALYSIS

MULTIPLAYER

EXTRAS

INDEX

USER INSTRUCTIONS

SEQUENCE 01

SEQUENCE 02

SEQUENCE 03

SEQUENCE 04

SEQUENCE 05

SEQUENCE 06

SEQUENCE 07

SEQUENCE 08

SEQUENCE 09

MEMORY 06: ESCAPE ROUTE

The escape from the smoke-filled underground settlement can be hugely disorienting. In the following sequence of screenshots, we show the quickest route out of the cavern.

I: From your starting position at the gate, run up the slope to your left. When you draw level with a building to Ezio's right, climb up to the left.

II: From the rooftop, run over the wooden beam to the east, hop over the beams protruding from the north wall of the cavern, then swing on a pole to reach a canopy.

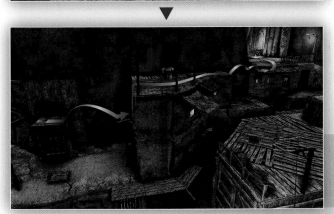

III: From the canopy, climb the wall directly ahead, then continue east. After hopping over another beam, the exit tunnel is just off to your left.

MEMORY 01

DISCOVERY: *Important!* Though you can return to Constantinople after seeing the story to its conclusion, this is your last real opportunity to complete Secondary Memories until the end of the final Sequence.

Memory 01 begins once you enter Sofia's bookshop. Walk into the back room and examine Yusuf. When play resumes, drop down to street level and run through the gate. This is the best position to complete the Full Synch requirement. You will find that Ezio's brother Assassins will rather get in the way, but it's not too difficult to achieve once you start a Kill Streak (📷 01).

You have an infinite number of Assassin Signals at your disposal during this Memory, so use Arrow Storms when you need them as you head to the waypoint where Ahmet awaits.

01

MEMORY 02

THE EXCHANGE: Ezio is now being hunted by every Ottoman patrol in the city, so it may be wise to use a Tunnel Entrance to travel to the Memory Start position inside the Assassin's HQ. This is your very last opportunity to send Assassins on contracts or buy equipment for a long time; with the Ottomans on high alert, all other activities are impractical.

After starting the Memory, travel to the graveyard close to Galata Tower. If you are short on Medicine, replenish your stocks with the Doctor standing just outside the entrance (📷 02). When the cutscene ends, travel to the waypoint to meet with Ahmet. Once the cinematic is over, you have two minutes to scale Galata Tower; experienced climbers should achieve this in half the time.

After Ahmet's deception is revealed, leap from the edge of the tower in the direction of the next waypoint and press the Primary Attack button to deploy a parachute. Steer left and right to avoid incoming bullets, then press the Empty Hand button to drop when you near Sofia; press it again to save her when the prompt appears.

MEMORY 03

END OF THE ROAD: This action-packed finale to Sequence 08 begins with Ezio riding a carriage and beset by two Templar vehicles on either side. You must collide with these and steer them into rough terrain to damage and eventually destroy them. Further along, there are positions where the "safe" part of the course narrows to the width of a single cart. When you reach these, time your movements carefully to ride through without damage.

Pay close attention when a cutscene begins and, once the prompt appears, press the Empty Hand button to deploy Ezio's parachute. In the set piece that follows, steer Ezio away from hazards with 🅛. When you fly above Templars on horseback, press the Primary Attack button to assassinate them, or press the Empty Hand button to perform a throw. The latter technique can be used to hurl an opponent's body into one of his peers, effectively disabling two assailants with a single attack. Use 🅛 to specify the direction that Ezio will throw his victim, though note that it is far easier to accomplish kills on Templars directly ahead than those to either side (📷 03).

The course becomes more difficult as you progress, with greater numbers of Templars and some technically demanding sequences of buildings and other obstacles to negotiate. Don't be frugal with Medicine: use it whenever it is needed.

When Ahmet and Ezio clash in a most unconventional fashion, press the High Profile button to defend whenever the prince draws his arm back to strike, and the Primary Attack button to pummel him at all other times.

02

03

PRIMER

WALKTHROUGH

SIDE QUESTS

REFERENCE & ANALYSIS

MULTIPLAYER

EXTRAS

INDEX

USER INSTRUCTIONS

SEQUENCE 01

SEQUENCE 02

SEQUENCE 03

SEQUENCE 04

SEQUENCE 05

SEQUENCE 06

SEQUENCE 07

SEQUENCE 08

SEQUENCE 09

SEQUENCE 09: REVELATIONS

MEMORY 01, 02 & 03

A HOMECOMING: Walk with Sofia until you reach a door, then press the Empty Hand button to pass through it. Approach the entrance to the secret library and tap the button again; now activate Eagle Sense to see the lines of the constellations. This begins a brief puzzle where you must use the five Masyaf Keys to unlock the way forward. The onscreen instructions and Sofia's insightful clues should make this an approachable brain-teaser, though you can find a full solution at the bottom of the page.

With the door open, stroll along the corridor; Ezio will light torches as he reaches them. Approach the chair to begin the next Memory (📷 01).

LOST LEGACY: As Altaïr, walk along the corridor; with an affecting symmetry, he will automatically extinguish each torch in turn. Walk to the back of the room, then approach the chair.

THE MESSAGE: Finally, back with Ezio, walk to the secret panel at the back of the room… then sit back to watch the closing cinematics.

Once the credit crawl ends, Desmond can reenter the Animus Island portal and return to Constantinople as Ezio. The Ottoman military returns to its pre-Sequence 08 state, and you are free to clear outstanding objectives and replay Memories as you see fit. If you have focused on Core Memories over optional tasks, turn the page to reach the Side Quests chapter and learn about the many further activities you can enjoy.

01

LIBRARY ENTRANCE SOLUTION

Pick up each Masyaf Key in turn, and move it to the position specified in this screenshot; rotate each one to complete missing sections of the constellation.

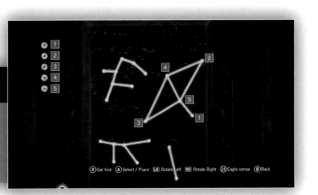

81

SIDE QUESTS

Packed with walkthroughs, analysis and tips covering every "optional" activity in Assassin's Creed Revelations, this chapter offers everything you need to complete all Secondary Memories and gain a maximum 100% Synch rating.

source\S16.anima.08082012.SSBBbSBOb3QgQWxpdmU=
source\S17.anima.09082012.QmFkV2VhdGhlcg==
source\S17.anima.10082012.TmluZVilYXJzQWxvbmU=
source\S17.anima.17092012.QXJIWW91RGVzbW9uZElpbGVzPw==

This diagram reveals the feature unlock progression in Assassin's Creed Revelations along a timeline of Core Memories. You can use this to plan your approach to optional activities separate to the main storyline, and as a jumping-off point to all guidance in this chapter.

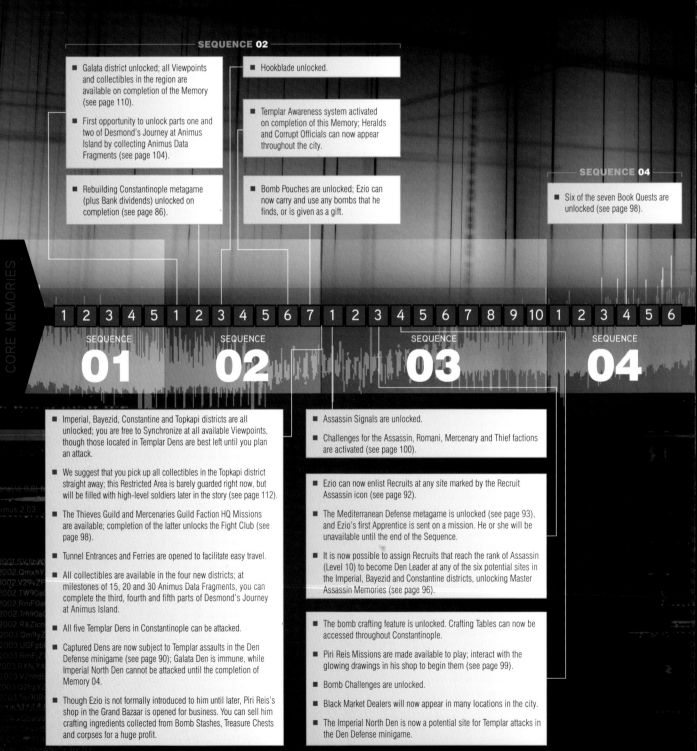

SEQUENCE 02

- Galata district unlocked; all Viewpoints and collectibles in the region are available on completion of the Memory (see page 110).

- First opportunity to unlock parts one and two of Desmond's Journey at Animus Island by collecting Animus Data Fragments (see page 104).

- Rebuilding Constantinople metagame (plus Bank dividends) unlocked on completion (see page 86).

- Hookblade unlocked.

- Templar Awareness system activated on completion of this Memory; Heralds and Corrupt Officials can now appear throughout the city.

- Bomb Pouches are unlocked; Ezio can now carry and use any bombs that he finds, or is given as a gift.

SEQUENCE 04

- Six of the seven Book Quests are unlocked (see page 98).

CORE MEMORIES

1 2 3 4 5 | 1 2 3 4 5 6 7 | 1 2 3 4 5 6 7 8 9 10 | 1 2 3 4 5 6

SEQUENCE **01**   SEQUENCE **02**   SEQUENCE **03**   SEQUENCE **04**

- Imperial, Bayezid, Constantine and Topkapi districts are all unlocked; you are free to Synchronize at all available Viewpoints, though those located in Templar Dens are best left until you plan an attack.

- We suggest that you pick up all collectibles in the Topkapi district straight away; this Restricted Area is barely guarded right now, but will be filled with high-level soldiers later in the story (see page 112).

- The Thieves Guild and Mercenaries Guild Faction HQ Missions are available; completion of the latter unlocks the Fight Club (see page 98).

- Tunnel Entrances and Ferries are opened to facilitate easy travel.

- All collectibles are available in the four new districts; at milestones of 15, 20 and 30 Animus Data Fragments, you can complete the third, fourth and fifth parts of Desmond's Journey at Animus Island.

- All five Templar Dens in Constantinople can be attacked.

- Captured Dens are now subject to Templar assaults in the Den Defense minigame (see page 90); Galata Den is immune, while Imperial North Den cannot be attacked until the completion of Memory 04.

- Though Ezio is not formally introduced to him until later, Piri Reis's shop in the Grand Bazaar is opened for business. You can sell him crafting ingredients collected from Bomb Stashes, Treasure Chests and corpses for a huge profit.

- Assassin Signals are unlocked.

- Challenges for the Assassin, Romani, Mercenary and Thief factions are activated (see page 100).

- Ezio can now enlist Recruits at any site marked by the Recruit Assassin icon (see page 92).

- The Mediterranean Defense metagame is unlocked (see page 93), and Ezio's first Apprentice is sent on a mission. He or she will be unavailable until the end of the Sequence.

- It is now possible to assign Recruits that reach the rank of Assassin (Level 10) to become Den Leader at any of the six potential sites in the Imperial, Bayezid and Constantine districts, unlocking Master Assassin Memories (see page 96).

- The bomb crafting feature is unlocked. Crafting Tables can now be accessed throughout Constantinople.

- Piri Reis Missions are made available to play; interact with the glowing drawings in his shop to begin them (see page 99).

- Bomb Challenges are unlocked.

- Black Market Dealers will now appear in many locations in the city.

- The Imperial North Den is now a potential site for Templar attacks in the Den Defense minigame.

PRIMER

WALKTHROUGH

SIDE QUESTS

REFERENCE &
ANALYSIS

MULTIPLAYER

EXTRAS

INDEX

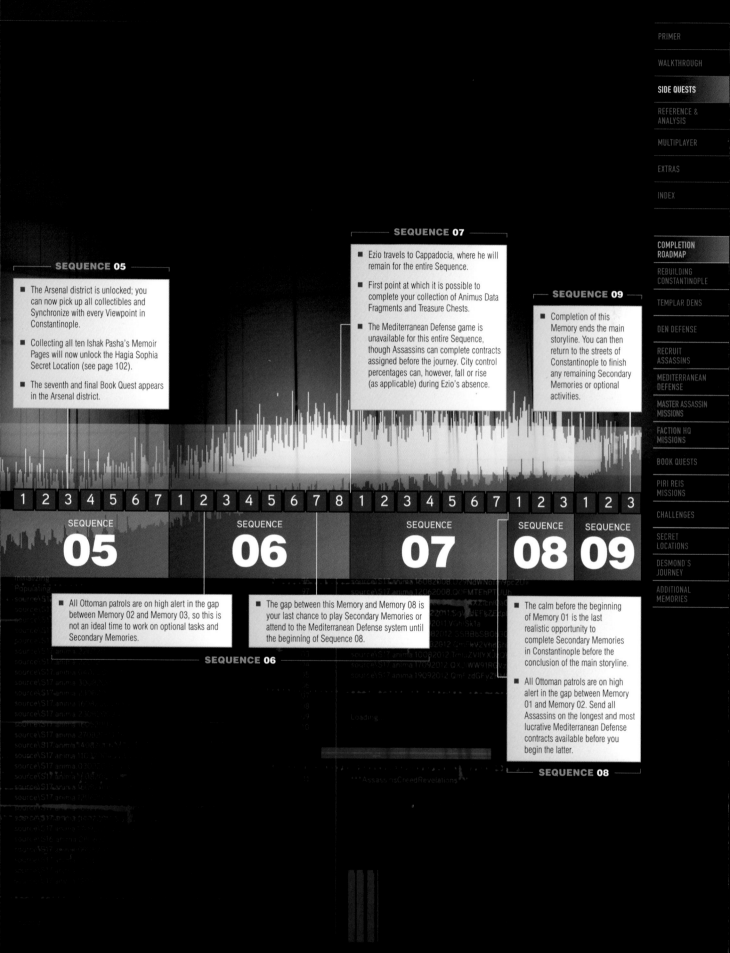

SEQUENCE 07

- Ezio travels to Cappadocia, where he will remain for the entire Sequence.

- First point at which it is possible to complete your collection of Animus Data Fragments and Treasure Chests.

- The Mediterranean Defense game is unavailable for this entire Sequence, though Assassins can complete contracts assigned before the journey. City control percentages can, however, fall or rise (as applicable) during Ezio's absence.

SEQUENCE 05

- The Arsenal district is unlocked; you can now pick up all collectibles and Synchronize with every Viewpoint in Constantinople.

- Collecting all ten Ishak Pasha's Memoir Pages will now unlock the Hagia Sophia Secret Location (see page 102).

- The seventh and final Book Quest appears in the Arsenal district.

SEQUENCE 09

- Completion of this Memory ends the main storyline. You can then return to the streets of Constantinople to finish any remaining Secondary Memories or optional activities.

1 2 3 4 5 6 7 | 1 2 3 4 5 6 7 8 | 1 2 3 4 5 6 7 | 1 2 3 | 1 2 3

SEQUENCE **05**

SEQUENCE **06**

SEQUENCE **07**

SEQUENCE **08**

SEQUENCE **09**

- All Ottoman patrols are on high alert in the gap between Memory 02 and Memory 03, so this is not an ideal time to work on optional tasks and Secondary Memories.

- The gap between this Memory and Memory 08 is your last chance to play Secondary Memories or attend to the Mediterranean Defense system until the beginning of Sequence 08.

SEQUENCE 06

- The calm before the beginning of Memory 01 is the last realistic opportunity to complete Secondary Memories in Constantinople before the conclusion of the main storyline.

- All Ottoman patrols are on high alert in the gap between Memory 01 and Memory 02. Send all Assassins on the longest and most lucrative Mediterranean Defense contracts available before you begin the latter.

SEQUENCE 08

Though you can complete the main story without involving yourself in this metagame, spending Akçe on Shops, Faction Buildings and (to a far lesser extent) Landmarks can provide a huge amount of income for comparatively little effort. Start building Ezio's property portfolio at an early stage, and the dividends you gradually accrue can be used to bankroll further investments and expensive equipment purchases.

GENERAL INFORMATION

- The ability to renovate buildings and businesses is unlocked early in Sequence 02, when Ezio will earn his first payment. You are awarded with one Bank, Blacksmith, Tailor, Doctor and Book Shop automatically, and these will lead to small dividends right from the start. To collect income, visit a Bank and select the Withdraw Money option. The Bank interface also enables you to view information on your progress in the Rebuilding Constantinople metagame.

- Though more expensive than other businesses, opening Banks increases the maximum Vault Capacity. If you do not make regular withdrawals from Banks, any Akçe held over this threshold will be lost. Bank deposits are made at intervals of every 20 minutes of play time – which represents an in-game "day" – with the clock frozen whenever an interface screen is open, such as the Pause menu or Mediterranean Defense interface.

- Shops and Banks provide by far the best profit return on your initial investment, but the cost of opening them increases with each successive site. Though Banks are necessary to increase the maximum Vault Capacity, opening shops also offers the convenience of always having a vendor nearby when you need to pick up supplies.

- In addition to providing a modest income, Empty Faction Buildings enable you to choose a Faction to inhabit the premises. Based on your decision, groups of Thieves, Mercenaries or Romanies will be made available to hire in the area surrounding the restored Faction Building.

- Landmarks are by far the most expensive property purchases and, given the relatively small payments Ezio receives from them, are best left until last.

- On the main map and mini-map, icons representing buildings that you have purchased are a bright white; those that are available for investment are gray. Ezio can only restore shops and buildings in regions free of Templar influence. Until the local Den has been captured, all potential renovations in its vicinity are represented by a padlock icon (🔒). If an Assassin Den is Contested or falls back into Templar hands after a failed Den Defense, no income can be accumulated from its surrounding region until you assert Assassin control.

- Investing in each building leads to a 20% increase in the Templar Awareness meter. When it reaches full Aware status, there is a small chance that each further renovation can trigger a Templar attack on an Assassin Den. In practice, though, the likelihood of causing a Den Defense situation is significantly lower than it is for starting a fight. It's often possible to renovate all buildings in an entire district without repercussions if you can also avoid open conflict.

- Though some might see it as cheating, leaving the game running with Ezio standing safely in a Den will enable you to make a large Bank withdrawal on your return.

RESTORATION STRATEGY

The strategy that we present here is designed for players seeking to achieve 100% completion in the most orderly and time-efficient manner possible.

Though it requires a not inconsiderable degree of extra time and effort, purchasing Treasure Maps from Book Shops and methodically working your way through the city to open the majority of them while liberating each Templar Den in turn will fund the early expansion of Ezio's business empire. You can efficiently combine this undertaking with other optional tasks, such as the Mediterranean Defense metagame, completing Secondary Memories and collecting Animus Data Fragments. Though the sums of hard currency you accumulate from Treasure Chests are rarely spectacular, the additional crafting ingredients you find can be sold for a *substantial* profit. If you also loot the Bomb Stashes you encounter during your journey, each district can lead to a comfortable five-figure return when you sell the raw materials to Piri Reis.

Treasure Chests: Per District Profits

TREASURE MAP	PRICE (A)*	TOTAL CHEST CONTENTS (A)
Galata District 1	704	2,774
Galata District 2	1,125	1,357
Imperial District 1	807	7,122
Imperial District 2	1,173	6,706
Bayezid District 1	743	5,687
Bayezid District 2	1,971	5,810
Constantine District 1	763	3,813
Constantine District 2	1,389	4,194
Arsenal District	1,203	4,159
Cappadocia 1	1,215	1,529
Cappadocia 2	1,936	2,690

*This is the adjusted price with the 15% Assassin district discount.

- **Sequence 02, Memory 02**: The end of this Memory marks the first occasion when you can head out and begin purchasing properties in the Galata district, and there is a benefit for doing so: at this point, the Templar Awareness system is disabled. Head to the open Book Shop and purchase both Treasure Maps for the Galata district. These make it easier to hunt Treasure Chests, as you can pinpoint their precise location and elevation with a Custom Marker on the Map screen. You will receive Bank deposits while you hunt for them, which will enable you to afford all but the Galata Tower Landmark before you continue. This will raise your 20-minute dividends to 2,850 A.

- **Sequence 03, Memory 03**: Once the Mediterranean Defense system is unlocked, visit Piri Reis to sell your stock of crafting ingredients, send your first Recruit on a mission, then purchase both Treasure Maps for the Imperial district and begin opening all available business premises and the sole Faction Building. Ignore the Templar Awareness Meter entirely for now: Galata Den cannot be attacked, while the Imperial North Den is granted temporary immunity until the completion of Memory 04. Once you have finished, your dividends will have increased to 6,500 Ａ every 20 minutes.

- **Before the end of Sequence 03**: Ideally, you should invest the time to conquer each Templar Den in turn, methodically unlocking all shops and Faction Buildings that you can afford after each success, and recruit Assassins to gain further income from the Mediterranean Defense game. With eleven Recruits working on contracts (Ezio's first Recruit is unavailable until the end of the Sequence), you can both generate plenty of income and work towards unlocking the Master Assassin Missions while you complete the Core Memories of this Sequence.

- **Sequence 04**: Unlock all remaining Banks, shops and Faction Buildings early in this Sequence. Once Ezio is receiving the lion's share of potential income from Constantinople, begin to purchase Landmarks as and when you can afford them.

- **Sequence 08**: This is your last opportunity to purchase buildings in Constantinople before the end of the story, so spend the funds accumulated during Ezio's stay in Cappadocia on any remaining Landmarks.

REFERENCE TABLES

Renovation Bonuses

RENOVATION	INCOME BONUS (Ａ)
Blacksmith	275
Doctor	250
Book Shop	275
Tailor	250
Bank	300
Faction Building	150
Landmark	See table to the right

Landmark Restorations

TYPE	RENOVATION	COST (Ａ)	INCOME BONUS (Ａ)
Landmarks 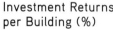	Gul Mosque	38,100	+600
	Myrelaion Church	45,600	+600
	Hagia Eirene	40,000	+600
	Hagia Sofia	60,000	+1,100
	Hippodrome	46,200	+900
	Grand Bazaar	42,350	+800
	Galata Tower	27,000	+350
	Column of Marcian	28,700	+350
	Valens Aqueduct	49,750	+1,100
	Forum of Constantine	29,750	+450
	Forum of OX	32,300	+450
	Fatih Mosque	35,000	+450
	Zeyrek Mosque	33,450	+600
	Little Hagia Sophia	44,400	+800
	Beyazid Mosque	37,250	+800
	Sub-totals	**589,850**	**+9,950**

Investment Returns per Building (%)

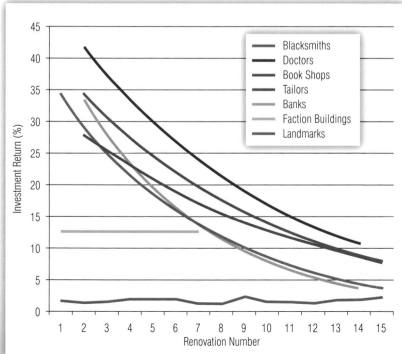

Shop & Building Restorations

SHOP/ BUILDING	RENOVATION	COST (Ａ)
Blacksmiths	#1	800
	#2	936
	#3	1,095
	#4	1,281
	#5	1,499
	#6	1,754
	#7	2,052
	#8	2,401
	#9	2,809
	#10	3,287
	#11	3,845
	#12	4,499
	#13	5,264
	#14	6,159
	#15	7,206
	Sub-total	**44,888**
Doctors	#1	-
	#2	600
	#3	672
	#4	753
	#5	843
	#6	944
	#7	1,057
	#8	1,184
	#9	1,326
	#10	1,486
	#11	1,664
	#12	1,864
	#13	2,087
	#14	2,338
	Sub-total	**16,817**
Tailors	#1	-
	#2	900
	#3	995
	#4	1,099
	#5	1,214
	#6	1,342
	#7	1,483
	#8	1,638
	#9	1,810
	#10	2,001
	#11	2,211
	#12	2,443
	#13	2,699
	#14	2,983
	#15	3,296
	Sub-total	**26,112**
Book Shops	#1	-
	#2	800
	#3	896
	#4	1,004
	#5	1,124
	#6	1,259
	#7	1,410
	#8	1,579
	#9	1,769
	#10	1,981
	#11	2,218
	#12	2,485
	#13	2,783
	#14	3,117
	#15	3,491
	Sub-total	**25,914**
Banks	#1	-
	#2	900
	#3	1,080
	#4	1,296
	#5	1,555
	#6	1,866
	#7	2,239
	#8	2,687
	#9	3,225
	#10	3,870
	#11	4,644
	#12	5,573
	#13	6,687
	#14	8,024
	Sub-total	**43,647**
Faction Buildings	#1	1,200
	#2	1,200
	#3	1,200
	#4	1,200
	#5	1,200
	#6	1,200
	#7	1,200
	Sub-total	**8,400**

TEMPLAR DENS

Liberating Templar Dens is the only way to enjoy the full benefits of the Mediterranean Defense and Rebuilding Constantinople metagames, or to play the twelve Master Assassin Missions. Before we begin, a few tips and observations:

- As revealed in the final Memory of Sequence 02, you must kill the Templar Captain in the Restricted Area surrounding a Den before lighting the Signal Fire to conquer a region. There are four distinct types of Captains: Some are **cowards** (icon) and will flee if they spot Ezio; if they reach an escape point before he can kill them, they will remain hidden for twenty minutes. Other Captains are **bold** (icon) and will gladly lock blades with Ezio. Finally, some Captains are **marked**, with their positions revealed by the corresponding icon the moment you enter the Restricted Area. Others are **unmarked**, and must be identified with Eagle Sense.

- A full stock of Throwing Knives and Poison is essential for each attack on a Templar Den. The Poison Dart weapon is extraordinarily efficient. Rooftop sentries in Templar Dens are extremely vigilant, and will frequently move to investigate even a brief sighting of Ezio. Use this to your advantage, luring Gunmen to positions where you can safely ambush them.

- Marksmen booths in Templar Dens make frontal assaults extremely inadvisable. Marksmen are removed immediately once the local Captain has been killed.

- Take the time to purchase buildings in other districts before you liberate a Den. As the Templar Awareness Meter is automatically set to Aware when you light the Signal Fire, this will save time spent tracking down Heralds and Corrupt Officials. However, avoid attacking a Den while at full Aware status: this will almost always trigger a Den Defense scenario.

IMPERIAL NORTH DEN

Captain Type: Bold, marked.

Strategy: Though Ezio liberates this Den at the conclusion of Sequence 02, it can fall back into Templar hands if you fail a Den Defense here at any time after Memory 04 of Sequence 03. The strategy required to kill the Captain is broadly the same as the one we suggested in the Walkthrough chapter for the earlier, story-mandated assault (see page 38), but with one key difference: he will now stay under the cover of the building marked in the screenshot. Approach the Restricted Area from the south and kill the two nearby sentries. You now need to lure the Captain into the open. A Cherry Bomb will achieve this immediately, but you can also throw one of the slain Gunmen to the ground. Punish the Captain's curiosity with a Poison Dart, then climb the tower and light the Signal Fire.

IMPERIAL SOUTH DEN

Captain Type: Bold, initially unmarked – and there are actually *two* of them. One holds a rifle, while the other favors a sword.

Strategy: The arrangement of Marksmen booths makes it difficult to approach the heart of this Den. Use a Tunnel Entrance to reach the South Port destination, then approach the Templar Den from the southwest and climb the building marked here. Kill the sentry on the rooftop above, then quickly move onto the ropes and use Eagle Sense to watch the path to the north. The patrol route of the two Templar Captains will take them past this position, so ready your Poison Darts and hit both once you have them in range. Climb to the top of the building to your right, and you can leap straight over to the Signal Fire tower to await their demise.

BAYEZID NORTH DEN

Captain Type: Coward, unmarked.

Strategy: This Coward is particularly vigilant, and has the ability to detect Ezio from a fair distance. Approach the Den from the south, and stand on the rooftop marked here; there may be an Ottoman Gunman that you must deal with first. The Captain's patrol route will take him past this position; he will be walking with a bodyguard. Identify him with Eagle Sense from a safe distance, then quickly drop down and target him with a Poison Dart when his back is turned. If he moves out of range before you open fire, you can run on top of the covered walkway and ambush him at the far side. In the event that he flees, you have a moderate chance of catching him in a footrace to his bolt-hole: use ranged weapons once you have a clear shot at his back.

BAYEZID SOUTH DEN

Captain Type: Coward, marked.

Strategy: Approach the southeast corner of the Restricted Area and climb the building shown here; there is a group of four Templars nearby that you may wish to distract, or you can start your initial climb further north, out of sight. On the rooftop, kill the Gunman without attracting attention. The Captain can be found walking around the central area, inspecting his troops. Wait until he moves to the south then, when he is facing away from you, hit him with a Poison Dart. There are Gunmen on the west side of the street, but you should be able to poison the Captain before they react. An alternative strategy is to perform a short Leap of Faith into the hay cart, then lie in wait and assassinate your target as he walks past.

CONSTANTINE NORTH DEN

Captain Type: Coward, marked.

Strategy: This Captain can be found on a rooftop in the south of the Restricted Area, and his tendency to stroll around can make it hard to catch him unawares. For that reason, a direct and aggressive strategy works best. We recommend that you wait until you have six Assassins free to perform an Arrow Storm before you begin. Follow the route highlighted in the accompanying screenshot, then jump straight over to the Captain's building and climb up. If he sees Ezio, use your Arrow Storm; if not, simply run over and perform an assassination.

CONSTANTINE SOUTH DEN

Captain Type: Bold, unmarked.

Strategy: Approach the Restricted Area from the east, and kill the Ottoman sentry and a Templar to reach a zipline. Ride it at full speed, then perform a zipline assassination on the individuals marked here – one of whom, fortuitously, is the Captain you seek. Like all best laid plans, there is a slight chance that this one can go awry: there are two Varangians who occasionally stop close to the Captain, and Ezio may target these instead. Should this occur, retreat to the nearby steps marked here: this provides cover from Marksmen, and therefore a place to finish off your target in a straight fight – or, of course, to incapacitate everyone with a bomb and end the conflict with a simple assassination.

Whenever the Templar Awareness Meter is in the Aware status, performing actions that lead to meter increases (see page 157) may provoke a Templar attack on an Assassin Den. This shifts the status of the Den to Contested. The region surrounding it will be populated with Templars, and Marksmen booths will be occupied by Gunmen. You must infiltrate the Restricted Area and interact with the front door of the Den to trigger the Den Defense minigame and attempt to repel the assault.

Successfully completing a Den Defense leads to monetary rewards, crafting ingredients, XP for Ezio's Assassins, and unit unlocks for future Den Defense scenarios. Failure will cause the Den to switch back to Templar control, and Ezio must once again kill the local Captain and light the Signal Fire to reassert Assassin dominance in the region.

If you have a particular penchant for this minigame, the quickest way to trigger a Den Defense is to fill the meter by any method you deem appropriate, then enter a Templar Den and kill a few Templars in open conflict. If all Dens are under Assassin control, you'll just need to pick on Ottomans instead. If you would prefer to avoid Den Defense situations, assigning an Assassin to a Den and completing both parts of his or her Master Assassin training (see page 96) will cause that Den to become "locked", rendering it immune to future Templar attacks.

DEFENSE STRATEGY

Preparations and Opening Tactics

- Before the battle, study the varieties and numbers of each enemy type you will face during the siege. This will enable you to decide which units to choose using the Edit function. Consult the reference tables for advice on the relationships between different Assassin and Templar units.

- When the battle begins, a slightly risky opening strategy will pay off over the course of the engagement. Depending on how many Morale points you start with, position at least two Leaders on rooftops immediately, then quickly position a handful of affordable Crossbowmen on the rooftops close to the first Templar wave. Aim to have all available rooftops occupied by a Leader after a couple of waves to maximize Morale generation: each one contributes two points every ten seconds, which soon stacks up.

- This tactic leaves you with very few units for the first few waves, so it's pivotal that you fire Ezio's Pistol constantly to support your Crossbowmen. If an early wave should feature a large group of opponents, use a single Cannon burst to destroy them as they arrive.

- As soon as you can afford it, drop your best Barricade to create a choke point close to your troops, but a few steps back to create an area where opponents can be slaughtered

before they reach the barrier. Barricades with weaponry will always be much more efficient. As a rule, try to save upgrades until a Barricade is damaged, as each one will instantly replenish its health gauge.

Midpoint Tactics

- Whenever you are not positioning units, constantly use the Pistol to shoot opponents and sweep the screen to loot enemy corpses (press the Empty Hand button) to gain Morale bonuses. Focus Pistol fire on enemies that your troops are weakest against, or those that present the greatest danger to your defense.

- Pay close attention to the display in the upper right corner of the screen, as it reveals which types of unit are incoming. This is especially useful for identifying Stalkers in advance, as these can cut through rooftop units at a ferocious rate. It will also enable you to be ready for enemy Bombmen, as they represent a huge threat to Barricades: these can be worth a Cannon attack if they appear before the final third of a battle where you face a Siege Engine.

- As units closest to the position where Templar forces arrive are most vulnerable to attack, you should generally position cheaper Assassins on these rooftops, such as Crossbowmen and Air Assassins. Fill the remaining rooftops around your principle choke point with more powerful units (especially Riflemen), and you will rarely encounter any difficulties during the middle part of a battle.

- Create a second choke point with a Barricade and begin to fill the nearby rooftops with additional troops. For battles where you face a Siege Engine, you may wish to take this preparation even further.

- Be liberal in your use of the Cannon during the first half of each Den Defense, then allow the gauge to recharge in the second half of the battle if the Templars have a Siege Engine. Fire it in single bursts: the big area-of-effect attack that empties all three segments of the gauge isn't nearly as efficient as three individual blasts.

Endgame

- If your build order is sound, you will accumulate more Morale than you need or can use. If you have a surplus, consider selling your weaker units to replace them with those more appropriate to the final third of the battle. If an enemy Siege Engine is due to arrive, for example, you can replace Air Assassins and Crossbowmen with the significantly more effective Splinter Bombers.

- Once a Siege Engine appears, hit it with Cannon blasts. While you wait for the meter to recharge, attrition is always the best tactic. Place Barricades armed with the best weapons available to you at tight intervals to slow its advance and, if possible, replace your barriers as soon as they are destroyed.

REFERENCE TABLES

Assassin Units

ICON	NAME	MORALE COST	HEALTH POINTS	MELEE DAMAGE	RANGED DAMAGE	NOTES
	Leader	10	150	50	-	Generates Morale every ten seconds. Place these on every rooftop early in the battle.
	Crossbowman	10	150	50	34	Position these close to where enemies arrive. This way, Templar Stalkers and Riflemen will attack them first, and they're cheap to replace.
	Rifleman	15	150	50	90	Great against armored foes; powerful but slow. Having a number fire in unison will often cause weaker opponents to break and flee. A staple unit type.
	Splinter Bomber	25	150	50	50	Good against large groups (has a 2.9 meter radius), and more likely to hit multiple opponents if used in conjunction with a Caltrop Bomber. A good choice of replacement for units that don't inflict damage on Siege Engines if you position them just before the Templar machines arrive.
	Caltrop Bomber	15	150	50	25	These slow down Templar forces within a 2.9 meter radius. Most efficient when positioned just in front of your main Barricade choke point and combined with Splinter Bombers.
	Bruiser	10	150	150	-	The best unit to place behind Barricades, with a 25% resistance to enemy damage. However, with a solid defensive strategy, these are more of a luxury than a necessity; note that they are easily squashed by Siege Engines, and so are best sold in advance of their arrival.
	Air Assassin	10	150	50	Kill	Only effective against human enemies, but will kill up to two of them instantly. Position them on rooftops closest to where Templar forces arrive.

Assassin Barricades

ICON	NAME	MORALE COST	HEALTH (LEVEL 1)	HEALTH (LEVEL 2)	HEALTH (LEVEL 3)	DAMAGE	NOTES
	Barricade	10 (upgrades: 15)	750	1,500	2,250	–	Effectively rendered obsolete once you gain Barricades with weapons, though you can use them in emergencies when funds are tight, or to slow down Siege Engines.
	Greek Fire Barricade	20 (upgrades: 20)	500	1,000	1,500	30 per second	Poor range and damage, but better than the standard Barricade – and it's cheap, too. Effective against large groups of weaker opponents.
	Multi-Barrel Gun Barricade	30 (upgrades: 20)	500	1,000	1,500	100 per shot	Better range and firepower than the Greek Fire Barricade, but less efficient against large groups of Templars.
	Cannon Barricade	40 (upgrades: 25)	750	1,500	2,250	200 per shot	The most expensive Barricade, but categorically the most powerful, with a 1.2 meter damage radius. Place it wisely, and it will hit most enemy waves before they even draw near: it's essentially a free Cannon shot every few seconds.

Templar Units

ICON	NAME	HEALTH POINTS	DAMAGE VS. ASSASSINS	DAMAGE VS. BARRICADES	NOTES
	Militia	34	35	7	Weak to Assassin Crossbowmen.
	Almogavar	100	75	7	Weak to Assassin Riflemen.
	Scout	80	75	–	Can climb Barricades and attack Assassins behind them.
	Infiltrator	68	50	–	Can climb Barricades, going straight for the Den. Eliminate them with your Pistol.
	Rifleman	68	50 (ranged) 25 (melee)	10	Weak to Air Assassins.
	Bombman	100	25	250	Left unchecked, these opponents can tear down a Barricade almost instantly. Focus fire on them with your Pistol, or use a Cannon shot if several appear at once. Air Assassins positioned at the forefront of your defense can help against these.
	Stalker	80	75	–	Kill them with your Pistol as an absolute top priority, or they will slaughter your assassins with great speed. You can track them by looking for their icon.

Templar Siege Engines

ICON	NAME	HEALTH POINTS	DAMAGE	NOTES
	Battering Ram	5,000	500 per attack	Can easily destroy even the strongest Barricade.
	Greek Fire	4,000	250 per second	Inflicts heavy damage to Barricades and defenders alike.
	Machine Gun	4,500	25 per shot	Provides covering fire for invading Templar troops.
	Cannon	4,500	800 per attack	Fires volleys at the Assassin Den from a great distance, dealing devastating damage. You can "distract" them by constantly replacing the armed Barricades that they destroy.

PRIMER

WALKTHROUGH

SIDE QUESTS

REFERENCE & ANALYSIS

MULTIPLAYER

EXTRAS

INDEX

COMPLETION ROADMAP

REBUILDING CONSTANTINOPLE

TEMPLAR DENS

DEN DEFENSE

RECRUIT ASSASSINS

MEDITERRANEAN DEFENSE

MASTER ASSASSIN MISSIONS

FACTION HQ MISSIONS

BOOK QUESTS

PIRI REIS MISSIONS

CHALLENGES

SECRET LOCATIONS

DESMOND'S JOURNEY

ADDITIONAL MEMORIES

After liberating Templar Dens, and whenever you have spaces free in your Mediterranean Defense roster, Recruit Assassin markers will appear in areas under Assassin control.

There are two types of potential Recruit Assassin scenarios: six short Secondary Memories (covered here) that tell the stories of individual Recruits and count towards the 100% Synch rating, and "generic" enlisting opportunities where you will find a prospective Recruit confronted by Templars. If you can kill these aggressors and save the citizen, they will automatically pledge themselves to the Assassin cause.

■ All Recruit Assassins Memories are technically available from the end of Sequence 03, Memory 03, though you will also need to capture Templar Dens in each region to unlock them (with the exception of The Avenger, which

appears automatically in the Galata district after you conquer the first Templar Den of your own choosing). There is a Recruit Assassins Memory to play in each region with the exception of the Imperial North and Arsenal districts.

■ Completing Recruit Assassins Memories will cause "generic" recruiting sites to spawn in the surrounding region.

■ There are only Templar Awareness penalties for recruiting Assassins from generic recruitment sites: Recruit Assassins Memories only contribute small increments based on your actions in combat.

■ The starting rank and weapon of the Assassin you receive is random, though the game code will take steps to ensure that you get a good balance of different weapon specialists.

MEMORY
THE BRAWLER

AVAILABILITY
Capture Constantine North Den

WALKTHROUGH
Talk to the highlighted individual outside the Fight Ring; Ezio must then beat a pugilist in a fistfight. The opponent evades punches, and regularly employs the Throw Sand technique. Use a kick or dodge to break his guard, then launch combos to weaken him. Kicks interrupt his attempts to use the Throw Sand move, so represent the quickest way to defeat him. Speak to the man at the waypoint marker to end the Memory.

MEMORY
THE ACROBAT

AVAILABILITY
Capture Beyezid South Den

WALKTHROUGH
This Memory is a short walk to the north after you light the Signal Fire to liberate Beyezid South Den, and starts immediately if you approach the area marked by the Recruit Assassin icon; you may wish to reduce your Templar Awareness status before you begin. Once you start the Memory, defend the Acrobat by killing the three marked targets. Follow her over the rooftops until she returns to ground level, then kill the guards who attack; when combat ends, speak to her to end the Memory.

MEMORY
THE PUPIL

AVAILABILITY
Capture Constantine South Den

WALKTHROUGH
This individual will automatically run to meet Ezio after you light the Constantine South Den Signal Fire and perform a Leap of Faith back to the ground. The Memory does not feature any conflict, so it's safe to complete it now and clear your Templar Awareness Meter afterwards. The prospective Recruit challenges Ezio to a race; beat him to the final waypoint to enlist him.

MEMORY
THE BEGGARS

AVAILABILITY
Capture Imperial South Den

WALKTHROUGH
Talk to the highlighted man to begin the Memory. Activate Eagle Sense, then follow the trail and identify your target within the green search zone. Chase after the thief and, avoiding citizens greedily rushing to collect the coins she liberally distributes, knock her from her feet with the Leg Sweep move.

MEMORY
THE AVENGER

AVAILABILITY
From Sequence 03, Memory 03

WALKTHROUGH
Speak to the injured man in the graveyard east of Galata Tower, then head south over the rooftops until you reach the green search zone. Activate Eagle Sense to identify the target in the courtyard below, then kill him by any method you please – a simple Throwing Knife will suffice if you would prefer to avoid conflict. Return to the man and speak to him to gain your new Recruit.

MEMORY
THE PICKPOCKET

AVAILABILITY
Capture Bayezid North Den

WALKTHROUGH
Walk into the marker a short distance south from the Bayezid North Den to begin the Memory. Use Eagle Sense to identify your target, then speak with the thief. You must then pickpocket 150 **A** before the timer expires. There are guard patrols in the area, so try to target civilians a safe distance away from them, changing positions in accordance with their movements.

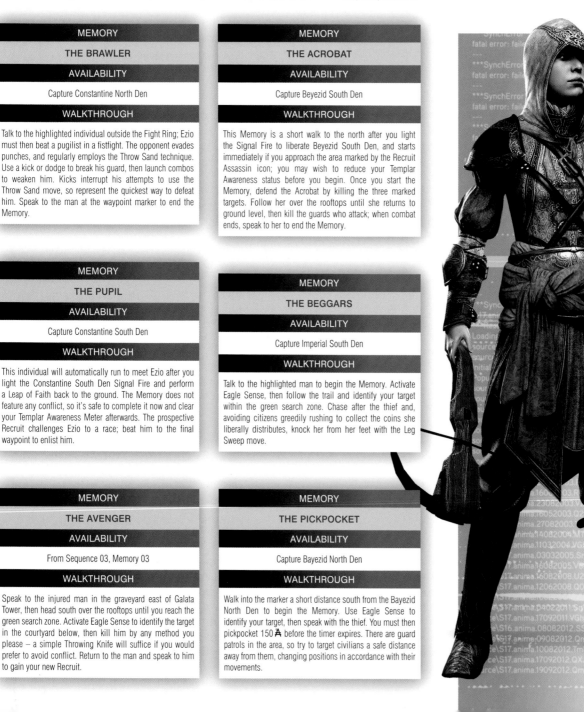

PRIMER

WALKTHROUGH

SIDE QUESTS

REFERENCE &
ANALYSIS

MULTIPLAYER

EXTRAS

INDEX

MEDITERRANEAN DEFENSE

THE BASICS

Unlocked in Sequence 03, the Mediterranean Defense metagame is both a great source of income and the means by which you can access the Master Assassin Missions: twelve significant episodes with fantastic rewards (see page 96).

Once you have acquired your first Assassin, we advise that you liberate all Templar Dens in Constantinople as a matter of urgency, as this will enable you to have a full twelve Recruits working on contracts (and, as a consequence, gaining in experience and levels) from an early stage in the story. To access the Mediterranean Defense interface, either visit a Pigeon Coop situated next to a Crafting Table in assorted locations throughout Constantinople, or interact with the maps found inside all Assassin Dens, the Assassin's HQ, or Piri Reis's shop in the Grand Bazaar.

When you open the interface, you have two options: Assassins and Mediterranean Defense. The **Assassins** menu enables you to study your current roster and spend Skill Points on armor and weapon upgrades. Assassins acquire Skill Points every time they gain a rank by accumulating experience points (XP). The most efficient method of earning XP is to send them on **Mediterranean Defense** contracts. This menu features a list of cities. Select these to study missions that Assassins can be sent on.

Every potential mission has up to six primary characteristics:

- **Requirement:** Certain unique missions require a cash investment from Ezio.

- **Difficulty:** A general indication of how hard the mission will be to complete; this is expressed with greater accuracy in the Odds of Success rating once you assign an Assassin (or multiple Assassins) to a contract. There are two main varieties of missions. *Generic missions* (marked by diamonds: ◆) are always replaced on completion, and are never in short supply. *Unique missions* (marked by stars: ✱) can only be undertaken once. It is an Assassin's rank alone that governs their Odds of Success in all missions.

- **Money:** The funds that Ezio will receive on successful completion of the mission.

- **XP:** The total experience points available on completion of the contract. If multiple Assassins are sent to complete a mission, this sum will be divided between the participants.

- **Synch Duration:** The number of minutes in active play time before the contract will be completed. As with the Rebuilding Constantinople system, the game clock is frozen whenever an interface screen is open. Assassins sent on contracts are unavailable for duties via the Assassin Signal button until they return.

- **Templar Control:** This indicates the effect that the mission will have on Templar hegemony in the city. See overleaf for details.

Once you have selected a mission, you can assign up to five Assassins to undertake it. After choosing an initial candidate, the Odds of Success bar will be filled to show the probability (as a percentage) that he or she will successfully complete it. If it is less than 100%, you can increase it by selecting additional Assassins. Any mission that you begin with an Odds of Success rating lower than 100% carries a chance, however slender, that the assignment will fail. Should this occur the Assassins will be killed (with the exception of Den Leaders – more on which overleaf), and must be replaced by new Recruits.

Each Assassin has a specific weapon specialty displayed beneath their portrait. Some generic missions can only be undertaken if you have a particular type of specialist available. However, after they have been assigned to the mission, you can boost the Odds of Success rating if required by adding Assassins of any type to the contract roster.

When you send Assassins on missions, you will receive a notification once the contract has been completed, plus information on any levels gained. To collect the rewards, study additional information and assign Skill Points (if applicable), visit the Mediterranean Defense interface via the nearest access point.

ASSASSINS GUILD: TRAINING STRATEGY

Once you have liberated Templar Dens, the most important task to accomplish in the Mediterranean Defense system is to rapidly advance six Recruits to Level 10. At this point, you can assign each of them to your Dens throughout Constantinople. This transforms them into Den Leaders. Complete the first Master Assassin Mission that this unlocks, and you can then level them up even further. When a Den Leader reaches Level 14 with a full XP gauge, you can complete the second part of their Master Assassin Mission to elevate them to Level 15. At this point, no further progress is possible.

■ To train Recruits rapidly – especially your first six raw enlistees, who will be the most likely candidates for Den Leader status – focus on contracts that offer the best XP return.

■ ◆ to ◆◆◆ generic contracts are only worthwhile if you have no other option at lower levels. Once your Recruits reach higher levels, start to send them in groups on more challenging ◆◆◆◆ generic contracts, or the easier unique contracts.

■ Save unique contracts with extremely high XP returns and ◆◆◆◆◆ generic contracts for Den Leaders alone until they all reach Master Assassin status. Those where you can send a single Den Leader on a mission with a 100% Odds of Success rating allow for very rapid advancement.

■ After focusing specifically on maxing out your Den Leaders (and turning them into Master Assassins), you can use these as "trainers" to vastly accelerate the development of all other Recruits. The XP gained

from a ◆◆◆◆◆ generic contract will cause a raw Recruit to gain several levels at once.

■ Complete Set 1 of the Assassins Guild Challenges (see page 100) to unlock a 10% bonus to the Odds of Success rating for the first Assassin assigned to a mission. Any subsequent Assassins added to the roster do not have this bonus applied.

Ezio can have a maximum of seven Master Assassins, including the individual assigned to you automatically during the events of Sequence 03. All other Recruitss can only reach Level 10: at that point, no further progress is possible. Den Leaders and Master Assassins also have a unique perk: they cannot die. Even if they fail a mission, or fall in combat while assisting Ezio, they will survive any wounds they sustain – though they will be unavailable for a period of convalescence.

Generic Mission Details

CONTRACT	AVERAGE DURATION (MM:SS)	AVERAGE A PER MINUTE	AVERAGE XP PER MINUTE
◆	4:00	162.50	3.13
◆◆	5:50	145.45	6.36
◆◆◆	7:00	142.86	17.14
◆◆◆◆	9:00	133.33	52.78
◆◆◆◆◆	10:50	128.57	204.76
◆◆◆◆◆◆	17:50	111.43	285.71

Assassin Ranks

LEVEL	RANK	XP
1	Recruit	0
2	Initiate	10
3	Apprentice	30
4	Novice	80
5	Footpad	180
6	Disciple	350
7	Mercenary	600
8	Warrior	1,000
9	Veteran	1,500
10	Assassin	2,500
11	Assassin, Second Rank	3,800
12	Assassin, Third Rank	5,600
13	Assassin, Fourth Rank	8,000
14	Assassin, Fifth Rank	11,000
15	Master Assassin	15,500

Assassin Upgrades*

TYPE	NAME	UPGRADE
	Default	Health = 60
	Upgrade 1	Health +15
	Upgrade 2	Health +30
ARMOR	Upgrade 3	Health +45
	Upgrade 4	Health +60
	Upgrade 5	Health +75
	Upgrade 1	■ Damage x1.5 ■ Unlocks the Combo and Kick moves
	Upgrade 2	■ Damage x2 ■ Unlocks the Special Attack and Combo Kill moves
COMBAT	Upgrade 3	■ Damage x2.5 ■ Unlocks Counter Dodge move
	Upgrade 4	■ Damage x3 ■ Unlocks Counter Kills
	Upgrade 5	■ Damage x4 ■ Improves Counter Kills

* Skill Points assigned to Assassins only govern their effectiveness when called into combat with the Assassin Signal button.

XP and Akçe Gains per Minute: Comparison*

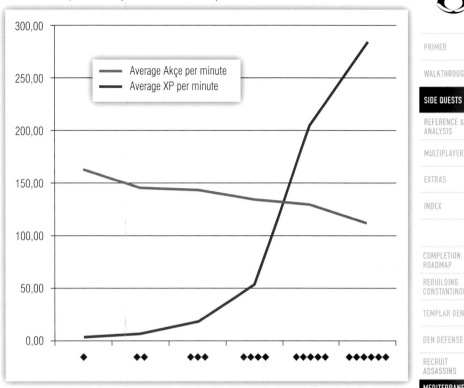

— Average Akçe per minute
— Average XP per minute

♦   ♦♦   ♦♦♦   ♦♦♦♦   ♦♦♦♦♦   ♦♦♦♦♦♦

There is a direct correlation between the time required to complete a contract and its XP reward: lengthier missions present the best returns. The opposite is true for money, where shorter assignments generally offer greater profitability. That said, constantly returning to the Mediterranean Defense interface to assign Assassins to ♦ and ♦♦ missions can be a little tiresome; we prefer to assign them to ♦♦♦, ♦♦♦♦ and ♦♦♦♦ ♦ contracts for the convenience. Protracted ♦♦♦♦♦♦ missions require more than one Master Assassin to complete, and so are inefficient as a method of generating income.

RECLAIMING CITIES

At the start of the Mediterranean Defense metagame, every city in the region has a 100% Templar Control rating. Each completed mission reduces Templar Control by the specified percentage, though the rating will slowly creep back up over time if you subsequently do not complete other contracts in the city. To liberate a city from Templar governance, select the Reclaim the City unique contract. The difficulty of this assignment is determined by the current Templar Control percentage; the lower this is, the higher the Odds of Success rating will be.

Successfully completing the Reclaim the City mission for each region will switch control from the Templars to the Assassins. On your next visit to the Mediterranean Defense menu, you will be asked to select a new leader for the city.

- Each liberated city has an Assassin Control rating. The rank of the Assassin you assign to the city determines the maximum possible percentage. An Assassin sent to a city is removed from your Mediterranean Defense roster, leaving a space for a new Recruit. You can swap Assassins not engaged in contracts with those assigned to cities at any time (press the Primary Attack button while selecting a city to do so).

- Cities living under the auspices of the Assassins generate XP for all Assassins garrisoned there, money for Ezio, and crafting ingredients. Funds accrued from a city are added to Bank deposits; the other rewards are credited directly.

- Reclaiming a city unlocks a host of new unique contracts. The majority of those require Ezio to spend money to upgrade the city's infrastructure. Installing each additional Assassin Den enables you to send another

person to the region, boosting the maximum potential Assassin Control rating. Most other unique contracts either offer a bonus to XP or Akçe dividends that the city provides every 20 minutes of play time.

- The Assassin Control rating declines steadily over time, and can only be replenished by completing contracts in the city; increasing the maximum Assassin Control rating by installing new Dens and assigning Assassins reduces the chance of Templar attacks.

- If you intend to conquer cities gradually, you could consider designating one city as a "training academy", with a maximum number of Dens and XP upgrades. As you conquer each city and enlist new Recruits, you could then send them to this locale to reach Level 10 until you swap them out and assign them to another region at a later date.

- Think hard before spending Akçe on unique contracts that contribute revenue increases. A mission that costs 1,500 Å for a 150 Å increment is a business venture that requires ten 20-minute dividend cycles (over three hours of game time) to break even. This is worth spending money on only if you still have plenty to do in Constantinople.

- If Assassin Control ever falls to 0%, the city will be Contested. Until you send Assassins to complete the Defend the City mission that appears, you will receive no further dividends from the region. If you fail in a Defend the City mission, the city will fall back into Templar hands. All Assassins assigned to the region will be held as hostages until you retake it.

- Sending Master Assassins to cities will not affect the status of their Den in Constantinople: it will remain immune to Templar attack.

MASTER ASSASSIN MISSIONS

Once you have a Level 10 Assassin available, and not currently occupied on a contract, visit an Assassin Den where the Master Assassin Mission icon appears (◭), and walk into the highlighted area. Pick him from the interface to assign him as Den Leader, then speak to him to begin the first part of the Master Assassin Mission unique to that Den.

You can assign Den Leaders to all six Dens in the Imperial, Bayezid and Constantine districts after removing Templar control from those areas. Completing Part 1 of all six missions unlocks the Master Assassin's Armor, and there are some rather fine weapons provided by individual Memories. Better still, completing Part 2 of each Den's Master Assassin Missions will cause that Den to become "locked", and immune to Templar attacks. Once you have finished them all, the Den Defense scenarios will cease to occur – which is something to bear in mind if you really enjoy the mini-game.

Note: There is a Challenge that requires you to provoke and win three Den Defense scenarios. If you would like to achieve 100% Synch, be sure to complete this requirement before you finish all Master Assassin Missions.

MISSION
THE DEACON, PART 1
AVAILABILITY
Assign a Leader to the Bayezid North Den.
BONUS REWARD
Unlocks Yusuf's Turkish Kijil at the Assassin's HQ.
WALKTHROUGH

Head to the waypoint, then run up the steps and scan the individual standing opposite a tree on the upper level to complete the Full Synch objective; speak to him to advance the story. When the conversation ends, travel to the next waypoint, avoiding the obvious route if you wish to skip conflict with the Templars in the area. Use Eagle Sense when prompted to identify the target to the right of the Tunnel Entrance, then escort your Den Leader to the waterfront via the waypoints.

MISSION
THE TRICKSTER, PART 1
AVAILABILITY
Assign a Leader to the Constantine North Den.
BONUS REWARD
Unlocks Mehmet's Dagger at the Assassin's HQ.
WALKTHROUGH

Walk with your Den Leader, then follow the marked Romanies. There are several potential ambushes along the path, but you can foil these by activating Eagle Sense; assassinate all targets marked by a light red glow. After the cutscene, you must use the Disarm technique to defeat the Ottoman Elites; to complete the Full Synch requirement, achieve this before any of the Romanies are killed. There is an easy way to meet this condition: if one of the onscreen Romani health meters falls below three blocks, kill one of the guards to cause immediate Desynchronization, then try again from the checkpoint.

MISSION
THE DEACON, PART 2
AVAILABILITY
Train the Bayezid North Den Leader to Level 14, with a full XP gauge.
WALKTHROUGH

After speaking with your Den Leader, head up the steps to the left of a Romani group, a short walk south from the Memory Start position. Scan the corpse with Eagle Sense, then follow the Deacon's trail until you reach a waypoint. When your Den Leader lures the target away, give chase but maintain a reasonable degree of distance. When you reach the ambush site, equip the Hidden Blade and run over to perform an assassination (to satisfy the Full Synch condition) before the fight can begin.

MISSION

THE TRICKSTER, PART 2

AVAILABILITY

Train the Constantine North Den Leader to Level 14, with a full XP gauge.

WALKTHROUGH

Ensure that you have at least two or three doses of Poison before you begin this Memory. Activate Eagle Sense and follow the trail – ignoring the red lines indicating guard patrols – until you reach The Trickster's position south of a Blacksmith on the west side of the Constantine district. Hit her with a Poison Dart to both complete the Memory and satisfy the Full Synch requirement.

MISSION

THE CHAMPION, PART 1

AVAILABILITY

Assign a Leader to the Bayezid South Den.

BONUS REWARD

Unlocks the Almogavar Axe at the Assassin's HQ.

WALKTHROUGH

Ownership of the Crossbow and capacity upgrades for Throwing Knives and the Hidden Gun are highly advisable. Walk with your Den Leader to hear their news, then ascend to the rooftop waypoint and follow from above; to complete the Full Synch objective, you must not touch the ground at any point in this part of the journey. Use ranged weapons to kill Templars as they attack (and Eagle Sense to identify them in advance, if you wish) until a brief cutscene begins. Chase after the Printer – the obligation to remain on the rooftops ends here – and defend him from the Templar attack, then return to the Den Leader.

MISSION

THE CHAMPION, PART 2

AVAILABILITY

Train the Bayezid South Den Leader to Level 14, with a full XP gauge.

WALKTHROUGH

To complete the Full Synch objective for this Memory, bombs crafted with Impact Shells are a necessity. Though Caltrop, Smoke Screen and Gold Bombs are all useful, the Stink Bomb is by far the most efficient choice; ensure that you have three, and sufficient ingredients to craft more if required. Walk with your Den Leader for an appraisal of the situation, then wait until the conversation with the Herald ends. When the Templar killers draw near, drop a Stink Bomb next to the Herald; dispatch the targets while they are incapacitated. As the clouds clear, use another bomb to prevent the next wave from reaching the Herald. Once your stocks are depleted, open the Weapon Selector screen and highlight the Stink Bomb; tap the Legs button to create more. This strategy makes a potentially infuriating Full Synch condition a formality. When the Champion arrives, move into the marked position to distract him, then tap the Assassin Signal button to instruct your Den Leader to make the kill.

MISSION

THE GUARDIAN, PART 1

AVAILABILITY

Assign a Leader to the Constantine South Den.

WALKTHROUGH

Ensure that you have plenty of Throwing Knives (and, optimally, own the Crossbow) before you begin this Memory. Kill the Templars who attack as you walk with your Den Leader, then approach the waypoint marker. Scan the chests in the market area, then speak with the highlighted merchant. After the cutscene, follow the Den Leader over the rooftops, killing any sentries or Templars who attack. When the final waypoint is revealed, you must sneak to that position without being detected to complete the Full Synch condition. Approach via the rooftops, eliminating Gunmen from range with projectiles, then stand on the roof directly above the waypoint. Watch the street below for patrols then, when the coast is clear, drop from the south face of the building and press forward on 🅛 to roll straight into the marker as you land.

MISSION

THE GUARDIAN, PART 2

AVAILABILITY

Train the Constantine South Den Leader to Level 14, with a full XP gauge.

WALKTHROUGH

Once the opening cinematic ends, follow the Rich Man from a safe distance. After the meeting, tail the Rich Man and the Byzantine soldier he meets until they head north through a guard post, then climb to the roof before the time limit expires; the Full Synch condition is satisfied at this point. Chase down and kill the soldier, then sprint to the waypoint and assassinate the Templar as he runs towards you.

MISSION

THE VIZIER, PART 1

AVAILABILITY

Assign a Leader to the Imperial North Den.

WALKTHROUGH

Walk with Ezio's Den Leader, then compete with him in a footrace through the streets; to complete the Full Synch objective, run to the north just after the race is suggested to gain a head start, then beat him to the ladder at the penultimate waypoint marker. After the cutscene on the rooftop, don't be too eager in your pursuit – follow the Templar Courier from a safe distance. Join the Den Leader to observe the events that unfold, then chase the Courier when instructed to do so. Killing him will immediately fill the Templar Awareness Meter completely, but there is a way to avoid this: perform the Leg Sweep move to knock your target from his feet, and the Den Leader will eventually catch up and inflict the mortal blow. With this task complete, speak to the individual at the waypoint marker to conclude the Memory.

MISSION

THE VIZIER, PART 2

AVAILABILITY

Train the Imperial North Den Leader to Level 14, with a full XP gauge.

WALKTHROUGH

This Memory begins with a frantic race against the clock, in which you have two minutes to locate your Den Leader. To complete the Full Synch condition, you must reach him within one minute without entering open conflict. Activate Eagle Sense and follow the trail; when you reach the Grand Bazaar entrance, hire the Thieves and instruct them to lure the guards away. Run along the first corridor leading south then take the first right; blend with the civilians to safely pass the Templar patrol, then take the next left, then a right. The location you are running towards is the small open-air courtyard slightly east of a Blacksmith. Performed at a reasonable speed (and perhaps with a practice run or two in advance), you can reach your Den Leader in approximately fifty seconds. Dive into the fray immediately, then follow your ally and fight further aggressors. When you kill the final two Almogavars, the Memory ends.

MISSION

THE THESPIAN, PART 1

AVAILABILITY

Assign a Leader to the Imperial South Den.

WALKTHROUGH

Though Ezio's Den Leader suggests that he should follow from the rooftops, it's easier to accomplish the Full Synch condition from street level. Once the target that you must track is revealed, stay out of sight until she walks to the east. You must now protect your Den Leader from attacks; fortunately, it is easy to identify prospective aggressors as they lie in wait by activating Eagle Sense; you can even assassinate them before they launch their attacks. Be careful not to move too close to the target you are tailing, as detection will return you to a previous checkpoint. When your Den Leader leaves street level, the immediate danger is over; once you hit a checkpoint, the completion of the Full Synch condition will be acknowledged. Follow your Den Leader into the Hippodrome until you reach a short cutscene. Walk through the opening leading to the outer area of the structure, then turn left; follow the path until you reach the corpses to end the Memory.

MISSION

THE THESPIAN, PART 2

AVAILABILITY

Train the Imperial South Den Leader to Level 14, with a full XP gauge.

WALKTHROUGH

Follow your Den Leader to reach a lofty vantage point. After the cutscene, you need to move swiftly to reach the target first. Your Den Leader will use a parachute to reach the ground, but you can ride the zipline to your left then leap from the rooftop; though Ezio will be injured in the fall, you can subsequently sprint to the target and assassinate her brazenly in front of the surrounding Templars. After the brief interlude, fight opponents in the immediate vicinity – an Arrow Storm can end this conflict almost instantly – then run along the dock to the west to escape.

MISSION
UNFORTUNATE SON

AVAILABILITY
From the start of Sequence 03.

WALKTHROUGH
Follow the Mercenaries out of their headquarters until you reach a green search zone; at this point, they will behave like a traditional Mercenary group. Order them to hold their position for the time being. Climb to the top of the building to the north and observe the Templars below; jump over to the roof above the captured Mercenaries to identify the individual you must save. There are several ways to complete this Memory without failing the Full Synch condition, but the most inventive is to wait for an Ottoman patrol on the road just south of this position to approach the street leading north, then throw a Cherry Bomb between the two groups of soldiers to cause them to clash. Target the Templars with ranged weapons from above – the capable Varangian in particular – then order your Mercenaries to finish off any survivors. Interact with the injured Mercenary, then pick him up with the Empty Hand button. Run straight to the waypoint, leaving the Templars stationed at the entrance to the courtyard for your hired group to fight. After conferring with the doctor, defeat the waves of Templar soldiers to end the Memory. Ezio can now partake in the Fight Club at the Mercenary HQ – see the box-out below for details.

MISSION
LOOSE LIPS

AVAILABILITY
From the start of Sequence 03.

WALKTHROUGH
Speak to the highlighted individual inside the Thieves HQ to begin this Memory, then rendezvous with the Thieves at the waypoint marker. Hire them as instructed, then climb to the rooftop above the guards. Order your faction to lure them away. Use Eagle Sense to identify the snitch in the crowd below; when he departs, follow him from a safe distance. Once you reach the Restricted Area, climb up and watch him from above (but out of sight) when you draw level with the group of Thieves above the street. After the cutscene, hire the Thieves and use a ladder to the south to reach the rooftop above the Benefactor. Target him, then order your hired group to lure him away. Follow via the rooftops and kill him by any method you desire once he moves outside the Restricted Area to complete both the Full Synch objective and the Memory.

▸ BOOK QUESTS

Six Book Quests become available from Sequence 04, Memory 04, with the seventh unlocked when the Arsenal district becomes available during Sequence 05. All Book Quests work in the same way: after reaching the Memory Start marker in a suitably lofty position, Ezio must scan his surroundings with Eagle Sense to locate a specific glowing Polo Symbol. With this initial task accomplished, travel to the waypoint and hold the Empty Hand button to retrieve the book. You can study notes on the books you have acquired in Book Quests in the library at the Assassin's HQ.

Completing all Book Quests and purchasing every book sold by merchants unlocks the Sage Achievement/Trophy. This includes the four books only available in Cappadocia which, at an incredible combined price of 352,303 Å,

might be somewhat beyond your means during your visit in Sequence 07. You can, however, return there (either via the Replay Memory feature or by taking the boat available on a dock on the east side of the Galata district) to purchase them after you have completed the main storyline.

⊗ FIGHT CLUB

Once you have completed the Unfortunate Son Faction HQ Mission, you can visit the dock south of the Mercenary HQ to participate in the Fight Club. There are five tiers of combat engagements to unlock, each with its own Award Multiplier that governs the return on the wager you can place before each bout. Neutralize all opponents within the tight time limits to win, and you can double your money at the highest tier; fail, and you leave the ring empty-handed.

QUEST	BOOK	REWARD (Å)
The Polo Symbols: Hippodrome	The Travels of Marco Polo	400
The Polo Symbols: Galata	One Thousand and One Nights	400
The Polo Symbols: Arsenal	The Book of Kings	400
The Polo Symbols: Forum of Ox	Nibelungenlied	400
The Polo Symbols: Aqueduct	Iliad	400
The Polo Symbols: Church I	The Canterbury Tales	400
The Polo Symbols: Church II	The Flute Girl	400

⊙ CITY EVENTS

City Events are random occurrences where Ezio can interact with civilians either in need of assistance or trying to pick a quarrel. These short, optional asides are not standard Memories, but offer a reward of 500 Å and crafting ingredients on completion. For example, if you find someone berating Ezio for "hiding behind a hood", look for a citizen with a distinct highlight; beat these braggarts up to claim your reward.

All Piri Reis Missions are available from the end of the Bomb Crafting Memory in Sequence 03. Each Memory will transport Ezio to a location in Constantinople, and acts as a tutorial on the use of different bombs. Interact with the boards to the right of his desk in his shop to begin these short missions. They all have (very simple) Full Synch conditions, so you can retry them at a later date via the Replay a Memory feature if required.

MISSION
PIRI REIS: SMOKE SCREEN
AVAILABILITY
After Sequence 03, Memory 04.
UNLOCKS
Phosphorus available for purchase from Piri Reis.
WALKTHROUGH
Follow the prompts to incapacitate the two groups of guards with Smoke Screen bombs – be warned that making contact with these soldiers will lead to Desynchronization – then activate Eagle Sense before you loot the specified container. Drop your third and final Smoke Screen bomb to temporarily neutralize the Janissaries at the front entrance, then sprint out of the highlighted area.

MISSION
PIRI REIS: SMOKE DECOY
AVAILABILITY
After Sequence 03, Memory 04.
UNLOCKS
Salt of Petra available for purchase from Piri Reis.
WALKTHROUGH
Throw a Smoke Decoy bomb at the target, then run past the guards and climb to the waypoint on the rooftop. After throwing the second bomb as prompted, perform a double air assassination on the two targets. Climb back to the rooftop from the alley and head south for an easy escape.

MISSION
PIRI REIS: STICKY SITUATIONS
AVAILABILITY
After Sequence 03, Memory 04.
UNLOCKS
Sticky Pouch available for purchase from Piri Reis.
WALKTHROUGH
At the waypoint marker, wait until a guard approaches your position, then throw the Sticky Splinter Bomb when he is highlighted. Immediately turn around and leave the zone marked on the mini-map to end the Memory.

MISSION
PIRI REIS: DATURA
AVAILABILITY
After Sequence 03, Memory 04.
UNLOCKS
Datura available for purchase from Piri Reis.
WALKTHROUGH
Follow the onscreen prompts to use Datura Bombs to kill the first two groups of guards, then climb onto the rooftop to the east and throw your final Datura Bomb to eliminate the marked target without being detected.

MISSION
PIRI REIS: CHERRY
AVAILABILITY
Complete Piri Reis: Smoke Decoy.
UNLOCKS
Sulfur available for purchase from Piri Reis.
WALKTHROUGH
Follow the instructions at the two waypoints, but don't rush straight out of the area when told to do so. Instead, jump over to the rooftop to the east, then look south to see a group of Ottoman guards. A glance at your mini-map will reveal that there are Templars further south. Aim your final Cherry Bomb between these two groups to complete the Full Synch objective, then head east to escape the marked area and end the Memory.

MISSION
PIRI REIS: THUNDER
AVAILABILITY
Complete Piri Reis: Datura.
UNLOCKS
Coal Dust available for purchase from Piri Reis
WALKTHROUGH
Move into the waypoint marker, then follow the prompts to throw a Fuse Shell Bomb at the wall. Once it explodes, sprint out of the highlighted zone to end the Memory.

MISSION
PIRI REIS: CALTROPS
AVAILABILITY
Complete Piri Reis: Smoke Screen.
UNLOCKS
Caltrops available for purchase from Piri Reis.
WALKTHROUGH
After throwing the bomb into the designated target area, run forward and use the Hidden Blade to assassinate all marked guards. To escape the area, run along the waterfront to the east, being careful not to enter the water – this will cause you to fail the Full Synch condition. When you clear the marked area, drop your two remaining Caltrop Bombs to deter pursuit, then seek refuge in a hiding spot until the Memory ends.

MISSION
PIRI REIS: TRIPWIRE
AVAILABILITY
Complete Piri Reis: Sticky Situations.
UNLOCKS
Trip Wires available for purchase from Piri Reis.
WALKTHROUGH
Walk to the waypoint and plant the Tripwire Bomb as directed, then retreat to the second waypoint. When the targeted individual triggers the explosive, kill him (and, to achieve Full Synch, him alone). Sprint along the boardwalk and dive into the water to escape.

CHALLENGES

ma.18082005.GEXp7EP9E60pc1ik2
ma.27082003.Tm9ORmFyRW5vdWdo
ma.14082004.MYUUsZYJ
ma.11032006.JGbleVdpbGxGaW5kTWU=
ma.03032005.SnVzdEFDdWx0IQ==

As well as contributing to your Total Synch rating, Challenges can lead to some interesting rewards. To complete them, achieve the requisite feat or activity the number of times specified in each table's Total column.

ASSASSINS GUILD

- The Set 1 reward can increase the profitability of the Mediterranean Defense metagame if you unlock it early enough. The easiest way to reach the totals is to start fights with Gunmen and Bombmen as you travel through the city, then call your Assassins into the fray to kill them – or simply use an Assassin Signal to designate them for assassination from afar.

- Once you have at least six Assassins at your disposal, use Arrow Storm on a random guard patrol prior to every visit to the Mediterranean Defense interface.

- The Den Defense requirement in Set 3 is the only Challenge that can be missed – thus preventing you from reaching 100% Synch. Be sure to provoke and complete three Den Defense situations before you complete all Master Assassin Missions.

SET	REQUIREMENT	TOTAL	REWARD
1	Call Assassins during a fight	x25	Increases the Odds of Success rating for the first Assassin assigned to a Mediterranean Defense contract by 10%.
1	Call Assassins on a target	x20	Increases the Odds of Success rating for the first Assassin assigned to a Mediterranean Defense contract by 10%.
2	Use Arrow Storm	x15	Increases the rate at which the Assassin Signal Meter recharges.
2	Call your Assassins within a story mission	x5	Increases the rate at which the Assassin Signal Meter recharges.
3	Recruit Assassins	x12	Unlocks Altaïr's Sword at the Assassin's HQ.
3	Train Recruits to the rank of Master Assassin	x7	Unlocks Altaïr's Sword at the Assassin's HQ.
3	Successfully perform a Den Defense	x3	Unlocks Altaïr's Sword at the Assassin's HQ.

✱ ROMANIES GUILD

SET	REQUIREMENT	TOTAL	REWARD
1	Use Romanies on guards	x10	Cost of hiring Romanies decreases.
1	Evade using stealth (crowd/hiding spots)	x10	Cost of hiring Romanies decreases.
1	Kill guards using the crossbow without being detected	x20	Cost of hiring Romanies decreases.
2	Use Tactical Bombs to escape guards	x10	Unlocks the Romani Faction Ability (any Romani who automatically peels away to distract guards will now poison all those that follow them). Also unlocks the Romanies Guild Crest at the Assassin's HQ.
2	Kill a Stalker without getting stabbed	x5	Unlocks the Romani Faction Ability (any Romani who automatically peels away to distract guards will now poison all those that follow them). Also unlocks the Romanies Guild Crest at the Assassin's HQ.
2	Kill guards using poison	x15	Unlocks the Romani Faction Ability (any Romani who automatically peels away to distract guards will now poison all those that follow them). Also unlocks the Romanies Guild Crest at the Assassin's HQ.
3	Kill guards using bombs without being spotted	x20	Unlocks the Romani Stiletto.
3	Assassinate a guard from behind	x10	Unlocks the Romani Stiletto.
3	Assassinate a guard from a blend spot	x5	Unlocks the Romani Stiletto.
3	Kill three enemies dazed by a single smoke bomb before it dissipates	x1	Unlocks the Romani Stiletto.

- This set of Challenges features activities that you should perform fairly regularly during the course of a standard playthrough.

THIEVES GUILD

- The "sprint uninterrupted" Challenge is more difficult than you might suspect if attempted in most areas of Constantinople. You can perform this feat without too much difficulty in the gardens around the Bayezid Mosque (Bayezid South district) and in the ruins to the south of the Constantine district.

- To perform a dive of over 30 meters, travel to the final tower on the north wall of Topkapi Palace, then jump towards the Golden Horn waterway. Don't forget to press the Legs button as soon as Ezio takes off to turn the leap into a dive.

- Whenever you see a wooden beam above a guard patrol, consider performing an air assassination to boost your total. The Yerebatan Cistern Memory in Sequence 03 presents a number of opportunities to perform this feat.

SET	REQUIREMENT	TOTAL	REWARD
1	Use Thieves on guards	x10	Cost of hiring Thieves decreases.
	Sprint uninterrupted for 300 meters	x1	
	Perform a Hook and Run	x15	
2	Perform a Leap of Faith	x40	Unlocks the Thief Faction Ability (any group of Thieves in Ezio's employ will automatically pickpocket civilians they encounter at street level and loot nearby dead bodies, with the profits passed immediately to Ezio). Also unlocks the Thieves Guild Crest at the Assassin's HQ.
	Climb a total distance of 1km	x1	
	Steal money with Counter Steal	250 𝔸	
3	Perform a dive of at least 30 meters	x1	Unlocks the Ottoman Mace.
	Kill a guard using Throwing Knives	x25	
	Perform an air assassination on guards from a beam	x5	
	Perform a zipline assassination	x10	

MERCENARIES GUILD

SET	REQUIREMENT	TOTAL	REWARD
1	Use Mercenaries on guards	x10	Cost of hiring Mercenaries decreases.
	Destroy a scaffold by throwing someone into it	x5	
	Kill an enemy using a thrown weapon	x5	
2	Disarm and kill a guard with his own weapon	x5	Unlocks the Mercenary Faction Ability (any group of Mercenaries in Ezio's employ will act as bodyguards, pushing harassers out of the way and fighting inquisitive guards). Also unlocks the Mercenaries Guild Crest at the Assassin's HQ.
	Kill a Byzantine Almogavar	x25	
	Perform a Hook and Throw	x10	
3	Perform a double assassination	x10	Unlocks the Broadsword at the Assassin's HQ.
	Kill five guards in under 10 seconds in melee	x1	
	Perform a Kill Streak of at least five kills	x10	
	Kill an Ottoman Janissary	x25	

- Whenever you notice a scaffold, look for a nearby guard patrol featuring either a Byzantine Militia or an Ottoman Agile. Both are vulnerable to the Grab move required for the related Set 1 Challenge.

- "Thrown weapon" means either Heavy or Long weapons types hurled forcefully into opponents bodies with a special attack move (see page 139). Throwing Knives do not count.

- Almogavar are actually rather rare. However, the Piri Reis: Datura mission is extremely short, and features several Almogavar targets that can be killed with great ease.

- Topkapi Palace is the best place to hunt Janissaries from Sequence 04. Travel to the main courtyard to encounter an angry abundance of them… and pack plenty of bombs.

- The Kill Streak Challenge requires a "pure" Kill Streak that isn't interrupted by a Counter Kill. As this is pretty much impossible when you face Janissaries in later Sequences, you can use the Replay Memory function to play the first Memory of Sequence 04. Instead of moving into the Memory Start position, head out into Constantinople and attract groups of Elites.

BOMBS

SET	REQUIREMENT	TOTAL	REWARD
1	Stick a bomb on a guard	x10	Extra bomb ingredients found within Dens.
	Kill a mission target with a bomb	x1	
	Distract a guard using bombs	x20	
	Kill five guards with a single bomb	x1	
	Kill guards with Tripwire bombs	x20	

SET	REQUIREMENT	TOTAL	REWARD
2	Craft a bomb with every shell type	x1	Bomb Capacity Upgrade. Also unlocks the Bomb Faction Crest at the Assassin's HQ.
	Use a bomb	x50	
	Kill a guard incapacitated by a bomb	x25	
	Craft one bomb of each effect type	x1	
	Use every bomb effect at least twice	x1	

- If you are methodical and start early in the story, when these Challenges first become available, you should have no problem in unlocking them before you complete all Core Memories.

PRIMER

WALKTHROUGH

SIDE QUESTS

REFERENCE & ANALYSIS

MULTIPLAYER

EXTRAS

INDEX

SECRET LOCATIONS

HAGIA SOPHIA'S SECRET

Requirement: Collect all 10 Memoir Pages; this can only be achieved after Memory 03 of Sequence 05.

After you have gathered all 10 Memoir Pages (see page 109), you can reach this location via a door to the right of the main Hagia Sofia entrance, found on the northeast side of this magnificent and commanding structure. As the free running and climbing skills required to reach the final waypoint aren't too demanding, completing the Full Synch objective is just a matter of being familiar with the required route. Pause to study our annotated screenshots and instructions before each part of the journey, and you might achieve it on your first attempt.

I: From the starting position, climb over the obstruction to the west and swing on the pole to reach a wooden beam. Climb along the outer walls of the corridor, using Back Eject when prompted, to reach a chandelier; from here, head through the opening to your right. Jump and swing down to the ground, then run to the north to trigger a cinematic sweep of the interior. When play resumes, follow the route illustrated here to reach a zipline, then ride it down. This will activate a checkpoint, and create a shortcut enabling you to return to this position in the event of a fall.

II: Scale the scaffold and traverse to the left to reach an opening in the railing, then climb up; if you are not on a speed run, or have moved with absolute precision so far, there is a Bomb Stash to open in the northwest corner. Run through the archway to the east, then perform a Long Jump on the hanging fixture to reach the opposite balcony; there is another Bomb Stash close to the east wall. Climb to the ledge to the south, then follow the route shown here. Ride the zipline down to reach the west balcony.

III: Use the wooden beams to cross the hole in the floor to the south, then perform a Long Jump to swing over another. Head through the archway, then climb over the obstruction to the east. Jump over to the beam to the north, then follow the route shown here. When you reach the final ledge, move to the far left and climb up a little to perform a Back Eject to reach a third zipline.

IV: After you land, ascend to the very top of the scaffold, then traverse to the right until you reach the ledges highlighted in the accompanying screenshot. Climb to the top, then Back Eject; when you land, leap over to the waypoint. Perform a Leap of Faith into the pool after the cutscene, then open the three Treasure Chests before you interact with the sarcophagus to claim Ishak Pasha's Armor (see page 147 for details). You can now return to Constantinople via the highlighted exit.

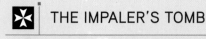

THE IMPALER'S TOMB

Requirement: Only available in special editions of Assassin's Creed Revelations, or as a preorder bonus.

Once you have unlocked this location, interact with the shimmering book in Sofia's Bookshop. With this initial task accomplished, head to the cemetery in the south of the Constantine district and enter the door at the Hidden Tomb marker (✠).

I: Once inside, free run on the short course directly ahead and to the left. When you reach the upper level, take a right, then a left. Swing down to the lower level, then continue west until you see an opening on the south wall. Follow the route illustrated here to bypass the locked gate; perform a Side Eject from the ledge to reach the platform to the right, then ride the zipline down. In the next area, follow the obvious climbing route to reach an opening in a wall, then swing via the pole to reach the lower level.

II: Follow the route illustrated in the accompanying screenshot. Execute a Long Jump when you get to the hanging fixture to reach the balcony, then perform a Leap of Faith from the perch. Swim to the ledge, then follow the tunnel (be wary of unseen pitfalls in the gloomy light) until you come to a room and, beyond it, a staircase.

III: Climb over the gate, then head west to reach a large room; climb the north wall. Use the ledges and platforms to get to the large arch to the south, then follow the route pictured here; from the right-hand side of the arch, make a Side Eject to reach the next ledge in line, and another Side Eject to the left from the ledge just below and to the side to arrive at the entrance. Jump onto the suspended cage, then traverse to the left, around the corner, and climb to the top via the door.

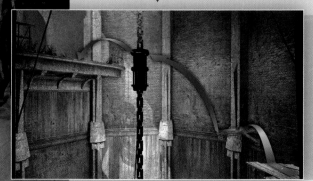

IV: The next task is to climb the shaft to reach a balcony up high. Jump over to the sewer opening to the south, then climb on top of the wooden beam above. From here, jump over to the north and ascend until the camera angle changes to reveal a Back Eject opportunity. Finally, use the wooden framework to the south to begin the last part of the climb to reach an opening to the north. Be careful when you arrive at the position shown in the accompanying screenshot: a chance misstep or accidental jump here will be fatal. Back Eject from the chain to get to the balcony, then run down the steps. Loot the stone container to obtain Vlad Tepes's Sword: a special weapon that will instill great fear in the hearts of Ezio's opponents, causing a 15% chance that an individual will flee with each blow he lands. Exit via the nearby gate to return to Constantinople.

These unique optional adventures reveal elements of Desmond's life via a first-person perspective, with a specific focus on action-oriented puzzles. They are unlocked by collecting Animus Data Fragments as Ezio, and can be accessed via the giant portals on Animus Island, entered from left to right in order of story progression. Select the Return to Animus Island option in the Pause menu to return there whenever you are not engaged in a Memory.

Use ⬅ to move, ➡ to control the camera, and the Legs button to jump. Desmond acquires the ability to spawn surfaces to walk on during the course of Part 1, a feature that becomes a mainstay from that point onward. Toggle between the two different types of surface with the Assassin Signal or Weapon Selector buttons, and press the High Profile button to spawn them. Facing a spawned surface, press the Primary Attack button to delete it.

Though the abilities at Desmond's disposal seem limited, it's how you apply them that matters. Once you can spawn them, *platforms* are flat surfaces used to cross open space, or descend without injury; *ramps* are sloped surfaces, used to gain altitude. Confused? Don't be. The best way to understand how they (indeed, this entire set of minigames) work in practice is to try them for yourself. And so, without further ado…

◆ PART 1: DOUBTS

Requirement: Collect 5 Animus Data Fragments.

I: Walk directly ahead to open the way forward, then follow the route in the screenshot to reach a room with an impassable barrier and a glowing switch. Activate the latter with the Empty Hand button, then pass through the newly opened exit.

II: Listen to Desmond's recollections, then follow the route pictured here to reach a switch. Activate it, then leave via the new exit. In the next room, walk up the slope and through the opening, then walk to the back of the black monolith and drop down. Use the moving platforms to reach an opening in the far wall, then continue on until you come to a large chamber.

III: Move to the switch, then activate it to create a new bridge (📷). Walk over this, then use the moving platform to reach a second switch. After pressing this, ride the moving platform to the top and follow the path to get to the portal. Pass through it to open the way forward.

IV: Desmond now acquires the ability to spawn surfaces at will; see the top of the page for guidance. Use flat platforms to navigate around the black Data Nodes; contact with these surfaces will return you to the previous checkpoint, so pay them a wide berth. The trick to successfully using platforms and ramps is to pay attention to the camera position, as this determines their precise placement and height (📷). Though your first steps will be a little tentative, you will soon master the art of spawning them swiftly, creating bridges or slopes to travel at great speed, or improvised surfaces below you as you're falling. On the far side, pick up the glowing cube to unlock **Multiplayer Emblem 1**, then switch to ramps and head up through the opening to the left of the collectible. This leads back to the chamber pictured in entry **I**. Walk through the portal to end the first Journey, or refer to **V** if you would like to pick up the second secret collectible in this area.

V: Instead of heading straight through the portal, retrace your steps to reach the chamber just beyond the room with the projection of The Farm on the wall. Collect **Multiplayer Emblem 2** from the top of the column (📷), then retrace your steps back to the exit portal.

PRIMER

WALKTHROUGH

SIDE QUESTS

REFERENCE &
ANALYSIS

MULTIPLAYER

EXTRAS

INDEX

COMPLETION
ROADMAP

REBUILDING
CONSTANTINOPLE

TEMPLAR DENS

DEN DEFENSE

RECRUIT
ASSASSINS

MEDITERRANEAN
DEFENSE

MASTER ASSASSIN
MISSIONS

FACTION HQ
MISSIONS

BOOK QUESTS

PIRI REIS
MISSIONS

CHALLENGES

SECRET
LOCATIONS

DESMOND'S
JOURNEY

ADDITIONAL
MEMORIES

PART 2: TRAINING

Requirement: Collect 10 Animus Data Fragments.

Note: This section of the Journey introduces two new features: "Particle Streams" that convey spawned surfaces in their direction of movement, and "Containment Fields": orange-tinted zones that cause spawned platforms and ramps within their effect radius to break up and fall into oblivion.

I: Walk along the corridor, then use ramps to reach an opening high on the opposite wall; you will be moving against the Particle Stream, so a little speed makes it easier. In the tunnel, walk into the vertical Particle Stream and spawn a platform beneath Desmond to ascend. In the next chamber, use ramps to reach the opening pictured here.

II: Travel through the Data Nodes until you reach the final, irregularly shaped Data Node moving downwards. Wait until a large Data Node descends, then quickly use platform blocks to drop down and pass through the opening on the other side (🎥). In the next room, you will encounter the first Containment Fields. After passing through the first, you will find that the second covers a sheer drop. Face down, then drop over the edge; wait a fraction of a second, then spawn a platform beneath Desmond to arrest his fall after you pass through the effect radius.

III: Move down to the walkway, then rapidly create and walk over ramps to ascend through the Particle Stream (🎥). On the other side, turn around to find **Multiplayer Emblem 3** on a ledge above. Continue forward until you reach a darkened chamber; use ramps to reach the opening.

IV: This chamber combines Particle Streams and Containment Fields to create a puzzle. Use ramps and platforms to reach a narrow ledge (🎥), then leap into the next Particle Stream area; even if you miss it and hit the ground to (temporarily) fatal effect, you will respawn at a checkpoint here. As you move inside the final Particle Stream, create a platform before you plummet to the ground. This Particle Stream moves diagonally, so quickly create platforms to reach solid ground.

V: The same principle applies in the next area: use Particle Streams to ascend, then drop through the Containment Fields to reach the next Particle Stream and spawn a platform to stop your descent (🎥). The final Particle Stream in this sequence veers left and right. Use ramps to ascend, then spawn a platform to ride up to reach the opening above. In the next chamber, you can find **Multiplayer Emblem 4** behind the walls where scenes from Desmond's childhood are projected. When you are ready, fall into the hole and spawn platforms to navigate the gaps in the Data Nodes as the Particle Stream conveys you downwards at speed. It may take a few attempts to memorize the course, but there is a checkpoint midway through the descent. Be economical with your movements and platform spawns, and this shouldn't be too much of a trial. At the bottom, follow the only available path to reach the exit portal.

PART 3: ESCAPE

Requirement: Collect 15 Animus Data Fragments.

Note: This third Journey section introduces orange "Containment Grids", moving barriers that destroy platforms and ramps.

I: Cross the initial gap with a platform or two and, when you reach the Containment Field, drop straight down and spawn a platform as soon as you pass through the effect area. Collect **Multiplayer Emblem 5** from the upper reaches of the chamber, then head for the panel shown in the accompanying screenshot. There is a Containment Field that prevents easy passage, but you can reach the other side with a jump from the beams. When the barrier has been disabled, use ramps to ascend to the rafters and travel to the opposite side of the room.

II: Create platforms over the Data Nodes below to safely get to the next chamber, where you will encounter a Containment Grid. Wait for it to move away from Desmond, then create platforms to reach solid ground on the left-hand side of the room before it returns. The next challenge is a room filled with Containment Grids. Though you might think that there is a need to find a particular path through them, you can actually just power through the center by creating platforms at speed. On the other side, ride through the Particle Streams in the tunnels; each solid surface you encounter in the Data Node rapids represents a restart position. When you near the end of the stream, quickly create platforms to reach solid ground to your right before you hit the Particle Stream "waterfall". Collect **Multiplayer Emblem 6** from its place of concealment () before you continue forward.

III: Drop down the shaft and use a platform to break your fall. Use the solid surfaces to reach the far side of the corridor filled with Containment Grids, then quickly use ramps to arrive at the exit. In the next room, wait until the lower Containment Grid moves towards Desmond, then spawn platforms to cross over it; once it passes beneath, descend quickly, then use ramps to reach safety on the opposite side. For the next run, just wait for the Containment Field to approach, then power through it at speed; take the Particle Stream into account as you move. The third trial adds two Containment Grids, a Particle Stream and three Data Nodes. Wait for the vertical Containment Grid to descend, then start your journey with a ramp or two, then immediately switch to platforms to finish the crossing (📷). Walk into the portal to exit.

Requirement: Collect 20 Animus Data Fragments.

Note: Part 4 introduces "Containment Arrays", red beams that destroy spawned platforms and ramps, and will send Desmond back to the previous checkpoint on contact.

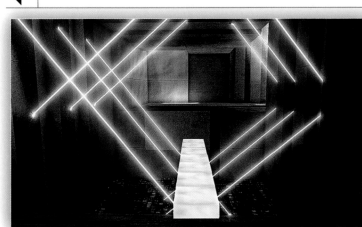

I: Create platforms to approach the center of the Containment Array pattern; when it opens up, quickly pass through. The next Containment Array is slightly more difficult. Wait until it opens up in the pattern pictured here, then spawn platforms at speed to negotiate it. By the third of these hazards, you should have the confidence to just stroll right through on platforms when the pattern opens up.

II: When you enter the room with the static Containment Arrays, look to your left to find **Multiplayer Emblem 7**. Make your way through the maze until you reach an intermittent Containment Array, then run through when it flicks off. Look down the deep shaft and wait for the Containment Array to activate (📷), then drop and create a platform beneath just before you reach it. When it deactivates, drop through. Repeat this process for those that follow, then head through the narrow opening at the bottom.

III: Walk over the light bridge to the far side; when Desmond's path is blocked, you must move around the chamber in a counterclockwise progression to reach the switch. The Particle Streams are less of a hindrance than you might expect -- the important thing is to identify the route to each crossing in advance, then move purposefully (📷).

IV: In the next room, you encounter an unusual new form of Containment Array. Spawn platforms to reach a position on your left, then wait for the beams to part by the solid surfaces; quickly run through, then drop down to collect **Multiplayer Emblem 8** from beneath (📷). This will almost certainly lead to a restart, but you only need pick it up once. The trick to completing the crossing is to move between the solid surfaces whenever gaps appear; while the movement of the Containment Arrays is hypnotic and disorienting, there's a knack to a quick crossing that you will soon acquire. In the final darkened area, you might suspect that you need ramps to cross the "traffic", but that's not the case: just stroll straight over and enter the portal.

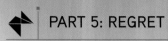

PART 5: REGRET

Requirement: Collect 30 Animus Data Fragments.

Note: Completing all five parts of Desmond's Journey unlocks the Desmond "avatar projection", which you can equip via the Outfits menu. This is a purely cosmetic skin change: he will still act and speak as Ezio.

I: Approach the doors and press the switch to activate a vertical Particle Stream; spawn a platform beneath your feet to ascend. At the top, use platforms and then ramps to proceed through two Particle Stream zones. After these, use the blocks that appear to cross the next chasm; look to your left to find **Multiplayer Emblem 9** (📷).

II: Use platforms to cross the next Particle Stream area, dodging the Containment Grids as they move towards you. Press the switch on the other side, then use platforms (and occasional ramps) to negotiate the moving blocks while fighting against the continual descent caused by the Particle Stream. The next hazard is a wall of Containment Grids that is too dense to penetrate. To cross safely, wait until the grid approaches, then follow it closely; towards the end of the corridor, take a right and wait for it to pass (📷).

III: Walk into the elevator and activate the switch; once again, ride the Particle Stream to the top. Head right from the elevator, then take a left. Cross the floor and bypass the Containment Grids by creating a platform path against either wall. In the next corridor, two Containment Grids mimic the classic "slamming gate" hazard; time your approach carefully to pass through safely. The remaining corridor is routine by comparison. When you reach the Abstergo laboratory, collect **Multiplayer Emblem 10** from the position pictured here, then head through the portal.

17.anima.08212002.TW9OeGVyU2Fk
17.anima.08212002.RmFOaGVyTWFt
17.anima.22072002.Tm9OaGLuZ0IzVHLj12G
17.anima.22072002.RXZIcnl0iHGluZ0zQ0zKyBWB
17.anima.04022003.Qm9vZWRBZkbmhJjdk1u1

PRIMER

WALKTHROUGH

SIDE QUESTS

REFERENCE & ANALYSIS

MULTIPLAYER

EXTRAS

INDEX

COMPLETION ROADMAP

REBUILDING CONSTANTINOPLE

TEMPLAR DENS

DEN DEFENSE

RECRUIT ASSASSINS

MEDITERRANEAN DEFENSE

MASTER ASSASSIN MISSIONS

FACTION HQ MISSIONS

BOOK QUESTS

PIRI REIS MISSIONS

CHALLENGES

SECRET LOCATIONS

DESMOND'S JOURNEY

ADDITIONAL MEMORIES

The following 18 pages reveal the locations of all collectibles and Viewpoints throughout Constantinople and Cappadocia.

Legend

Viewpoint	Animus Data Fragment	Ishak Pasha's Memoir Page	Treasure Chest

Before you read any further, we suggest that you digest the following short selection of tips and tricks.

- There are a number of rewards for hitting Animus Data Fragment collection milestones. At 5, 10, 15, 20 and 30, you will unlock episodes in the Desmond's Journey side quest on Animus Island (see page 104). Collecting 25 Data Fragments unlocks a unique Treasure Map that marks the location of all Memoir Pages on the main map and mini-map. Similarly, picking up 50 Animus Data Fragments leads to the automatic award of a Treasure Map that marks the locations of all remaining Data Fragments on all maps. Unlocking the 10 Memoir Pages enables access to the Hagia Sofia Secret Location. This cannot be accomplished until Ezio can enter the Arsenal district in Sequence 05.

- Our primary goal in this section is to help you to find Animus Data Fragments, as these are the hardest collectibles to locate until you hit the magic 50 benchmark. However, we also provide assistance (in the rare instances where it is necessary) to help you find Treasure Chests. Eight of the Memoir Pages are located on rooftops or towers, and therefore easy to find; to enable you to avoid the 10,000 **A**+ expense of purchasing the associated map, we offer captions on the two Memoir Pages that are concealed with greater cunning.

- Treasure Chests count towards your overall Total Synch rating, and naturally contribute incremental rewards, but there is no final bonus for collecting all of them. Some of these are protected by stationary guards who will react with violence if you attempt to go near them, though there are instances where you can avoid conflict by climbing to approach from a different position. It should go without saying that containers located in Templar Dens are much easier to pick up once you assert Assassin control in the region. There are also three Treasure Chests to open at the very end of each of the five Secret Locations, documented in the corresponding section of the DNA menu.

- All collectibles picked up when you use the Replay Memory feature are automatically saved – even if you do not complete the Memory. This includes funds and crafting ingredients acquired from Treasure Chests and Bomb Stashes.

- An interesting and useful feature of the Custom Marker function at the main map screen is that selecting collectible items will not merely direct you to the object in question, but will also provide information on its elevation relative to Ezio's current position. For this reason, Treasure Maps purchased from Book Shops are worth every last coin if you are seeking 100% completion – the time saved makes the expense absolutely justifiable.

- Glancing at any form of collectible with Eagle Sense active will make an icon representing its position appear on in-game maps.

- There is a subtle sound effect that plays whenever Ezio moves close to a collectible.

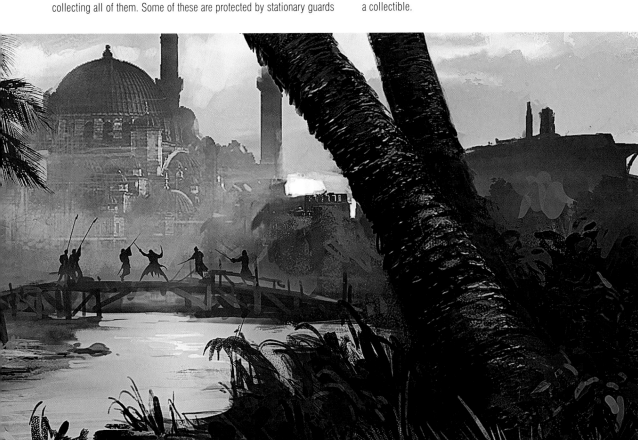

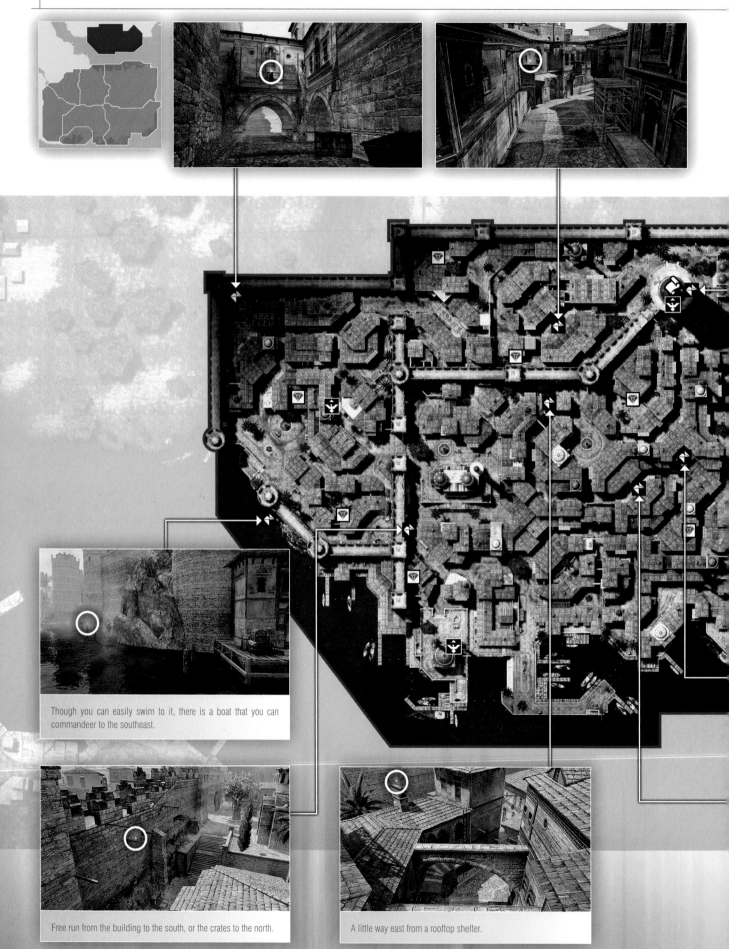

Though you can easily swim to it, there is a boat that you can commandeer to the southeast.

Free run from the building to the south, or the crates to the north.

A little way east from a rooftop shelter.

Climb Galata Tower, then leap off the south face and use a parachute to reach this platform. It doesn't matter if Ezio plummets to his death as a consequence: as long as he collides with the wall above and makes contact with it as he falls, the Animus Data Fragment will be credited to your collection.

Located not far west from a Bank.

Drop from the ledge above.

High on a rooftop just south of a Tailor, situated between two ziplines.

PRIMER

WALKTHROUGH

SIDE QUESTS

REFERENCE & ANALYSIS

MULTIPLAYER

EXTRAS

INDEX

Note: We suggest that you pick up collectibles in the Topkapi district at the start of Sequence 03, as this Restricted Area is almost entirely free of guards at that stage in the story.

Jump over from the nearby wooden canopy, or drop from the roof above.

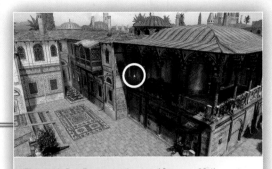

Pick up this Data Fragment at the start of Sequence 03. If you return here later in the story, you will need to avoid countless guards to reach this Fragment and the other collectibles in the Topkapi district.

Perform a Leap of Faith to the north to safely return to ground level after you collect this.

Perform a Leap of Faith to the northwest to return to ground level.

This is tucked away out of sight from most angles of approach. There is a domed roof slightly to the west of it.

Tucked away on top of an arch, between two buildings. If you approach via the rooftops, there is a rooftop shelter just to the east of it.

If you approach this Animus Data Fragment from the rooftops, you can find it just to the north of a zipline.

Scale one of the building on either side of the archway to reach it.

Slightly north of a covered walkway; approach it from the rooftops to spot it easily.

On the spire of the tower with a Viewpoint; face south for the Leap of Faith back to the ground, and you can collect the two nearby Treasure Chests after you land.

This Treasure Chest is on top of the tower. Jump over from the adjacent building after collecting the nearby Animus Data Fragment.

Though revealed by purchasing the Bayezid District Treasure Map 2, this Treasure Chest is actually located here in the Imperial district. It is found on top of this tower, which you must reach by scaling one of two positions on the wall to the northwest. There are actually two Animus Data Fragments in Bayezid South that lead you close to this position; see page 118 for details.

PRIMER

WALKTHROUGH

SIDE QUESTS

REFERENCE & ANALYSIS

MULTIPLAYER

EXTRAS

INDEX

COMPLETION ROADMAP

REBUILDING CONSTANTINOPLE

TEMPLAR DENS

DEN DEFENSE

RECRUIT ASSASSINS

MEDITERRANEAN DEFENSE

MASTER ASSASSIN MISSIONS

FACTION HQ MISSIONS

BOOK QUESTS

PIRI REIS MISSIONS

CHALLENGES

SECRET LOCATIONS

DESMOND'S JOURNEY

ADDITIONAL MEMORIES

You can reach this tower via the rooftops to the east and west.

Either free run on the column sections to reach it, or make a straight jump from the building to the north.

On a rooftop connected to the Viewpoint tower.

PRIMER

WALKTHROUGH

SIDE QUESTS

REFERENCE & ANALYSIS

MULTIPLAYER

EXTRAS

INDEX

Note that the ship here is not visible on the in-game map.

If you approach from the rooftop to the north, note that Ezio will often fail to make the jump to the column from that position; it's safer to reach it via the beam to the south (pictured here).

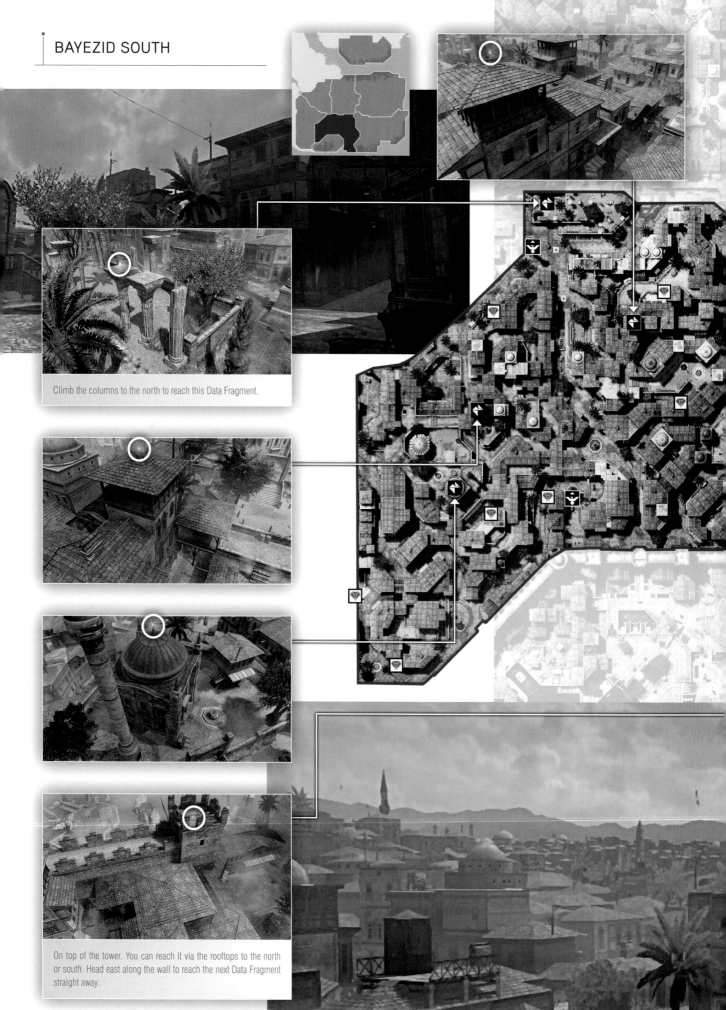

Climb the columns to the north to reach this Data Fragment.

On top of the tower. You can reach it via the rooftops to the north or south. Head east along the wall to reach the next Data Fragment straight away.

PRIMER

WALKTHROUGH

SIDE QUESTS

REFERENCE &
ANALYSIS

MULTIPLAYER

EXTRAS

INDEX

COMPLETION
ROADMAP

REBUILDING
CONSTANTINOPLE

TEMPLAR DENS

DEN DEFENSE

RECRUIT
ASSASSINS

MEDITERRANEAN
DEFENSE

MASTER ASSASSIN
MISSIONS

FACTION HQ
MISSIONS

BOOK QUESTS

PIRI REIS
MISSIONS

CHALLENGES

SECRET
LOCATIONS

DESMOND'S
JOURNEY

**ADDITIONAL
MEMORIES**

Ezio cannot scale the southeast (rear) face of Little Hagia Sophia, so ascend to the rooftop from a different position.

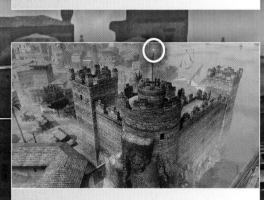

If you approach this from ground level, there are rock ledges to the north of it that allow easy access; run west along the wall to collect the Data Fragment on the nearby tower if you have yet to do so.

Located in the heart of a Templar Den, at the top of the Viewpoint tower.

Though not marked as a Restricted Area, this courtyard is guarded by a large number of Ottoman troops who don't take kindly to trespassers. Scale a wall, jump down from above and make good your escape after grabbing the Data Fragment.

Climb onto the wooden roof to the right, then perform a Wall Run and Side Eject to reach the beam.

Ride the zipline from the high rooftop further south to reach this Data Fragment.

PRIMER

WALKTHROUGH

SIDE QUESTS

REFERENCE & ANALYSIS

MULTIPLAYER

EXTRAS

INDEX

COMPLETION ROADMAP

REBUILDING CONSTANTINOPLE

TEMPLAR DENS

DEN DEFENSE

RECRUIT ASSASSINS

MEDITERRANEAN DEFENSE

MASTER ASSASSIN MISSIONS

FACTION HQ MISSIONS

BOOK QUESTS

PIRI REIS MISSIONS

CHALLENGES

SECRET LOCATIONS

DESMOND'S JOURNEY

ADDITIONAL MEMORIES

This is directly below the Viewpoint perch on the tower.

This is located within an Ottoman Janissary camp – another location that, while not formally a Restricted Area, is a place where the (numerous) local soldiers will take exception to his presence. There are also two Treasure Chests that you can collect during your visit. If you would like to sneak inside, turn to page 160 and refer to the annotated screenshot that accompanies the Mosh Pit Achievement/Trophy. The zipline on the tower offers an easy escape if you attract attention.

Climb to the top of the southeast end of the Valens Aqueduct then, after jumping the gap between the two sections – extend Ezio's Hookblade to be safe – run along the aqueduct to reach this Data Fragment. You could also parachute to it from a tower on the Fatih Mosque.

Climb to the top of the archway to the south, then free run to this Data Fragment; extend the Hookblade during the first jump.

CONSTANTINE SOUTH

From the Crafting Table located almost directly to the north of this position, head through the archway to the south and run in that direction until you reach a dead end; you can find this Memoir Page to your right.

Perform a Wall Run from the beam to the left, then Side Eject to reach the wooden platform.

This Treasure Chest is a little harder to find than most, even if you have purchased the appropriate map. You can either drop through one of the holes in the wooden roof sections to enter this hard-to-reach back alley, or enter from street level to the north.

A rare Animus Data Fragment at ground level. From the rooftops, look for the two trees in close proximity to locate it.

Climb the rooftop to the east, then stand on the fixture pointing almost directly towards the beam where the Data Fragment rests. Leap over, and extend the Hookblade as Ezio flies through the air to land without damage.

This Data Fragment hovers tantalizingly above Ezio's head, so you may assume that a parachute jump is required. There is a more prosaic solution: stand directly beneath it, hold the High Profile button, then tap the Legs button to hop.

At the top of the Viewpoint tower; this is at the center of a Templar Den.

If you approach this via the rooftops, look for a rooftop shelter; this Data Fragment is beneath a wooden canopy just to the north.

ARSENAL

NOTE: The Arsenal district is cloaked by a Desynchronization boundary until Sequence 05.

This is situated below a pole over an archway. If you have completed Memory 03 of Sequence 05, and followed our suggested route closely (see page 64), you may have collected this automatically.

This Memoir Page is hidden inside this building. Walk inside and climb the northwest wall, then Back Eject to reach it.

Board the ship via the gangplank to the south, then run to the aft section. Hop over the railing, then climb down to collect this Data Fragment.

PRIMER

WALKTHROUGH

SIDE QUESTS

REFERENCE &
ANALYSIS

MULTIPLAYER

EXTRAS

INDEX

Climb to the top of the crane and drop onto the platform.

When you reach the crow's nest, you will need to climb the rigging on the outside of it to reach the very top of the mast.

In the rafters of this building. Climb the east interior wall and Back Eject to reach it.

CAPPADOCIA

Note: This region is visited in Sequence 07. If you do not pick up all collectibles before you leave, you can return to do so at a later date either by taking the boat available on a dock on the east side of the Galata district, or by replaying Memory 01, 02 or 03 (you do not actually need to complete the Memory you chose).

This Treasure Chest is located on a high platform on the west side of the central rock spire, close to a zipline.

Climb the central spire, then use the rope bridge to reach the north wall of the cavern. When you reach the zipline, look to your left to locate this Data Fragment.

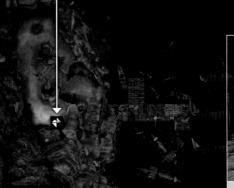

Hidden behind a Blacksmith store; you can reach it via an opening to the north, or steps leading down from the rooftop.

This lies inside a Restricted Area. Either fight your way in via the steps if there are guards stationed here, or use the elevated free run course on the south wall of the cavern to reach it without causing a commotion.

The only entrance to the cul de sac where this Treasure Chest can be found is located to the west at street level.

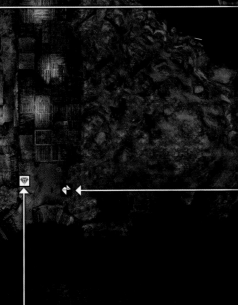

PRIMER

WALKTHROUGH

SIDE QUESTS

REFERENCE & ANALYSIS

MULTIPLAYER

EXTRAS

INDEX

REFERENCE & ANALYSIS

Packed with tables, parameters and expert guidance, this chapter is designed to provide a concise overview of the many systems and features in Assassin's Creed Revelations, with a particular focus on equipment, weapons and combat. It also covers all Achievements and Trophies, and reveals the order in which weapons, armor and upgrades are made available for purchase from merchants.

SPOILER WARNING! Though we make no reference to specific plot developments, this chapter contains references to features that are unlocked throughout the main storyline.

MOVES OVERVIEW

Basic Moves & Functions

MOVE	XBOX 360	PS3	DETAILED DESCRIPTION
Walk/Move	Hold **L**	Hold **L**	Tilt the Movement Stick in the required direction.
Fast Walk	Hold **L** + **A**	Hold **L** + **X**	Tilt the Movement Stick in the required direction and hold the Legs button.
Look/Control Camera	**R**	**R**	Use the Camera Stick to look around and control the game camera.
Run	Hold **L** + **RT**	Hold **L** + **R1**	Tilt the Movement Stick in the required direction and hold the High Profile button.
Sprint/Free Run/Jump	Hold **L** + **RT** + **A**	Hold **L** + **R1** + **X**	Tilt the Movement Stick in the required direction while holding the High Profile and Legs buttons.
Jump Up	Hold **RT**, press and release **A**	Hold **R1**, press and release **X**	Hold the High Profile button in a stationary position; press the Legs button to crouch, then release to jump.
Breaking A Fall (Forward Roll)	Hold **L** forward	Hold **L** forwards	Hold the Movement Stick forward when falling to roll on contact with the surface below.
Target Lock	**LT** (Toggle On/Off)	**L1** (Toggle On/Off)	Press the Target Lock button to lock on a target; press the button again to exit Target Lock.
Eagle Sense	**T** (Toggle On/Off)	**L3** (Toggle On/Off)	Press the Eagle Sense button to activate the ability; press the button again to deactivate.
Interact	**B**	**◎**	Press the Empty Hand button to interact with the environment (such as doors or shops) whenever a prompt appears.
Steal/Pickpocket	Hold **A**	Hold **X**	Hold the Legs button and collide with pedestrians to steal from them.
Loot	Hold **B**	Hold **◎**	Hold the Empty Hand button while standing by a corpse or chest until the Loot Icon has filled.
Pick Up/Drop Weapon	**B**	**◎**	To pick up a weapon, press the Empty Hand button while standing over it.
Pick Up/Drop Dead Body	**B**	**◎**	To pick up a dead body, tap the Empty Hand button while standing over it. Press the button again to drop it.
Gentle Push	Hold **L** + **B**	Hold **L** + **◎**	Hold the Movement Stick to walk and use the Empty Hand button to push through crowds.
Shove	Hold **L** + **RT** + **B**	Hold **L** + **R1** + **◎**	Hold the Movement Stick and High Profile button to run, then press or hold the Empty Hand button to barge civilians or guards aside.
Throw Money	**Y**	**△**	Press the Secondary Attack button when the money pouch is equipped.
Quick Inventory	**✛**	**✛**	Use the Quick Inventory buttons to instantly equip or use weapons and items. The four available slots can be customized.
Weapon Selector	Hold **RB**, select with **L** or **R**	Hold **R2**, select with **L** or **R**	Open the menu by holding the Weapon Selector button. Use the Movement Stick and Camera Stick to assign weapons or items for use with the Primary Attack and Secondary Attack buttons respectively.
Customize Quick Inventory	Hold **RB**, select with **L/R**, choose direction on **✛**	Hold **R2**, select with **L/R**, choose direction on **✛**	Open the menu by holding the Weapon Selector button. Use the Movement Stick or Camera Stick to highlight the weapon or item you wish to assign to a Quick Inventory slot, then select the required direction on the directional pad (or equivalent PC keystroke).

Climbing and Leaping

MOVE	XBOX 360	PS3	DETAILED DESCRIPTION
Start Climbing	Hold **LS** + **RT** + **A**	Hold **LS** + **R1** + **✕**	Tilt the Movement Stick in the required direction, hold the High Profile button and the Legs button.
Climb	**LS**	**LS**	Tilt the Movement Stick in the required direction.
Climb Faster/Hook Leap	Hold **LS** + **RT** + **A**	Hold **LS** + **R1** + **✕**	If an arrangement of continuous surface features allows it, hold the Legs button while climbing to ascend at maximum speed. To perform a Hook Leap, tap the Legs button while climbing. This enables Ezio to reach ledges outside his usual range with the Hookblade.
Climb Ladder/Switch Side	**LS**	**LS**	Push the Movement Stick up/down to climb or descend, and left/right to switch sides.
Ride Zipline	Hold **LS** + **RT** + **A**	Hold **LS** + **R1** + **✕**	Jump onto a zipline to ride it. Release the High Profile button to descend slowly, and press the Empty Hand button to let go.
Look Down From Raised Surface	Hold **LS** forward	Hold **LS** forward	Push the Movement Stick forward while standing close to the edge of a surface.
Ledge Drop/Beam Drop	Hold **LS**, press **B**	Hold **LS**, press **◯**	Push the Movement Stick towards the edge of a surface or a beam, then press the Empty Hand button to drop down on the specified side.
Drop/Let Go	**B**	**◯**	While hanging from a ledge or a beam, tap the Empty Hand button.
Extended Reach/Catch Back	Hold **B**	Hold **◯**	While jumping or falling, hold the Empty Hand button to grab the closest handhold within range.
Wall Run	Hold **LS** + **RT** + **A**	Hold **LS** + **R1** + **✕**	Hold the High Profile button and the Legs button to free run up a wall.
Beam Shimmy	**LS**	**LS**	Hanging from beam or pole, use the Movement Stick to shimmy along.
Free Run Drop	Hold **LS** + **RT** + **A**, release **A**	Hold **LS** + **R1** + **✕**, release **✕**	During a Sprint or Free Run, release the Legs button before you reach the end of a surface to drop down instead of jumping.
Back Eject	Release **LS**, hold **RT**, press **A**	Release **LS**, hold **R1**, press **✕**	While climbing, release the Movement Stick, hold the High Profile button, then tap the Legs button to jump backwards.
Side Eject	Hold **RT**, tilt **LS** left/right, press **A**	Hold **R1**, tilt **LS** left/right, press **✕**	While hanging or climbing, hold the High Profile button and push the Movement Stick left/right; now tap the Legs button to jump sideways.
Back Eject/Side Eject While Wall Running	Hold **RT**, tilt **LS** in required direction, press **A**	Hold **R1**, tilt **LS** in required direction, press **✕**	While running up a wall, push the Movement Stick and press the Legs button to jump in the chosen direction.
Advanced Catch Back	**LS** toward wall + **B**	**LS** toward wall + **◯**	After a Side Eject, push the Movement Stick in the direction of a surface and hold the Empty Hand button to grab an available ledge or handhold.
Swing On Pole	Hold **RT** + **A**, push **LS**	Hold **R1** + **✕**, push **LS**	Hold the High Profile and Legs buttons, then push Movement Stick forward to swing from pole to pole.
Turn On Pole	**LS** backwards	**LS** backwards	While hanging from a pole, press the Movement Stick backwards to turn around.
Ride Lift	**LS** + **RT**	**LS** + **R1**	Run (or sprint) into a Lift to ride it.
Leap Of Faith	**LS** + **RT** + **A**	**LS** + **R1** + **✕**	Push the Movement Stick towards a suitable landing spot, then press the High Profile and Legs buttons.
Long Jump	**B**	**◯**	Press the Empty Hand button while in mid-air before performing a lamp turn.

Combat

MOVE	XBOX 360	PS3	DETAILED DESCRIPTION
Enter/Exit Combat Mode	**LT**	**L1**	Press the Target Lock button to enter/exit Combat Mode when facing a hostile target.
Step Dodge	Tap **LS** sideways	Tap **LS** sideways	While in Combat Mode, tap the Movement Stick to quickstep sideways.
Attack	**X**	**□**	Press the Primary Attack button to attack; mostly employed to use blades.
Combo	**X**, repeat in sequence	**□**, repeat in sequence	Press the Primary Attack button repeatedly to perform combo attacks. If successful, the final blow will be an automatic kill.
Special Attacks	Hold and release **Y**	Hold and release **△**	Hold, then release the required button to perform the Sweep, Throw, Throw Sand or Flying Knives special attacks (depending on the weapon currently equipped – see page 135).
Kick	**A**	**✕**	While locked on, press the Legs button to kick an opponent within range.
Deflect/Block	Hold **RT**	Hold **R1**	Hold the High Profile button; press the Movement Stick towards an attacking opponent if they are standing behind you.
Dodge	Hold **RT**, press **A**	Hold **R1**, press **✕**	Hold the High Profile button and tap the Legs button just before an enemy attack lands.
Counter Kill	Hold **RT**, press **X**	Hold **R1**, press **□**	With a weapon equipped, hold the High Profile button and press the Primary Attack button just before an opponent's blow lands.
Counter Hook And Throw	Hold **RT**, press **B**	Hold **R1**, press **◯**	Hold the High Profile button and tap the Empty Hand button just before an enemy attack lands.

PRIMER

WALKTHROUGH

SIDE QUESTS

REFERENCE & ANALYSIS

MULTIPLAYER

EXTRAS

INDEX

MOVES OVERVIEW

GENERATING INCOME

WEAPONS

ARMOR

SHOPS

ENEMIES

TEMPLAR AWARENESS

ACHIEVEMENTS & TROPHIES

MISSION CHECKLIST

Combat (continued)

MOVE	XBOX 360	PS3	DETAILED DESCRIPTION
Counter Hook And Run	Hold (RT), hold (B)	Hold (R1), hold (O)	This requires the same input on the controller as the previous move, but you must instead keep the Empty Hand button held. On completion, you automatically exit Combat Mode to facilitate an escape.
Counter Steal	Hold (RT), press (Y)	Hold (R1), press (△)	Hold the High Profile button and press the Secondary Attack button just before an enemy attack lands. This enables you to pickpocket an assailant as he attacks you.
Disarm	Hold (RT), press (X)	Hold (R1), press (□)	While unarmed, hold the High Profile button and press the Primary Attack button just before an enemy blow lands.
Grab Opponent	(B)	(O)	While sufficiently close, press the Empty Hand button.
Grab: Position Opponent	(L)	(L)	During a Grab, push the Movement Stick to move an opponent or aim for a throw.
Grab: Throw Opponent	(B)	(O)	During a Grab, press the Empty Hand button.
Grab: Headbutt	(Y)	(△)	During an unarmed Grab, press the Secondary Attack button to perform up to three attacks.
Grab: Punch	(X)	(□)	During an unarmed Grab, press the Primary Attack button to perform up to three attacks.
Grab: Knee	(A)	(✕)	During an unarmed Grab, press the Legs button to perform up to three attacks.
Grab: Kill	Release (L), press (X)	Release (L), press (□)	During a Grab, with a weapon equipped and the Movement Stick neutral, press the Primary Attack button.
Counter Grab	Hold (RT), press/hold (B)	Hold (R1), press/hold (O)	Press the High Profile and Empty Hand buttons to counter an enemy Grab; hold the buttons to perform a throw. If Grabbed, tap the Empty Hand button rapidly to escape.
Finish Enemy On Ground	(X)	(□)	With a weapon equipped, press the Primary Attack button while standing over a prone opponent.
Stomp Enemy On Ground	(X)	(□)	While unarmed, repeatedly press the Primary Attack button while standing over a prone opponent.
Escape Fight	Hold (L) + (RT) + (A)	Hold (L) + (R1) + (✕)	Hold the Movement Stick, High Profile button and Legs button to break away from a fight.
Standing Tackle	(RT) + (B)	(R1) + (O)	Press the High Profile button and Empty Hand button when within range.
Running Tackle	Hold (L) + (RT), press (B)	Hold (L) + (R1), press (O)	While chasing a highlighted target, press the Empty Hand button when you move within range.
Air Tackle	(RT) + (B)	(R1) + (O)	From a platform, wall or beam, press the High Profile and Empty Hand buttons.
Hook And Run	Hold (L) + (RT), hold (B)	Hold (L) + (R1), hold (O)	Run towards a target and hold the Empty Hand button. This non-lethal ability is particularly effective when you need to bypass an opponent while fleeing combat.
Hook And Throw	Hold (L) + (RT), tap (B)	Hold (L) + (R1), tap (O)	Run towards a guard and tap the Empty Hand button when close to him. This automatically puts Ezio into Combat mode on completion.
Leg Sweep	Hold (L) + (RT), tap (B)	Hold (L) + (R1), tap (O)	Primarily used to disable non-combatants without causing any harm (such as Templar Couriers). Can also be employed against guards from behind; rather useful against Gunmen and Bombmen when they back away.

Ranged Attacks

MOVE	XBOX 360	PS3	DETAILED DESCRIPTION
Drop/Throw Bomb	(Y) (+ (L))	(△) (+ (L))	Press the Secondary Attack button to drop a Bomb. To aim manually, hold the button and use the Movement Stick to aim; release the button to throw.
Throw Knives/Shoot Pistol/Shoot Poison Darts	(Y)	(△)	Press the Secondary Attack button to fire or throw ranged weapons at the highlighted target. Use Target Lock to improve the accuracy of Throwing Knives.
Focus (Pistol, Poison Darts)	Hold and release (Y)	Hold and release (△)	Hold the button for accurate aim; release it to shoot/throw.
Cancel Shot/Throw	(B)	(O)	Used to cancel all ranged attacks while you are aiming. Note that the Throw Sand ability cannot be aborted once charged up.
Throw Long or Heavy weapon	Hold and release (X)	Hold and release (□)	Hold the Primary Attack button; release to throw at the highlighted target.

Assassinations

MOVE	XBOX 360	PS3	DETAILED DESCRIPTION
Stealth Assassination	(X)	(□)	Performed in close proximity to a target. Hold the High Profile button as well to knock a target to the ground as you perform the kill.
Assassinate From Zipline	(X)	(□)	Performed on enemies situated below your position as you ride a zipline.
Assassinate From Hiding Spot	(X)	(□)	Press the Primary Attack button as a highlighted enemy walks by. Add the High Profile button to leap from the hiding spot to perform the kill.
Assassinate From Ledge	(X)	(□)	Hanging from a ledge below your target, press the Primary Attack button to stab and throw them down. Hold the High Profile button as well to jump up and assassinate them where they stand.
Air Assassination	(X)	(□)	Highlight or lock your target and press the Primary Attack button.

Assassinations (continued)

MOVE	XBOX 360	PS3	DETAILED DESCRIPTION
Double Assassination/Double Air Assassination	✗	□	Press the Primary Attack button while standing between two opponents in close proximity. Can be performed from above as a Double Air Assassination.
Assassinate With Poison	✗	□	Move close to an opponent with the Poison Blade equipped, then tap the Primary Attack button.
Knock Out	✗	□	While unarmed, sneak up behind an opponent and tap the Primary Attack button to perform a non-lethal takedown.

Swimming

MOVE	XBOX 360	PS3	DETAILED DESCRIPTION
Swim	L	L	Tilt the Movement Stick in the required direction.
Front Crawl	Hold L + RT	Hold L + R1	Tilt the Movement Stick in the required direction and hold the High Profile button.
Fast Swim	Hold L + RT + Ⓐ	Hold L + R1 + ✗	Tilt the Movement Stick in the required direction and hold the High Profile and Legs buttons.
Hide/Swim Underwater	Hold Ⓐ (+ L)	Hold ✗ (+ L)	Hold the Legs button to dive below the water's surface. Tilt Movement Stick to swim while submerged.
Dive	Ⓐ (while jumping towards water)	✗ (while jumping towards water)	While jumping towards water, tap the Legs button to dive.
Climb Out Of Water	L + RT + Ⓐ	L + R1 + ✗	Press the Movement Stick, the High Profile button and the Legs button to climb onto a ledge within range.
Throw Knives	Lock on enemy with LT, press Ⓨ	Lock on enemy with L1, press △	On the surface, lock on to an enemy with Target Lock, then press the Secondary Attack button.
Assassination (From Water)	✗	□	On the surface below a target within range, press the Primary Attack button.

Faction Controls

MOVE	XBOX 360	PS3	DETAILED DESCRIPTION
Assassin Signal	LB	L2	Tap the button to order an assassination on a highlighted individual. In Combat mode, tap the button to summon available Assassins to lend assistance.
Arrow Storm	Hold LB	Hold L2	With three Assassin Signals available, hold the button to order the Arrow Storm attack.
Hire/Stop/Follow	Ⓑ	○	Press the Empty Hand button to hire a Faction Group. While they remain within your employ, use the button to order them to Stop or Follow.
Issue Faction Order	Lock on to a target with LT, press Ⓑ	Lock on to a target with L1, press ○	Lock on to an enemy with the Target Lock button, then press the Empty Hand button to use their unique ability.

Vehicle Controls

MOVE	XBOX 360	PS3	DETAILED DESCRIPTION
Boat: Enter Rowing Position	Ⓑ	○	Press the Empty Hand button to begin rowing a boat.
Boat: Exit Rowing Position	Ⓐ	✗	Press the Legs button to stop rowing.
Boat: Steer	L	L	Tilt Movement Stick left and right to steer. Pull back to reverse the rowing direction.
Boat: Row	Ⓑ (repeatedly)	○ (repeatedly)	Press the Empty Hand button rhythmically.
Parachute: Deploy	✗	□	Press the Primary Attack button in midair to deploy a parachute.
Parachute: Release	Ⓑ	○	Press the Empty Hand button to release a parachute.
Carriage: Steer	L	L	Tilt the Movement Stick left and right.

Camera & Interface

MOVE	XBOX 360	PS3	DETAILED DESCRIPTION
Center Camera	R	R3	This immediately positions the camera behind your avatar.
Display Map/Database; Begin Tutorial	BACK	SELECT	Press the Map button to access the main map. When Database or tutorial prompts appear, hold the button to access them.
Access Animus Desktop	START	START	Press the Pause button.
Synchronize At Viewpoint	L	L3	Press the Eagle Sense button while perched on a Viewpoint.

PRIMER

WALKTHROUGH

SIDE QUESTS

REFERENCE & ANALYSIS

MULTIPLAYER

EXTRAS

INDEX

MOVES OVERVIEW

GENERATING INCOME

WEAPONS

ARMOR

SHOPS

ENEMIES

TEMPLAR AWARENESS

ACHIEVEMENTS & TROPHIES

MISSION CHECKLIST

GENERATING INCOME

Unlike Assassin's Creed Brotherhood and (especially) Assassin's Creed II, it is absolutely essential to at least partly involve yourself in optional tasks to acquire currency for equipment and upgrades in Revelations. The following brief rundown offers a simple guide to the principle ways in which Ezio can accumulate Akçe.

 Mission Rewards: As in previous episodes, the vast majority of Core Memories and Secondary Memories offer a cash sum on completion. However, once you progress into Sequence 03, you will find that these payments are actually rather negligible.

 City Events: Offering a standard reward of 500 Å per task, these optional challenges can supplement Ezio's limited income during early Sequences.

 Pickpocketing & Looting: Pickpocketing can be useful in Sequence 02, where Ezio's financial reach is limited, but soon becomes something of an irrelevance once he begins to accumulate revenue from properties and the Mediterranean Defense metagame. The sum of coins he obtains from each "lift" depends on the class of the individual he targets. Those clad in finery yield more than those wearing rags, but not by a great deal. Though Pickpocketing does not lead to Templar Awareness penalties (in a departure from Brotherhood's Notoriety system), male victims may seek to fight Ezio on discovery of the crime, while Ottoman soldiers in the region of the act will often attack. For this reason, it's a petty act best forgotten once Ezio is established in Constantinople.

By contrast, looting corpses can be highly profitable – though only occasionally in a financial sense. Almost every opponent that Ezio defeats will surrender a small sum of coins when he rifles through their pockets but, more importantly, will yield varying numbers of consumable items (such as Throwing Knives, Medicine and crafting ingredients). This can enable you to keep Ezio's supplies stocked up at all times, removing the need to visit merchants; surplus crafting materials can be sold to Piri Reis for a tidy profit. Stalkers and the Templar Captains stationed in Dens are the most lucrative targets to loot, as they each carry in the region of 1,000 Å. Note that Looting is a reprehensible act, and will invite expressions of disgust and disdain from nearby civilians – and raw aggression from passing patrols. You can optionally perform the Counter Steal technique (see page 132) to divest opponents of their valuables before you disable them.

 Treasure Chests & Bomb Stashes: The ornate, rectangular Treasure Chests offer variable sums of money in addition to occasional crafting items; they also contribute to the Total Synch rating. The vast majority of them are located in Constantinople, though there are a further 12 in Cappadocia in Sequence 07, and 15 in five "Secret Locations" (the four destinations that Ezio visits in Core Memories to obtain Masyaf Keys, plus the unlockable Hagia Sofia). You can purchase Treasure Maps that reveal their locations in Constantinople and Cappadocia at Book Shops. Bomb Stashes, containers that are either made from wood or have rounded corners, hold crafting ingredients only – though these can, naturally, be converted into currency via Piri Reis.

 Templar Couriers: These individuals can be robbed of the Templar tax revenue they carry, usually in the region of 1,000 Å to 1,500 Å. The difficult process of catching these fleet-footed individuals, however, ensures that Ezio will usually earn every last coin before the conclusion of the chase. Be sure to use the Tackle, Leg Sweep or Grab techniques to incapacitate them without lasting injury, as killing them will instantly elevate your Templar Awareness level to full "Aware" status.

 Mediterranean Defense: From early in Sequence 03, sending Assassin recruits and apprentices on missions not only enables you to improve their standing, but also leads to noteworthy cash bounties. When you eventually liberate cities from Templar control, you will also accumulate a steady stream of additional revenue from Brotherhood activities in each region. See page 93 to learn how the Mediterranean Defense metagame can become a cash machine.

 Rebuilding Constantinople: Ezio's liberation of city districts from Templar influence and taxation opens up business opportunities. Investment in retail establishments and other properties will lead to a regular income and, in time, substantial profits. It will also enable you to gain discounts on purchases from merchants in zones under Assassin control. Turn to page 86 for a full guide to this lucrative metagame.

PRIMER

WALKTHROUGH

SIDE QUESTS

REFERENCE & ANALYSIS

MULTIPLAYER

EXTRAS

INDEX

MOVES OVERVIEW

GENERATING INCOME

WEAPONS

ARMOR

SHOPS

ENEMIES

TEMPLAR AWARENESS

ACHIEVEMENTS & TROPHIES

MISSION CHECKLIST

Every melee weapon is rated in three categories (Damage, Speed and Deflect) that define its effectiveness in combat. The higher the rating in each category, the better the weapon will perform.

- **Damage:** This attribute is used to determine the strength of each successful attack.

- **Speed:** Weapons with a high speed rating enable Ezio to attack faster and more frequently.

- **Deflect:** Governs a weapon's effectiveness when used to block enemy assaults.

Special attacks and the number of blows required to kill an opponent with a combo assault are also important factors to take into account when assessing the overall efficiency of each class of weapon.

- **Special Attacks:** These "charge-up" techniques are unique to certain weapon classes. Heavy and Long weapons share the Throw move, with Long weapons also offering the Sweep attack; armed with fists alone, Ezio can perform the Throw Sand move.

- **Combo Efficiency:** Weapon classes differ in the number of hits required for a finishing blow, while the size of a weapon will also have a bearing on its efficiency in both combos and Kill Streaks.

Finishing Blows: Combo Requirements

WEAPON	HITS REQUIRED
Fists	5
Hidden Blade/Hookblade	4
Small Weapons	3
Medium Weapons	3
Heavy Weapons	2
Long Weapons	2

Every time you acquire a weapon as a purchase or as a reward, Ezio equips it immediately. You can switch to other weapons in your collection via any Blacksmith store (with the exception of those that they do not hold in stock), or by collecting them from the display racks inside the Assassin's HQ.

FISTS

Fist-fighting enables Ezio to attack at speed, but the vast majority of opponents will foil his attempts to initiate combos unless you begin with a Dodge. Even if you have an enemy off-balance, Ezio inflicts very little damage with individual blows. It also renders him highly vulnerable to enemy attacks, even if you diligently block. The principle reason to use unarmed combat is to employ the Disarm move, especially when you face the Varangian enemy archetype: their Long weapons are unparalleled in large-scale brawls. However, fist-fighting can also be employed when you must disable opponents without killing them. If stealth and mercy are called for, sneak up behind an opponent and tap the Primary Attack button to incapacitate them with a non-lethal finishing move.

Fists Attributes

NAME	DAMAGE	SPEED	DEFLECT	PRICE (A)	AVAILABILITY
Fists	✖	✖✖✖✖✖	✖	-	Available from the start

Special Attack: Throw Sand

While unarmed, hold the Primary Attack button to grab a handful of dirt, sand or dust; release the button to hurl it in the faces of your opponents (📷01). This will temporarily stun opponents who stand within the effect radius, though it has no effect on Janissaries and Almogavar. Ezio is immobilized while powering up this attack, and it cannot be cancelled once you begin.

- The Throw Sand move renders susceptible opponents vulnerable to combo attacks, even if they would usually dodge or block them.

- When enemies prepare to perform this attack – it's a particular favorite of the Varangian archetype – use the Dodge move to jump clear.

HIDDEN BLADES

Against all but the mighty Janissaries, the Hidden Blade is viciously efficient – but only if you can master the precise timing required to perform Counter Kills. Set up a Kill Streak, and you can dance a whirlwind of death to neutralize all hostiles in range. However, its short range and poor damage on individual combo strikes makes it unsuited to pummeling aggressors in a conventional manner. It is a weapon that lends itself to artistry, not brute force.

- Only Janissaries have the ability to consistently resist Hidden Blade Counter Kills or instant-death attacks during a Kill Streak, though at the expense of a sizable hit to their health gauge.
- When Ezio acquires the Hookblade in Sequence 02, he recovers the ability to perform Double Assassinations.
- The Poison Blade can only be used to inject targets with Poison at close range – an act that will usually pass without notice. If you enter combat, Ezio will automatically switch to the Hidden Blade.

NAME	DESCRIPTION	PRICE (Å)	AVAILABILITY
Hidden Blade	Enables Assassination techniques; wickedly effective when employed for quick Counter Kills and Kill Streaks.	–	Available from the start
Poison Blade	Slim secondary blade. Enables Assassination by Poison.	–	Available from the start
Hookblade	Endows its user with a wider range of navigational and combat maneuvers.	–	Sequence 02, Memory 03

SMALL WEAPONS

Small weapons enable Ezio to attack with tremendous speed, but offer poor reach and relatively low damage with individual combo blows. That said, Ezio's fighting style and a selection of grizzly finishing attacks can make them enjoyable to use.

Small Weapon Attributes

NAME	DAMAGE	SPEED	DEFLECT	PRICE (Å)	AVAILABILITY
Macedonian Dagger	✖✖	✖✖	✖✖	518	Sequence 02
Kurdish Jambiya	✖	✖✖	✖✖	345	Sequence 02
Standard Stiletto	✖	✖✖✖	✖✖	805	Sequence 03
Arabian Dagger	✖✖	✖✖✖✖	✖	2,185	Sequence 04
Butcher's Knife	✖✖✖	✖✖✖✖✖	✖✖✖	5,750	Sequence 05
Bayezid's Knife	✖✖✖✖✖	✖✖✖	✖✖✖✖	13,248	Sequence 06
Afghani Khyber Blade	✖✖✖✖	✖✖✖✖	✖✖	11,040	Sequence 07
Romani Stiletto	✖✖✖✖✖	✖✖✖	✖✖✖✖	–	Complete all Romani Challenges (see page 100)
Mehmet's Dagger*	✖✖✖✖✖	✖✖✖✖✖	✖✖✖✖✖	–	Complete The Trickster, Part 1 (see page 96)

* Each hit with this weapon has a chance to poison the target.

PRIMER

WALKTHROUGH

SIDE QUESTS

REFERENCE & ANALYSIS

MULTIPLAYER

EXTRAS

INDEX

MEDIUM WEAPONS

Balance is the watchword of the Medium weapon category, offering a good blend of range, speed, damage and defense. Swords are especially effective for combo attacks and Kill Streaks. Brooms and fishing poles dropped by civilians count as Medium weapons if you collect and utilize them in combat.

Medium Weapon Attributes

NAME	DAMAGE	SPEED	DEFLECT	PRICE (A)	AVAILABILITY
Assassin Yataghan Sword	✗	✗ ✗	✗	–	Available from the start
Prussian War Hammer	✗	✗ ✗ ✗	✗ ✗ ✗	2,990	Sequence 02
Persian Shamshir	✗	✗ ✗ ✗ ✗	✗ ✗ ✗	3,163	Sequence 02, Memory 05
Florentine Falchion	✗	✗ ✗ ✗	✗ ✗ ✗ ✗	6,555	Sequence 03
Merovingian Axe	✗	✗ ✗ ✗ ✗ ✗	✗ ✗ ✗ ✗ ✗	7,326	Sequence 03, Memory 04
Mercenario War Hammer	✗ ✗	✗	✗ ✗	7,360	Sequence 04
Condottiero Mace	✗ ✗	✗ ✗	✗ ✗	10,120	Sequence 04, Memory 04
Syrian Sabre	✗ ✗	✗ ✗ ✗ ✗	✗ ✗ ✗	11,960	Sequence 05
Sledgehammer	✗ ✗ ✗	✗ ✗ ✗ ✗	✗	13,340	Sequence 05, Memory 03
Sicilian Rapier	✗ ✗ ✗	✗ ✗ ✗ ✗ ✗	✗ ✗ ✗ ✗ ✗	23,736	Sequence 06
Janissary's Kijil	✗ ✗ ✗ ✗	✗ ✗	✗ ✗	28,290	Sequence 06, Memory 04
Byzantine Arming Sword	✗	✗ ✗	✗	1,610	Sequence 07
Byzantine Mace	✗ ✗ ✗	✗ ✗ ✗ ✗ ✗	✗ ✗ ✗	18,055	Sequence 07
Ottoman Mace	✗ ✗ ✗ ✗	✗ ✗ ✗ ✗	✗ ✗	–	Complete all Thieves Guild Challenges (see page 101)
Altair's Sword	✗ ✗ ✗ ✗ ✗	✗ ✗ ✗	✗ ✗ ✗ ✗	–	Complete all Assassin Guild Challenges (see page 100)
Yusuf's Turkish Kijil*	✗ ✗ ✗ ✗ ✗	✗ ✗ ✗ ✗ ✗	✗ ✗ ✗ ✗ ✗	–	Complete The Deacon, Part 1 (see page 96)
Vlad Tepes's Sword	✗ ✗ ✗ ✗	✗ ✗ ✗ ✗	✗ ✗ ✗ ✗	–	Complete the Impaler's Prison Secret Location (see page 103)
Captain's Sword	✗ ✗	✗ ✗ ✗	✗ ✗ ✗	–	Unlocked through Uplay website
Milanese Sword	✗ ✗ ✗	✗ ✗ ✗	✗ ✗	–	Unlocked through Uplay website
Schiavona	✗ ✗ ✗	✗ ✗	✗ ✗ ✗	–	Unlocked through Uplay website

MOVES OVERVIEW

GENERATING INCOME

WEAPONS

ARMOR

SHOPS

ENEMIES

TEMPLAR AWARENESS

ACHIEVEMENTS & TROPHIES

MISSION CHECKLIST

* Every time you unsheathe this weapon at the start of a fight, there's a chance that some enemies will flee.

HEAVY WEAPONS

Heavy weapons are carried by the Byzantine Almogavar, and can be collected after you kill them. Once you acquire the Heavy Sheath from a Tailor, though, Ezio can purchase and carry one of these mighty axes or swords at all times, with it occupying the inventory slot usually reserved for his Medium weapon.

Weapons in the Heavy category may be slow and cumbersome, but their reach and high damage makes them a perfect choice when you need to brutalize Janissaries in a conventional battle. They are especially effective when these opponents draw their sidearms to fire on Ezio, with the increased range foiling their attempts to back away; two hits in these situations will severely weaken them. Indeed, you may find it worthwhile to sacrifice the use of a Medium weapon entirely for the express purpose of using a long sword or axe for encounters with Janissaries.

Heavy Weapon Attributes

	NAME	DAMAGE	SPEED	DEFLECT	PRICE (Ａ)	AVAILABILITY
	Bearded Axe	✖✖	✖✖✖	✖✖✖✖	8,050	Sequence 02
	French Bastard Sword	✖✖✖	✖✖✖✖	✖✖✖	14,260	Sequence 04
	Condottiero Axe	✖✖✖	✖✖	✖✖✖✖✖	23,460	Sequence 06
	Prussian Long Sword	✖✖✖	✖✖✖✖✖	✖✖✖✖✖	30,015	Sequence 07
	Broadsword	✖✖✖✖✖	✖✖✖✖	✖✖✖✖	-	Complete all Mercenaries Guild Challenges (see page 101)
	Almogavar Axe	✖✖✖✖✖	✖✖✖✖✖	✖✖✖✖✖	-	Complete The Champion, Part 1 (see page 97)

Special Attack: Throw

With a Heavy weapon equipped, hold and release the Primary Attack button to throw it at a targeted opponent, killing them instantly (📷 02). If you perform this attack with a Heavy weapon owned by Ezio (and not appropriated from a defeated Almogavar), don't forget to collect it afterwards. If you leave it behind, or pick up another weapon by mistake, visit a Blacksmith or return to the Assassin's HQ to grab a replacement.

PRIMER

WALKTHROUGH

SIDE QUESTS

REFERENCE & ANALYSIS

MULTIPLAYER

EXTRAS

INDEX

MOVES OVERVIEW

GENERATING INCOME

WEAPONS

ARMOR

SHOPS

ENEMIES

TEMPLAR AWARENESS

ACHIEVEMENTS & TROPHIES

MISSION CHECKLIST

 # LONG WEAPONS

Though Ezio cannot purchase or permanently equip Long weapons, these polearms can be acquired whenever you face the Byzantine Varangian archetype, principally in Core Memories or while passing through Templar Dens. With their unrivalled range and the devastating "Sweep" special attack, we suggest that you make use of these whenever you find them.

Though their slow speed makes them broadly unsuited to combos and Kill Streaks, Long weapons can be used to perform spectacular Counter Kills on all opponents. However, the way in which Ezio employs them is a little unusual: he will often execute killing blows that leave the polearm embedded within a victim's body. You can retrieve it by standing over the corpse, but this can be dangerous when you are surrounded by a variety of assailants.

Long weapons have a special relationship with weapons in the Heavy category. They are the only weapon of any kind that enable you to block the Almogavar's Smash assault. Though the Long weapon will be broken as a consequence, Ezio may continue to wield one half of it; functionally, it will now operate as a Medium weapon. Performing a Counter Kill on an Almogavar will also break a polearm, though Ezio will subsequently plunge both halves into his victim's body.

Long Weapon Attributes

	NAME	DAMAGE	SPEED	DEFLECT	PRICE (Ⓐ)	AVAILABILITY
	Spear	✖✖✖	✖✖✖✖✖	✖✖✖	-	Obtained from Varangians only
	Halberd	✖✖✖✖	✖✖✖✖	✖✖✖	-	

Special Attacks: Sweep & Throw

Exclusive to polearms and only available in Combat mode, the power-up Sweep move (hold then release the Primary Attack button) kills all surrounding opponents within a wide radius as Ezio swings the halberd or spear in a circle at neck height (📷 03). With a little practice, this technique effectively makes you invincible; the only drawback, alas, is that polearms are usually hard to come by.

When Ezio is not locked in Combat mode, Sweep is replaced by the Throw technique. With this, Ezio will hurl the polearm at a highlighted target; the results are always fatal.

03

BOMBS

Bombs can be created by interacting with crafting tables at the Assassin's HQ, at an Assassin's Den, and at various locations throughout Constantinople and certain external destinations.

Ezio can carry three different types of bomb at once, each contained in its own specific pouch:

- **Lethal Bombs:** Designed to kill enemies.
- **Tactical Bombs:** Designed to give an advantage in a fight or when escaping from enemies.
- **Diversion Bombs:** Designed to distract or misdirect guards.

Bombs are made of three elements that, once combined, determine the nature of the bomb: an **Effect**, a **Casing**, and **Gunpowder**. These three types of crafting ingredients can be acquired in various ways: looted from the bodies of enemies, bought from certain shops, purloined from Bomb Stashes, as rewards for defending Dens, and as "profits" in the Mediterranean Defense metagame.

Bomb Effects

Your choice of Effect ingredient determines the precise nature of a bomb, and is the most critical component.

ICON	INGREDIENT	BOMB	DESCRIPTION	TIPS
	Caltrop	Caltrop Bomb (Tactical)	Impedes enemy movement by dispersing small spikes across the ground, rendering its victims vulnerable during a fight.	■ Great for ending enemy pursuits as you run through narrow streets or alleyways. ■ Ezio is immune to their effects, so it can also be employed to impede opponents during a fight.
	Lamb's Blood	Blood Bomb (Tactical)	Expels a thick spray of blood over its victims, stunning them briefly with the fear that they have been badly injured.	■ These bombs incapacitate guards, but only very temporarily. They will soon resume their assault on Ezio unless he escapes. ■ If all aggressors are caught in a Blood Bomb explosion during a fight, Ezio will automatically exit Combat mode to facilitate a rapid departure.
	Shrapnel	Splinter Bomb (Lethal)	Kills or injures by dispersing deadly shrapnel with its explosion.	■ The default bomb with a bang; used for killing groups of enemies. ■ Be very careful when you use this in areas crowded with pedestrians.
	Salt of Petra	Smoke Decoy (Diversion)	Releases a quiet but persistent smoke signal that lures all soldiers who catch sight of it.	■ Used to lure guards to a particular location. ■ This is a more discrete diversion than the noisy Cherry Bomb, as enemies will usually only investigate if they can actually see the smoke. This makes it perfect when you need to move a sentry or two from a very specific position without attracting too much attention from elsewhere.
	Phosphorous	Smoke Screen (Tactical)	Blinds its victims and breaks their line of sight.	■ This replicates the effects of the classic Assassin's Creed Smoke Bomb. ■ Activate Eagle Sense to see clearly while running through the smoke. ■ Enemies incapacitated by a Smoke Screen are pitifully easy to kill, no matter their individual prowess under normal combat situations. This makes these bombs a powerful tool if you are surrounded by Janissaries.
	Datura	Datura Bomb (Lethal)	Releases a poisonous cloud that slowly cripples all those who inhale its fumes.	■ All unfortunates within the radius of a Datura Bomb explosion will experience the effects of the poisonous fumes. This makes it ill-suited to areas with large numbers of civilians.
	Coal Dust	Thunder Bomb (Lethal)	Cripples or injures foes with an intense explosive force.	■ The Thunder Bomb is less damaging than other explosives in the Lethal category, but also temporarily disables opponents caught within the blast radius. ■ Ezio can only carry three units of Coal Dust at a time. If you decide to use this bomb regularly, be prepared to pay for the privilege.
	Skunk Oil	Stink Bomb (Diversion)	Drenches its victims with a foul odor, repelling all those who come too close.	■ Useful for separating a marked target from innocent crowds. ■ Any enemy who comes into contact with the effect radius of a Stink Bomb will stop in their tracks. This means that you can create temporary impassable "barriers" in all but the widest thoroughfares.
	Sulfur	Cherry Bomb (Diversion)	Explodes with a loud bang, luring all guards within earshot.	■ Cherry Bombs are fantastically effective, but far from subtle. You may find they attract more enemies than you might anticipate – which isn't always a good thing.
	Pyrite Coins	Gold Bomb (Diversion)	Disperses chunks of glittering Pyrite Coins, attracting hordes of scrounging citizens who will become aggressive towards any guard who approaches.	■ When deployed in combat, citizens in the vicinity will attempt to grab guards, restraining them to facilitate Ezio's escape. ■ Though ostensibly designed for hurried departures, you can instead opt to stalk through the crowd, executing the helpless Ottomans or Byzantines. ■ Ezio's carrying capacity for Pyrite Coins is extremely low, so you should refrain from selling this ingredient if you intend to craft this bomb.

Bomb Casing

The type of Casing used determines how a bomb is triggered, or the delay before it detonates.

ICON	CASING	DESCRIPTION	TIPS
	Fuse Shell	Rebounds off surfaces; detonates after three seconds.	■ Perfect when you need a brief delay before the bomb explodes. The distraction of the device landing can be an additional bonus when it is used to cover Ezio's movements.
	Impact Shell	Explodes on impact.	■ Best used for immediate results. ■ If used with bombs in the Lethal category, be careful not to drop them at Ezio's feet. This style of deployment is often desirable for Diversion and Tactical bombs, however.
	Trip Wire	Detonates when enemies walk near it.	■ Most commonly used to set up traps. ■ Extremely effective when you have used Eagle Sense to identify a patrol route followed by an individual you need to kill, such as a Templar Captain.
	Sticky Pouch	Sticks to surfaces and individuals, and detonates after five seconds.	■ Though it has many tactical applications, the Sticky Pouch is also great fun to use. ■ The delay before the fuse burns means that it enables Ezio to put distance between himself and the explosion before the device detonates.

Bomb Gunpowder

Your choice of Gunpowder only affects the blast radius, represented by a small gauge display below a bomb's icon. As a rule, use Indian Gunpowder for precision attacks on a single target – or, to employ the classic euphemism, minimize collateral damage – and British Gunpowder for maximum effect.

ICON	GUNPOWDER	BLAST RADIUS
	Indian Gunpowder	2 meters
	Arabic Gunpowder	3 meters
	British Gunpowder	4 meters

Bomb Pouches

Though Ezio can carry three bombs in the Lethal, Tactical and Diversion pouches by default, you can increase his overall capacity.

NAME	CAPACITY/UPGRADE	AVAILABILITY
Small Bomb Pouch	3	Sequence 02, Memory 06
Medium Bomb Pouch	+1	Complete Bomb Challenges (see page 101)
Large Bomb Pouch	+1	Only available in specific Assassin's Creed Revelations editions, or as a preorder bonus

PRIMER

WALKTHROUGH

SIDE QUESTS

REFERENCE & ANALYSIS

MULTIPLAYER

EXTRAS

INDEX

MOVES OVERVIEW

GENERATING INCOME

WEAPONS

ARMOR

SHOPS

ENEMIES

TEMPLAR AWARENESS

ACHIEVEMENTS & TROPHIES

MISSION CHECKLIST

RANGED WEAPONS & CONSUMABLES

When an objective calls for subtlety, or the odds are set against you, ranged weapons provide the means to strike decisively from a distance. Indeed, many Full Synch requirements can be prohibitively difficult unless you make good use of projectiles.

While supplies for all consumables can be purchased from merchants, regularly looting defeated foes will enable you to replenish your stocks without expense (with the exception of Parachutes, which can only be bought from a Tailor). We suggest that you invest in all capacity upgrades for your ranged weapons when you can afford them.

⚔ Crossbow

This powerful and silent weapon is perfect for stealth kills from a safe distance or elevation, but represents a substantial investment when it first becomes available for purchase on Ezio's arrival in Constantinople. We would advise that funds acquired during Sequences 02 and 03 are better spent on opening businesses and Banks. Once dividends from Ezio's property acquisitions and Mediterranean Defense missions begin pouring in during Sequence 04, though, it's a worthwhile purchase – and one that, by that stage, won't render Ezio a pauper for a time. The visit to the Yerebatan Cistern in Sequence 03 (with its exacting Full Synch requirement) is the only Core Memory prior to Sequence 05 where the Crossbow might be a boon. Interestingly, though, once you have purchased it, the weapon is made available whenever you use the Replay Memory feature.

To aim the Crossbow, hold the Primary Attack button until the line-of-sight indicator is fully focused (04). Fire too early, and the bolt may miss the target entirely, or skid harmlessly off their armor or clothes. Though the Crossbow is most efficient when employed from range against oblivious opponents, it can be used to perform Counter Kills on certain adversaries in close combat. The timing window for these lethal rebuttals is similar to Hidden Blade Counters. Though these are enjoyable to perform, Ezio will usually be better served by switching to an alternative weapon in open conflict.

🔫 Pistol

As with the Crossbow, the Pistol is used by holding the Primary Attack button to aim. Once Ezio's focus has steadied, release the button to fire, or press the Empty Hand button to cancel the shot. While a single bullet will be lethal against all but the strongest Ottomans or Byzantines, the violent noise of each discharge will attract attention in a wide radius. For this reason, it is wise to only employ this weapon when there are no patrols or sentries in range to hear it. One ideal application is using it to slay fleeing Stalkers from a distance: the near-instantaneous impact of the bullet makes it more reliable than the slower Crossbow bolts, Poison Darts or Throwing Knives.

Pistol & Upgrades

NAME	CAPACITY	PRICE (A)	AVAILABILITY
Pistol	6	–	Available from the start
Bullets	–	242	Available in Blacksmith stores from the start of Sequence 02
Capacity Upgrade	+2	–	Only available in specific Assassin's Creed Revelations editions, or as a preorder bonus

Crossbow & Upgrades

NAME	CAPACITY/ UPGRADE	PRICE (A)	AVAILABILITY
Crossbow	15	22,080	Sequence 02
Crossbow Bolt	–	242	Once you have bought the Crossbow
Medium Quiver	+5	7,705	Once you have bought the Crossbow
Large Quiver	+5	14,950	Sequence 05
Extra-Large Quiver	+5	–	Only available in specific Assassin's Creed Revelations editions, or as a preorder bonus

Throwing Knives

Though other projectiles are faster and inflict greater damage, Throwing Knives are a staple that you will use more frequently than any other ranged weapon. With the rooftops of Constantinople dotted with Gunmen and, later, Bombmen, Throwing Knives enable you to near-effortlessly clear a path of troublesome sentries while free running from one destination to another. They can be nigh-essential when Ezio must infiltrate an area without being seen.

Though Throwing Knives can be thrown at targets once they are highlighted, acquiring a Target Lock will significantly increase their accuracy. This is especially important against assailants who are moving or climbing. With practice, you will gain the ability to perform perfunctory kills on guards who might detect Ezio while barely breaking stride.

In open combat, Throwing Knives can be a useful addition to standard combat strategies. You can hurl them whenever opponents are content to circle Ezio, when a Gunman or Janissary prepares to fire a weapon, or to kill or weaken adversaries as they run in to engage you.

05

Special Attack: Flying Knives

With the Throwing Knives equipped, hold the Secondary Attack button to power up the Flying Knives ability, then release it to hurl blades at up to three targets (📷 05). Though rarely effective in an established battle, this technique is most efficient when used to initiate hostilities, potentially killing a trio of targets before they can lay hands on their weapons. This is particularly useful when you fight guards who are surrounding potential recruits.

Throwing Knives & Upgrades

NAME	CAPACITY/ UPGRADE	PRICE (Ⱥ)	AVAILABILITY
Initial Knife Belt	5	-	Available from the start
Throwing Knife	-	86	Sequence 02
Knife Belt Upgrade	+5	2,185	Sequence 02
Knife Belt Upgrade	+5	3,565	Sequence 04
Knife Belt Upgrade	+5	7,015	Sequence 06
Knife Belt Upgrade	+5	11,845	Sequence 08

PRIMER

WALKTHROUGH

SIDE QUESTS

REFERENCE & ANALYSIS

MULTIPLAYER

EXTRAS

INDEX

MOVES OVERVIEW

GENERATING INCOME

WEAPONS

ARMOR

SHOPS

ENEMIES

TEMPLAR AWARENESS

ACHIEVEMENTS & TROPHIES

MISSION CHECKLIST

Poison Darts

Don't underestimate Poison Darts: these tiny projectiles are one of Ezio's most devastating weapons, and have unique tactical applications that can make challenging objectives far, far easier. As with the Pistol and Crossbow, Poison Darts must be aimed before they are fired to successfully penetrate armor and puncture skin; release the Secondary Attack button too soon, and they will harmlessly rebound from the target. A successful shot, however, will have an immediate effect on all Ottoman and Byzantine soldiers – including the redoubtable Janissaries and Templar Captains (📷 06).

06

The beauty of Poison Darts is that they enable Ezio to strike a target without raising the alarm. Even inside a Templar Den, nearby soldiers will simply look on with bemusement as their ally begins to behave in a bizarre fashion; it should go without saying that the effects of the lethal payload make Poison Darts an excellent diversionary technique. A convenient solution to many difficult situations in Core and Secondary Memories, this weapon is a must for Den Attacks.

The Fast Poison upgrade dramatically reduces the delay before a victim succumbs to the deadly effect of a dart or a stab from the Poison Blade. However, this rather diminishes the effectiveness of both weapons as a method of creating diversions. If that does not deter you from a purchase, there is an Achievement/Trophy that you should definitely unlock before buying this upgrade: see page 159 for details.

Poison & Upgrades

NAME	CAPACITY/ UPGRADE	PRICE (A)	AVAILABILITY
Small Poison Vial	5	–	Available from the start
Poison Dose	–	201	Sequence 02
Fast Poison	–	8,625	Sequence 02
Medium Poison Vial	+5	3,220	Sequence 05
Large Poison Vial	+5	9,315	Sequence 08

Medicine

Medicine can be purchased from any Medical Shop or stall operated by a Doctor, though players who diligently loot opponents will rarely have cause to spend money on these miraculous restorative tinctures. You can acquire two Medicine Pouch upgrades during the course of the story.

Medicine & Upgrades

NAME	CAPACITY/ UPGRADE	PRICE (A)	AVAILABILITY
Medicine	–	86	Sequence 01, Memory 05
Small Medicine Pouch	5	–	Available from the start
Medium Medicine Pouch	+5	2,875	Sequence 03
Large Medicine Pouch	+5	7,130	Sequence 07

Parachute

Parachutes are the only consumable item that cannot be replenished through looting, though the cost of individual refills is trifling once Ezio begins to accrue income from Constantinople and the Brotherhood's activities in the Mediterranean region.

Parachute & Upgrades

NAME	CAPACITY/ UPGRADE	PRICE (A)	AVAILABILITY
Small Parachute Bag	5	–	Sequence 01, Memory 04
Parachute Refill	–	230	Sequence 02
Medium Parachute Bag	+5	5,980	Sequence 04
Large Parachute Bag	+5	9,718	Sequence 06

VyU2Fk
VyTWFk
IuZ0lzVHJ1ZQ==
0aGluZ0lzUGVybWl0dGVk
VRPZidhclN0h3JoZXM=

OUTFITS

From the Inventory ▶ Outfits menu, you can select skins unlocked through gameplay milestones or provided as preorder bonuses or special edition perks. These are purely aesthetic changes, having no effect on Ezio's capabilities.

ARMOR OF BRUTUS

Only available in specific Assassin's Creed Revelations editions, or as a preorder bonus.

DESMOND OUTFIT

Unlocked by completing Desmond's Journey #5 (see page 108).

TURKISH ASSASSIN ARMOR

Only available in specific Assassin's Creed Revelations editions, or as a preorder bonus.

OLD EAGLE

Activate the Old Eagle cheat (see page 201 for details).

ARMOR

Most suits of armor are separated into four distinct sections that can be purchased separately: bracers, greaves, spaulders, and a chest plate or guard. Each piece has two ratings. Health reveals the number of blocks that the protective garb will add to Ezio's Health Meter. Resistance indicates how much damage the armor can withstand before it breaks, necessitating a trip to a Blacksmith for (easily affordable) repair work.

The Assassin's Creed combat system does not distinguish between hit locations,

with every injury sustained by Ezio affecting all armor parts equally; every hit point of damage he sustains is shared by his armor. Once the cumulative damage exceeds the maximum Resistance (revealed in Hit Points in the tables that follow), an armor section will break. At this point, the Health benefits it contributes will be removed, as represented by red "broken" blocks on the Health Meter.

There are three grades of armor to unlock over time, plus two complete suits of secret armor that cannot be purchased from merchants (see overleaf).

| AZAP ARMOR SET | MAMLUK ARMOR SET | SEPAHI ARMOR SET |

Arms Armor

NAME	HEALTH BLOCKS	RESISTANCE	HIT POINTS	PRICE (Ⱥ)	AVAILABILITY
Azap Leather Bracers	I	✖✖	200	1,150	Sequence 03
Mamluk Metal Bracers	I	✖✖✖	300	4,002	Sequence 05
Sepahi Riding Bracers	II	✖✖✖✖	400	12,696	Sequence 06, Memory 05

Legs Armor

NAME	HEALTH BLOCKS	RESISTANCE	HIT POINTS	PRICE (Ⱥ)	AVAILABILITY
Azap Leather Greaves	I	✖✖)	250	1,265	Sequence 04
Mamluk Metal Greaves	II	✖✖✖)	350	4,416	Sequence 05
Sepahi Riding Greaves	II	✖✖✖✖)	450	13,662	Sequence 06, Memory 05

Shoulder Armor

NAME	HEALTH BLOCKS	RESISTANCE	HIT POINTS	PRICE (Ⱥ)	AVAILABILITY
Azap Leather Spaulders	I	✖✖✖	300	1,675	Sequence 02
Mamluk Metal Spaulders	II	✖✖✖✖)	450	7,038	Sequence 06
Sepahi Riding Spaulders	III	✖✖✖✖✖)	550	15,456	Sequence 07

Chest Armor

NAME	HEALTH BLOCKS	RESISTANCE	HIT POINTS	PRICE (Ⓐ)	AVAILABILITY
Azap Leather Guard	II	✖✖✖✖	400	2,875	Sequence 04, Memory 04
Mamluk Chest Plate	III	✖✖✖✖✖	500	7,866	Sequence 06
Sepahi Chest Guard	IIII	✖✖✖✖✖✖	600	16,560	Sequence 07

Master Assassin's Armor Set*

NAME	HEALTH BLOCKS	RESISTANCE	HIT POINTS	SPECIAL FEATURE	AVAILABILITY
Master Assassin's Bracers	III				
Master Assassin's Greaves	III			Makes Ezio more silent: he won't cause enemies to turn around when performing High Profile moves on rooftops	Train seven Assassin recruits to Level 11
Master Assassin's Spaulders	IIII	∞	∞		
Master Assassin's Chest Guard	IIIII				

Ishak Pasha's Armor Set*

NAME	HEALTH BLOCKS	RESISTANCE	HIT POINTS	SPECIAL FEATURE	AVAILABILITY
Ishak Pasha's Bracers	III				
Ishak Pasha's Greaves	III			Has a chance to deflect bullets and reduce the damage from enemy bombs	Complete the Hagia Sophia Secret Location (see page 102)
Ishak Pasha's Spaulders	IIII	∞	∞		
Ishak Pasha's Chest Guard	IIIII				

* This armor set must be worn as a complete suit. It cannot be damaged, and therefore need never be repaired.

17.anima.23082003.RmFjZXNJbiN0b25l
17.anima.16082003.RXNjYXBl
17.anima.23082003.V2hhdElzVGhpc1BsYWNl
17.anima.16052003.Q2hpY2Fnb0dpcmxxz
17.anima.27082003.Tm90RmFyRW5vdWdo

In this section, we examine the wares and services that Ezio can procure from the merchants he encounters in Constantinople and Cappadocia. For information on the Rebuilding Constantinople metagame, see page 86 of the Side Quests chapter.

We specify base prices throughout this chapter. If a store is in a region controlled by Templars, an additional 10% premium will be charged. If it is governed by the Brotherhood, Ezio will receive a 15% discount.

BLACKSMITHS

Note: Ezio will automatically equip weapons or armor bought from a Blacksmith. You can also use this feature to switch between equipment he has purchased at an earlier date.

Blacksmiths: Shop Selections

CATEGORY	NAME	PRICE (Ⱥ)	AVAILABILITY	LOCATION
Small Weapons	Kurdish Jambiya	345	Sequence 02	Constantinople
	Macedonian Dagger	518	Sequence 03	Constantinople
	Standard Stiletto	805	Sequence 03	Constantinople
	Arabian Dagger	2,185	Sequence 04	Constantinople
	Butcher's Knife	5,750	Sequence 05	Constantinople
	Afghani Khyber Blade	11,040	Sequence 07	Cappadocia
	Bayezid's Knife	13,248	Sequence 06	Constantinople
Medium Weapons	Assassin Yataghan Sword	-	Sequence 01, Memory 02	Constantinople
	Byzantine Arming Sword	1,610	Sequence 07	Cappadocia
	Prussian Warhammer	2,990	Sequence 02	Constantinople
	Persian Shamshir	3,163	Sequence 02, Memory 05	Constantinople
	Florentine Falchion	6,555	Sequence 03	Constantinople
	Merovingian Axe	7,326	Sequence 03, Memory 04	Constantinople
	Mercenario War Hammer	7,360	Sequence 04	Constantinople
	Condottiero Mace	10,120	Sequence 04, Memory 04	Constantinople
	Syrian Sabre	11,960	Sequence 05	Constantinople
	Sledgehammer	13,340	Sequence 05, Memory 03	Constantinople
	Byzantine Mace	18,055	Sequence 07	Cappadocia
	Sicilian Rapier	23,736	Sequence 06	Constantinople
	Janissary's Kijil	28,290	Sequence 06, Memory 04	Constantinople
Heavy Weapons	Bearded Axe	8,050	Sequence 02	Constantinople
	French Bastard Sword	14,260	Sequence 04	Constantinople
	Condottiero Axe	23,460	Sequence 06	Constantinople
	Prussian Long Sword	30,015	Sequence 07	Cappadocia
Ranged Weapons	Crossbow	22,080	Sequence 02	Constantinople
Armor	Azap Leather Bracers	1,150	Sequence 03	Constantinople
	Azap Leather Greaves	1,265	Sequence 04	Constantinople
	Azap Leather Spaulders	403	Sequence 02	Constantinople
	Azap Chest Guard	2,875	Sequence 04, Memory 04	Constantinople
	Mamluk Metal Bracers	4,002	Sequence 05	Constantinople
	Mamluk Metal Greaves	4,416	Sequence 05	Constantinople
	Mamluk Metal Spaulders	7,038	Sequence 06	Constantinople
	Mamluk Chest Plate	7,866	Sequence 06	Constantinople
	Sepahi Riding Bracers	12,696	Sequence 06, Memory 05	Constantinople
	Sepahi Riding Greaves	13,662	Sequence 06, Memory 05	Constantinople
	Sepahi Riding Spaulders	15,456	Sequence 07	Constantinople
	Sepahi Chest Guard	16,560	Sequence 07	Constantinople
Bomb Ingredients	Fuse Shell	115	Sequence 03	Any
	Indian Gunpowder	288	Sequence 03	Any
	Pyrite Coins	144	Sequence 03	Any
Ammunition	Pistol Bullet	242	Sequence 02	Any
	Throwing Knife	86	Sequence 02	Any
	Crossbow Bolt	242	After buying the Crossbow	Any
Repairs	Azap Leather Armor	30	-	Any
	Mamluk Metal Armor	60	-	Any
	Sepahi Riding Armor	100	-	Any

TAILORS

Though the ability to dye clothes is a purely aesthetic consideration, Tailors also sell a variety of vital upgrades and Parachute Refills.

BOOK SHOPS

Most Books in Revelations are acquired by purchasing them from these merchants, with an Achievement/Trophy for acquiring all of them. Book Shops also sell Treasure Maps, which helpfully mark the locations of Treasure Chests on the main map and mini-map.

CATEGORY	NAME	PRICE (Ꭺ)	AVAILABILITY
Dye Clothes	Original Grey	–	Sequence 02
	Byzantium Red	184	Sequence 02
	Algerian Silver	196	Sequence 02
	Janissary Green	196	Sequence 02
	Egyptian Blue	322	Sequence 02
	Mediterranean Cobalt	460	Sequence 02
	Aegean Marble	575	Sequence 02
	Topkapi Gold	817	Sequence 02
	Syrian Ash	943	Sequence 02
	Caspian Teal	1,116	Sequence 02
	Cappadocian Amber	1,173	Sequence 02
	Yemen Copper	1,725	Sequence 02
	Royal Violet	2,496	Sequence 02
	Masyaf White	2,703	Sequence 02
	Bosnian Indigo	3,301	Sequence 02
Capacity Upgrades	Medium Parachute Bag	5,980	Sequence 04
	Large Parachute Bag	9,718	Sequence 06
	Medium Medicine Pouch	2,875	Sequence 03
	Large Medicine Pouch	7,130	Sequence 07
	Medium Poison Vial	3,220	Sequence 05
	Large Poison Vial	9,315	Sequence 08
	Medium Quiver	7,705	After buying the Crossbow
	Large Quiver	14,950	Sequence 05
	Knife Belt Upgrade 1	2,185	Sequence 02
	Knife Belt Upgrade 2	3,565	Sequence 04
	Knife Belt Upgrade 3	7,015	Sequence 06
	Knife Belt Upgrade 4	11,845	Sequence 08
Misc	Heavy Sheath	9,488	Sequence 02
	Parachute Refill	230	Sequence 02

CATEGORY	NAME	PRICE (Ꭺ)	AVAILABILITY
Constantinople Books	The Odyssey	201	Sequence 02
	Aeneid	242	Sequence 02
	Mu'allaqat	334	Sequence 02
	Geography	483	Sequence 02
	The History of the Kings of Britain	529	Sequence 02
	Heimskringla	1,840	Sequence 03, Memory 02
	The Book of Prophecies	3,220	Sequence 03, Memory 02
	The Golden Ass	3,588	Sequence 03, Memory 02
	Parallel Lives	9,085	Sequence 03, Memory 02
	Metamorphoses	9,315	Sequence 03, Memory 02
	Opus Majus	9,775	Sequence 05
	The Secret History of the Mongols	24,725	Sequence 05
	Anabasis Alexandri	27,600	Sequence 05
	Record of the Grand Historian	44,505	Sequence 05
Cappadocia Books	Digenes Akritas	59,800	Sequence 07
	Cronica	76,475	Sequence 07
	Tirant Lo Blanch	86,250	Sequence 07
	Bibliotheca	97,750	Sequence 07
Treasure Maps	Imperial District Treasure Map 1	949	Sequence 03
	Imperial District Treasure Map 2	1,380	Sequence 03
	Galata Treasure Map 1	828	Sequence 02
	Galata Treasure Map 2	1,323	Sequence 02
	Beyazid District Treasure Map 1	874	Sequence 03
	Beyazid District Treasure Map 2	1,495	Sequence 03
	Constantin District Treasure Map 1	897	Sequence 03
	Constantin District Treasure Map 2	1,633	Sequence 03
	Arsenal Treasure Map	1,415	Sequence 03
	Cappadocia Treasure Map 1	1,104	Sequence 07
	Cappadocia Treasure Map 2	1,760	Sequence 07
	Ishak Pasha's Memoir Pages Map	12,075	Gather 25 Animus Data Fragments

PRIMER

WALKTHROUGH

SIDE QUESTS

REFERENCE & ANALYSIS

MULTIPLAYER

EXTRAS

INDEX

MOVES OVERVIEW

GENERATING INCOME

WEAPONS

ARMOR

SHOPS

ENEMIES

TEMPLAR AWARENESS

ACHIEVEMENTS & TROPHIES

MISSION CHECKLIST

PIRI REIS

Introduced to Ezio in Sequence 03, Piri Reis is a unique merchant in two important respects. Most of the wares in his Grand Bazaar establishment are unavailable until you complete his missions (see page 99), or fulfill specific assignments in the Mediterranean Defense metagame (see page 93). Perhaps more importantly, he will also purchase surplus crafting ingredients from Ezio for the same price he charges to supply them. This can provide income that you can invest in making great progress in the Rebuilding Constantinople metagame from an early stage in the story.

CRAFTING INGREDIENT	SALE & PURCHASE PRICE (Ⱥ)	AVAILABILITY
Indian Gunpowder	200	Sequence 03
Arabic Gunpowder	315	Sequence 03
Sticky Pouch	300	After completing Sticky Pouch Bomb Mission for Piri Reis
Trip Wire	200	After completing Trip Wire Bomb Mission for Piri Reis
Sulfur	100	After completing Cherry Bomb Bomb Mission for Piri Reis
Salt of Petra	80	After completing Smoke Decoy Bomb Mission for Piri Reis
Phosphorous	150	After completing Smoke Screen Bomb Mission for Piri Reis
Caltrop	165	After completing Caltrop Bomb Mission for Piri Reis
Datura	210	After completing Datura Bomb Mission for Piri Reis
Coal Dust	185	After completing Thunder Bomb Mission for Piri Reis
Impact Shell	150	After completing the survey mission in Marseille for Piri Reis (Mediterranean Defense)
Fuse Shell	80	After completing the survey mission in Tunis for Piri Reis (Mediterranean Defense)
British Gunpowder	420	After completing the survey mission in Alexandria for Piri Reis (Mediterranean Defense)
Lambs Blood	125	After completing the survey mission in Tripoli for Piri Reis (Mediterranean Defense)
Skunk Oil	55	After completing the survey mission in Madrid for Piri Reis (Mediterranean Defense)
Shrapnel	235	After completing the survey mission in Genoa for Piri Reis (Mediterranean Defense)
Pyrite Coin	105	After completing the survey mission in Lisbon for Piri Reis (Mediterranean Defense)

BLACK MARKET DEALERS

Though their services are useful in an emergency, you will often find that it is better to construct your own purpose-built explosives at a Crafting Table than hand your hard-earned coins to a Black Market Dealer. If money is tight in Sequence 03, however, patient players can turn a profit by bulk purchasing the Fuse Cherry Bomb and Impact Caltrop Bomb, dismantling them, then selling the components to Piri Reis.

BOMB	PRICE (Ⱥ)	AVAILABILITY
Fuse Cherry Bomb	250	Sequence 03
Tripwire Datura Bomb	1,000	Sequence 03
Sticky Splinter Bomb	750	Sequence 03
Impact Splinter Bomb	500	Sequence 03
Impact Caltrop Bomb	400	Sequence 03

DOCTORS

You never have to travel far in Constantinople to find a Doctor – especially as opening Medical Shops will also mean that the local practice will open mobile carts in the surrounding region.

CATEGORY	NAME	PRICE (Ⱥ)	AVAILABILITY
Consumables	Medicine	86	Sequence 02
	Poison	201	Sequence 02
Upgrades	Fast Poison	8,625	Sequence 02
Bomb Ingredients	Skunk Oil	86	Sequence 03
	Salt of Petra	115	Sequence 03

ENEMIES

All opponents in Assassin's Creed Revelations belong to one of several specific enemy archetypes, and will exhibit behaviors, proficiencies and weaknesses specific to their class. In this section, we examine the strengths and weaknesses of each archetype, offer combat strategies, and reveal the inner workings of the morale system.

ENEMY ARCHETYPES

BYZANTINE MILITIA

The Byzantine Militia enemy type is roughly analogous to the Ottoman Elite, in that both are rank-and-file opponents who should fall quickly to Ezio's attacks.

- Militia opponents are extremely susceptible to projectiles: a single Throwing Knife is enough to put them on their backs. They can dodge kicks, but this is pretty much irrelevant, as they can be defeated easily with a combo or Counter Kill.

- Whenever they appear in mixed groups with more dangerous allies, Militia provide an easy way to start a Kill Streak.

- Though they have a degree of free running prowess, Militia are slower than Ezio in a straight-line sprint and cannot scale walls.

MILITIA FACT SHEET	
Health Points	36
Strength	3
Morale	25
Melee Weapon	One-handed sword or mace
Ranged Weapon	Rocks
Notes	■ Can dodge kicks ■ Vulnerable to everything else

LOOT TABLE	
Drop	**Chance (%)**
Bullets	25
Throwing Knives	100
Medicine	40
Crossbow Bolts	25
Poison	30
Akçe (Ⓐ)	12-17
Bomb Ingredients	90

ALMOGAVAR FACT SHEET	
Health Points	84
Strength	7
Morale	1,000
Melee Weapon	Heavy weapons
Ranged Weapon	Rocks
Notes	■ Resistant to Disarm and immune to Hook and Throw ■ Can block grabs and standard weapon attacks ■ Final combo attack cannot be blocked ■ Can knock Ezio down with the Smash attack ■ Vulnerable to everything else, including kicks and Kill Streaks

LOOT TABLE	
Drop	**Chance (%)**
Bullets	40
Throwing Knives	35
Medicine	50
Crossbow Bolts	40
Poison	40
Akçe (Ⓐ)	41-49
Bomb Ingredients	90

BYZANTINE ALMOGAVAR

Slow but relentlessly aggressive, the armor-plated Almogavar are easily identified by their enormous stature.

- Almogavar can perform the Smash special attack after a distinct wind-up animation; on impact, it knocks Ezio to the ground and causes massive damage. Attack or kick the target to interrupt the assault before it is launched, or perform a Dodge to evade the blow before unleashing a combo while they are off-balance.

- You must either evade an Almogavar's attack or perform a kick to break their guard and initiate a combo. They are extremely vulnerable to Counter Kills, though the Smash special attack cannot be countered. While they are ostensibly immune to the Disarm technique, there is actually a way to divest them of their Heavy weapon. Wait until they begin their three-hit combo, and allow the first blow to hit Ezio; as they launch the second strike, press the required button to claim your prize.

- Almogavar are ponderously slow and cannot climb. From a higher vantage point or a safe distance, you can dispatch them easily with ranged weapons.

- Due to their incredible strength and tendency to move to the forefront of every battle, the Almogavar should always be a priority target once you begin a Kill Streak.

PRIMER

WALKTHROUGH

SIDE QUESTS

REFERENCE & ANALYSIS

MULTIPLAYER

EXTRAS

INDEX

MOVES OVERVIEW

GENERATING INCOME

WEAPONS

ARMOR

SHOPS

ENEMIES

TEMPLAR AWARENESS

ACHIEVEMENTS & TROPHIES

MISSION CHECKLIST

BYZANTINE VARANGIAN

One of the least common archetypes, and rarely encountered once you have captured all Templar Dens, the Varangian can cause great difficulties in large-scale brawls unless neutralized swiftly.

- In a combat situation the Varangian will generally put the extended reach of his Long weapon to good use, remaining at the periphery of a battle and striking from afar. Most, but not all, Varangians are immune to the Counter Kill move. As there is no way to ascertain which category each opponent falls into, it's best to use other techniques to defeat them.

- A Varangian soldier will regularly use the Throw Sand attack to temporarily incapacitate Ezio. You can avoid the effects of this by dodging, or by moving outside the effect radius. The sheer nuisance value of this means that you will often decide to kill these opponents before their allies.

- The Disarm move is the best way to tackle the Varangian. If you turn his polearm on him immediately after taking it, you can initiate a Kill Streak. Better still, hold and release the Primary Attack button to perform a lethal Sweep special attack to kill all nearby guards.

- The Varangian can search hiding spots and detect Ezio while he is blending with civilians, which will always lead to a fight if they encounter him in a Templar Den area. If Ezio attempts to escape one of these soldiers by moving to a different elevation, they may draw a pistol and fire at him.

VARANGIAN FACT SHEET	
Health Points	60
Strength	5
Morale	60
Melee Weapon	Long weapons
Ranged Weapon	Pistol
Notes	■ Most individuals are immune to Counter Kills ■ Can block grabs and standard weapon attacks ■ The final attack in his combo cannot be blocked ■ Vulnerable to everything else, including Disarm and Kill Streaks

LOOT TABLE	
Drop	Chance (%)
Bullets	30
Throwing Knives	30
Medicine	50
Crossbow Bolts	30
Poison	100
Akçe (A)	41-49
Bomb Ingredients	100

GUNMEN (BYZANTINE & OTTOMAN)

Gunmen are almost always encountered on walls or rooftops, where they act as sentries commissioned to punish all trespassers severely. After an initial barked warning they will draw their weapons and fire on Ezio, giving chase if he flees.

- Once engaged in combat, Gunmen will take aim at Ezio and fire at regular intervals. They have a tendency to back away as he approaches them, and will stand at the outer edge of a melee featuring other opponents. As their bullets will interrupt Kill Streaks, you should always target these foes first when you encounter them in open combat against a mixture of different adversaries.

- Though you can use any weapon you please, Throwing Knives are perfect for cutting down Gunmen before they can draw their rifles while free running over rooftops. Be sure to secure a Target Lock beforehand to ensure optimal accuracy. As Gunmen are reasonably fast and adept at climbing, and can be rather dogged in the way that they pursue Ezio, it's usually advisable to slay them if they give chase – or, ideally, beforehand.

- If stealth is desirable or mandatory, be careful when you attack Gunmen standing on the edges of rooftops, platforms and walls. If necessary, you can run over and pick up their bodies before they slide and fall to the ground.

- Marksmen are Gunmen stationed in armored booths situated in Templar Dens. These eagle-eyed sharpshooters will identify Ezio quickly, then fire at regular intervals. They can only be killed with well-placed projectiles and bombs, though it is advisable to avoid detection entirely.

GUNMAN FACT SHEET	
Health Points	24
Strength	2
Morale	60
Melee Weapon	-
Ranged Weapon	Rifle
Notes	■ No special resistances ■ Vulnerable to everything

LOOT TABLE	
Drop	Chance (%)
Bullets	100
Throwing Knives	50
Medicine	30
Crossbow Bolts	30
Poison	35
Akçe (A)	32-37
Bomb Ingredients	90

PRIMER

WALKTHROUGH

SIDE QUESTS

REFERENCE &
ANALYSIS

MULTIPLAYER

EXTRAS

INDEX

MOVES
OVERVIEW

GENERATING
INCOME

WEAPONS

ARMOR

SHOPS

ENEMIES

TEMPLAR
AWARENESS

ACHIEVEMENTS &
TROPHIES

MISSION
CHECKLIST

BOMBMAN FACT SHEET

Health Points	24
Strength	2
Morale	25
Melee Weapon	Small weapons
Ranged Weapon	Bombs
Notes	■ No special resistances ■ Vulnerable to everything

LOOT TABLE

Drop	Chance (%)
Bullets	30
Throwing Knives	50
Medicine	30
Crossbow Bolts	100
Poison	35
Akçe (Ꭺ)	32-37
Bomb Ingredients	100

BOMBMEN (BYZANTINE & OTTOMAN)

Though they often favor a short sword in close-range combat, Bombmen are only a true danger when they employ their explosives to assail Ezio from a distance.

■ Bombmen are relatively uncommon, and tend only to appear as sentries in elevated positions. As such locations are usually the sole preserve of Gunmen, you can distinguish them from a fair distance by noting the lack of a rifle on their back.

■ Though individual bombs do not inflict major damage, they will briefly incapacitate Ezio – and may cause him to stagger over the edge of a rooftop. Bombmen will throw their explosives with frustrating regularity unless you deal with them quickly. Do not attempt to run in and engage them in melee combat in these situations: just equip the Throwing Knives and fell them with a single blade.

OTTOMAN ELITES

Elites are the standard Ottoman patrol unit in earlier Sequences, but are soon supplanted by Agiles and Janissaries later in the story.

■ Though they can resist Grab attempts, Elites are susceptible to combos or Counter Kills. As with Byzantine Militia and Agiles, you can rely on their regular attacks to set up opportunities for Kill Streaks.

■ Elites can kick Ezio, briefly stunning him. Be wary of this at close range, especially if surrounded by a number of them.

ELITE FACT SHEET

Health Points	48
Strength	4
Morale	60
Melee Weapon	One-handed sword or mace
Ranged Weapon	Rocks
Notes	■ Can block grabs ■ The final attack in his combo cannot be blocked ■ Vulnerable to everything else

LOOT TABLE

Drop	Chance (%)
Bullets	30
Throwing Knives	40
Medicine	100
Crossbow Bolts	40
Poison	50
Akçe (Ꭺ)	21-29
Bomb Ingredients	90

AGILE FACT SHEET

Health Points	36
Strength	3
Morale	60
Melee Weapon	Small weapons
Ranged Weapon	Throwing Knives
Notes	■ Can dodge kicks and standard weapon attacks ■ Use Throwing Knives to stagger Ezio

LOOT TABLE

Drop	Chance (%)
Bullets	25
Throwing Knives	100
Medicine	60
Crossbow Bolts	25
Poison	40
Akçe (A)	21-29
Bomb Ingredients	90

As their name might suggest, Agiles are fleet-footed adversaries defined by their speed and swift reactions both in and out of direct conflict.

■ Though their free running and climbing prowess is not quite a match for Ezio, they can easily outpace him in a footrace. As they run behind him, they will lash out with their daggers to stagger him. There is, however, a great trick that you can use to avoid this. As you see an Agile moving in to strike, quickly release and then press the Legs button to perform a short jump. This will confuse your pursuer, who will slow down and lose ground.

■ Agiles cannot withstand much punishment in combat, but you will need to use specific techniques to successfully land a blow. As they can evade kicks and combo attempts (unless preceded by a successful Dodge), employ Counter Kills or target them in Kill Streaks.

■ As they are vulnerable to the Grab move, Agiles can be grappled and used as human shields – and summarily executed if you equip a Short or Medium weapon. You can throw them at surrounding adversaries to temporarily knock other hostiles from their feet.

■ Agiles will periodically use Throwing Knives to stagger Ezio, making them a nuisance in large battles. Try to disable them quickly.

■ Agiles are the only archetype immune to the Counter Steal technique.

OTTOMAN JANISSARY

The Janissary is the ultimate enemy archetype, combining the strength and resilience of the Almogavar, the pursuit speed and athleticism of the Agile, and special abilities shared by other classes – they even regularly draw firearms to perform ranged attacks. Resistant to many combat techniques, they are the toughest enemies you will meet.

■ Janissaries can successfully withstand up to three cumulative Counter Kill attempts or Kill Streak attacks. If you strike one during a Kill Streak, target another assailant to continue the streak; attacking the same Janissary twice will end it. If you strike a different Janissary with the next blow, the Streak will also end.

■ Dangerous when encountered individually, Janissaries are incredibly difficult to beat when fought in large numbers – as anyone foolish enough to loiter in the main Topkapi Palace courtyard will discover. The best strategy is often to avoid combat with these opponents entirely.

■ If you must fight them in open conflict, beating Janissaries is a matter of selecting the right weapons for the task. Unusually, Ezio's Hidden Blades are an extremely poor choice, lacking the required range and damage; the protracted struggle animations that ensue on Counter Kill or Kill Streak attacks also work against you. In conventional combat, a Heavy sword or axe is by far the best choice. The extended range means that you can strike Janissaries who draw firearms, while you maximize the damage inflicted by individual blows. If you want to take no chances, just throw a Tactical Bomb and assassinate them instantly while they are stunned by the effect.

■ Strangely, the Crossbow can be an amazingly efficient weapon when employed against Janissaries – though not quite in the manner you might expect. The speed of Counter Kills performed while wielding it can enable you to disable them more quickly than with the majority of blades and ranged assaults. You can combine this with a strategy where you back away at all times, weakening them with individual bolts.

■ Though Janissaries can resist multiple projectiles before they fall, a single Poison Dart will always incapacitate and then kill them.

■ Though calling on the assistance of Assassins while facing Janissaries can be helpful, most recruits (and even apprentices) can struggle against these deadly opponents.

■ Janissaries may yield bombs when looted – either one of a type that Ezio is carrying, or a random bomb if he has at least one empty pouch.

JANISSARY FACT SHEET

Health Points	84
Strength	7
Morale	2,000
Melee Weapon	One-handed sword or mace
Ranged Weapon	Firearm
Notes	■ Immune to Disarm and Hook and Throw techniques ■ Can block grabs, kicks and standard weapon attacks ■ Final combo attack cannot be blocked ■ Have access to several special attacks ■ Will sustain damage from Counter Kills and Kill Streak attacks; it takes up to three of each to disable them

LOOT TABLE

Drop	Chance (%)
Bullets	100
Throwing Knives	40
Medicine	100
Crossbow Bolts	40
Poison	40
Akçe (A)	81-89
Bomb Ingredients	100
Bombs	40

PRIMER

WALKTHROUGH

SIDE QUESTS

REFERENCE & ANALYSIS

MULTIPLAYER

EXTRAS

INDEX

MOVES OVERVIEW

GENERATING INCOME

WEAPONS

ARMOR

SHOPS

ENEMIES

TEMPLAR AWARENESS

ACHIEVEMENTS & TROPHIES

MISSION CHECKLIST

Enemy Overview

This table offers an at-a-glance guide to the strengths and weaknesses of all enemy archetypes.

	WEAPON/ MOVE	JANISSARY (OTTOMAN)	ELITE (OTTOMAN)	AGILE (OTTOMAN)	BOMBMAN (BYZANTINE/ OTTOMAN)	GUNMAN (BYZANTINE/ OTTOMAN)	MILITIA (BYZANTINE)	VARANGIAN (BYZANTINE)	ALMOGAVAR (BYZANTINE)
WEAKNESSES	Crossbow	3 to kill	Kill	Kill	Kill	Kill	Kill	Kill	3 to kill
	Hidden Gun	3 to kill	Kill	Kill	Kill	Kill	Kill	Kill	3 to kill
	Throwing Knives	3 to kill	2 to kill	Kill	Kill	Kill	Kill	2 to kill	3 to kill
	Lethal Bomb	2 to kill	Kill	Kill	Kill	Kill	Kill	Kill	2 to kill
	Finishing Blow	3 to kill	Kill	Kill	Kill	Kill	Kill	Kill	Kill
SKILLS	Resist Hook and Throw	Yes	No	No	No	No	No	No	Yes
	Resist Combo	Yes	No	Yes	No	No	No	Yes	Yes
	Resist Throw Sand	Yes	No	No	No	No	No	No	Yes
	Resist Grab	Yes	Yes	No	No	No	No	Yes	Yes
	Resist Kick	Yes	No	Yes	No	No	Yes	No	No
	Resist Sweep	No	No	Yes	No	No	No	No	No
	Resist Counter-Kill	3 to kill	No	No	No	Yes	No	Yes	No
	Resist Disarm	Yes	No	No	No	No	No	No	Yes
	Resist Counter-Steal	No	No	Yes	No	No	No	No	No
	Resist Dodge	No	No	No	No	No	No	No	No
	Search hiding spots	No	No	No	No	No	No	Yes	No
	Ranged Attack*	Yes	No	Yes	Yes	Yes	No	Yes	No
	Grab Attack	Yes	No	No	No	No	Yes	No	No
	Kick Attack	Yes	Yes	No	No	No	No	No	No
	Knock down player	No	No	No	No	No	No	No	Yes

*This refers to conventional firearms (or, with Agiles, Throwing Knives), and does not include the Throw Rock attack that opponents may use when Ezio is climbing.

UNIVERSAL COMBAT TIPS

■ Though less relevant in later Sequences once you have liberated all Templar Dens, don't forget Yusuf's advice that the Byzantine and Ottoman soldiers share no love for each other. Indeed, engineering any form of commotion in an area where both appear can cause the two sides to clash. You could achieve this with a simple projectile from a safe elevation, leading to deadly false assumptions, or by sending Mercenaries in to cause trouble. Just use a little imagination, and it's easy to set up interesting confrontations without getting directly involved in the fracas that ensues.

■ If you must start a fight, rather than respond to aggression, don't feel obliged to do so fairly. Use the Flying Knives technique to eliminate stock troops, Poison Darts to incapacitate stronger archetypes… and, of course, don't be frugal with bombs. Ezio's new arsenal of explosives can be employed creatively in a wide variety of ways, and require very little effort to craft.

■ Kill Streaks are the best way to end all combat encounters that include no more than one Janissary. Remember that you can often Counter Kill at any time during a Streak to foil an incoming enemy attack without breaking the chain.

■ Keep your guard up with the High Profile button to deflect enemy attacks by default, as you can instantly Dodge, Disarm or perform a Counter Kill from this stance.

01

■ Byzantine Militia and Ottoman Agiles are both susceptible to the Grab technique, which enables you to hold them as human shields (📷 01). This can be a great way to maneuver Ezio into a more convenient fighting position, and to engineer a brief break in combat as enemies evaluate the situation. Later in the story, when you regularly encounter Ottoman patrols featuring Agiles and Janissaries, grab the former and throw them to knock the giant Janissaries from their feet. You can then dart over and strike the more dangerous foes while they lie prone for an automatic one-hit assassination.

02

■ Use the environment to your advantage. You can kill opponents instantly by barging, bludgeoning or, in some instances, throwing them from rooftops or into water. Ezio can also use a new Hookblade-based trick whenever he is close to a scaffold: press the Empty Hand button as he runs by to bring the structure crashing down, crushing any opponents behind him (📷 02).

■ All enemies are vulnerable to instant kill attacks from behind. By briefly dropping your defense to Step Dodge, you can sometimes move directly behind their backs – especially when they are stunned or preparing an attack.

ENEMY MORALE

Morale is the (hidden) factor that determines the bravery or cowardice of your enemies, and the likelihood that they will flee combat. The morale of all enemies is constantly updated during a battle, as illustrated in the "Enemy Morale Adjustments" table. If you effortlessly cut through stronger opponents, you will break the resolve of their subordinates by reducing their morale to zero. Demoralized enemies may cease their attack and sheathe their weapons before running away (📷 03).

03

Note that killing Templar Captains in open combat while assaulting enemy Dens can automatically cause all Byzantines within the immediate vicinity to turn and flee, irrespective of their morale level.

Morale Values

UNIT	MORALE
Ottoman Elite	60
Ottoman Agile	60
Ottoman Janissary	2,000
Byzantine Militia	25
Byzantine Varangian	60
Byzantine Almogavar	1,000
Byzantine & Ottoman Bombman	25
Byzantine & Ottoman Gunman	60
Templar Stalker	2,000

Enemy Morale Adjustments

EVENT DURING COMBAT	VARIATION
Ezio exits Combat mode	+20
Ezio aims the Pistol at an opponent	-5, then -1 per second
Ezio performs an assassination	-5
Ezio performs a Counter Kill	-5
Ezio performs a Disarm	-5
Ezio performs a kill with the Pistol	-5
Ezio kills a Gunman	-5
Ezio kills a Militia	-5
Ezio kills an Agile	-5
Ezio kills a Bombman	-5
Ezio kills a target with their own weapon after Disarm	-10
Ezio kills an Elite	-10
Ezio kills an Almogavar	-15
Ezio kills a Janissary	-15
Ezio attacks with Vlad Tepes's Sword	15% chance to make the enemy flee

PRIMER

WALKTHROUGH

SIDE QUESTS

REFERENCE & ANALYSIS

MULTIPLAYER

EXTRAS

INDEX

MOVES OVERVIEW

GENERATING INCOME

WEAPONS

ARMOR

SHOPS

ENEMIES

TEMPLAR AWARENESS

ACHIEVEMENTS & TROPHIES

MISSION CHECKLIST

TEMPLAR AWARENESS

12002.TW90aGVyU2Fk
12002.RmF0aGVyTWFk
72002.Trh90aGluZ0lzVHJ1ZQ==
72002.RXZlcnl0aGluZ0lzUGVybWl0dGVk
22003.Qm9yZWRRPZldhclNQb3.JnZXM

| 0% | 25% | 50% | 75% | 100% |

Activated late in Sequence 02, the Templar Awareness system will be a constant thorn in your side unless you take steps to keep it under control.

- The accompanying table reveals all situations that can lead to increases or decreases in the Templar Awareness meter. We find that preventative maintenance is best in early Sequences: plan your journeys to pass Heralds and reduce it whenever possible.

- The Templar Awareness Meter is deactivated or frozen during certain Memories – for example, those taking place in Altaïr's time, or in locations outside or beneath Constantinople.

- Once the meter switches to the Aware status, avoid conflict and other activities that lead to Templar Awareness penalties until you have completely emptied it – unless, that is, you actively want to trigger a Den Defense.

- The Templar Awareness system acts as a subtle deterrent to gratuitous violence. You can start fights and brutalize your way to success in Memories whenever you like – but be prepared to pay a penalty.

- Whenever you encounter Corrupt Officials, they and their bodyguards will attack Ezio on sight. For easy kills, and to negate the need for Templar Awareness increments, try to hit Officials with a Poison Dart from a safe distance. You do not need to stay to observe your victim's demise: the 50% reduction will be credited when they finally succumb to the deadly toxin.

- Every Assassin Den in the Imperial, Bayezid and Constantine districts can be rendered immune to Templar attacks by completing their unique Master Assassin missions. See page 96 for further details.

- You can find further tips and tricks for reducing labor due to Templar Awareness penalties in the Rebuilding Constantinople section of the Side Quests chapter: see page 86.

Templar Awareness Penalties & Reductions

ACTION	VARIATION
Killing a Templar Courier	+100%
Liberating a Templar Den	+100%
Allowing a Stalker to escape after he has stabbed Ezio	+25%
Enlisting a recruit	+20%
Buying a new Shop, Bank, Faction Building or Landmark	+20%
Killing an important target	+15%
Failing a mission in the Mediterranean Defense metagame	+15%
Killing a guard with a bomb	+5%
Every five enemies killed in continuous open conflict	+5%
Killing a Janissary or an Almogavar	+4%
Killing a regular enemy	+2%
Killing a Stalker	-25%
Bribing a Herald	-25%
Killing a Corrupt Official	-50%
Triggering a Den Defense	-100%

ACHIEVEMENTS & TROPHIES

The following tables offer a range of prompts and tips to help readers obtain a full haul of Achievements and Trophies. Where extended guidance is required or might prove useful, we've also supplied page references to relevant information elsewhere in the guide.

MAIN STORY MILESTONES

ICON	NAME	Ⓖ	TROPHY	UNLOCK CONDITION
	Best Served Cold	20	Silver	Complete Sequence 01.
	Istanbul and Constantinople	20	Silver	Complete Sequence 02.
	Seal the Deal	20	Silver	Complete Sequence 03.
	The Prince	20	Silver	Complete Sequence 04.
	The Plot Thickens	20	Silver	Complete Sequence 05.
	Successes and Failures	20	Silver	Complete Sequence 06.
	Old Boss, New Boss	20	Silver	Complete Sequence 07.
	Priorities	20	Silver	Complete Sequence 08.
	Revelations	50	Gold	Complete Sequence 09.

SECONDARY MEMORIES & OPTIONAL ACCOMPLISHMENTS

ICON	NAME	Ⓖ	TROPHY	UNLOCK CONDITION
	Fond Memories	20	Silver	Achieve 100% Synchronization in all Sequences.
	Holy Wisdom	20	Bronze	Complete the Hagia Sofia Secret Location. See page 102.
	Capped	20	Bronze	Collect all Animus Data Fragments. See page 109.
	Worth A Thousand Words	20	Bronze	Collect all of Ishak Pasha's Memoir Pages. See page 109.
	Pyromaniac	20	Bronze	Complete all Piri Reis missions. See page 99.
	Armchair General	20	Bronze	Control all cities (except Rhodes) simultaneously in the Mediterranean Defense game. See page 93.
	A Friend Indeed	20	Bronze	Complete all Challenges from a single faction. See page 100.
	My Protégé	20	Bronze	Have one trainee reach the rank of Master Assassin. See page 94.
	The Mentor	20	Silver	Have seven trainees reach the rank of Master Assassin. See page 94.
	Sage	20	Bronze	Complete all Book Quests. See page 98.
	The Early Years	20	Bronze	Complete Desmond's Journey, Part 1: Doubts. See page 104.
	The Reluctant Assassin	20	Bronze	Complete Desmond's Journey, Part 2: Training. See page 105.
	Escape To New York	20	Bronze	Complete Desmond's Journey, Part 3: Escape. See page 106.
	The Rotten Apple	20	Bronze	Complete Desmond's Journey, Part 4: Metropolis. See page 107.
	Are You Desmond Miles?	20	Bronze	Complete Desmond's Journey, Part 5: Regret. See page 108.

PRIMER

WALKTHROUGH

SIDE QUESTS

REFERENCE &
ANALYSIS

MULTIPLAYER

EXTRAS

INDEX

MOVES
OVERVIEW

GENERATING
INCOME

WEAPONS

ARMOR

SHOPS

ENEMIES

TEMPLAR
AWARENESS

ACHIEVEMENTS &
TROPHIES

MISSION
CHECKLIST

MULTIPLAYER

ICON	NAME	G	TROPHY	UNLOCK CONDITION
	Mastering the Art	30	Silver	Earn the Incognito bonus.
	Tools of the Templar	10	Bronze	Purchase your first Ability in the Abstergo Store.
	Achiever	10	Bronze	Complete a Challenge.
	True Templar	20	Silver	Reach Level 20.
	Looking Good	10	Bronze	Customize a Persona.
	There Is No "I" in Team	20	Bronze	Win a session of a team mode.
	Make the Headlines	30	Silver	Obtain 13 different Accolades.
	The Way I Like It	20	Bronze	Edit your Templar Profile to change your title, emblem, and patron.
	Explorer	20	Silver	Finish a session of each game mode.
	Tactician	30	Silver	Score at least 2,505 points in a multiplayer session.

UNIQUE FEATS

ICON	NAME	G	TROPHY	UNLOCK CONDITION
	Iron Curtain	20	Bronze	Perform a perfect Den Defense without using the Cannon attack. See page 39.
	Spider Assassin	20	Bronze	Climb Hagia Sofia from the ground to the pinnacle in under 25 seconds (see overleaf).
	Tax Evasion	10	Bronze	Simply wait until you spot a Templar Courier (see page 47), then give chase and use either the Tackle or Leg Sweep technique to catch them at close range.
	Lightning Strikes	20	Bronze	Kill five guards in five seconds using only your Hidden Blades. The trick to this is to amass a large entourage of guards who do not wish you well, then incapacitate them in a huddle with a Smoke Screen bomb. Start with a double assassination on two opponents in close proximity, and you have a chance to hit the total before five seconds elapse. This requires more than a little luck to accomplish.
	Overkiller	20	Bronze	Assassinate 50 guards with the Hidden Blade; a milestone you should easily hit during the course of the story.
	Show-Off	20	Bronze	Parachute onto a zipline (see overleaf).
	Fast Fingers	20	Bronze	Have Thieves loot the bodies of 50 guards for you. This requires the Thief Faction Ability (see page 101).
	Mosh Pit	20	Bronze	Have 10 guards poisoned at the same time (see overleaf).
	Mouse Trap	20	Bronze	Kill five guards with a scaffold after they have been stunned by Caltrop Bombs (see overleaf).
	Craft Maniac	20	Bronze	Craft 30 bombs.
	Almost Flying	20	Bronze	Parachute directly from the top of the Galata Tower to the Golden Horn waterway. From the very summit, flying directly south, you have just enough height to reach the water.
	Silent but Deadly	20	Bronze	Kill three guards simultaneously with Throwing Knives. This is simple: just use the Flying Knives technique (see page 143).
	I Can See You	20	Bronze	Kill five guards while under the cover of a Smoke Screen bomb. Craft a tactical explosive that offers maximum smoke dispersal (British Gunpowder + Phosphorous), then lure five opponents to a suitably enclosed location before you strike – ideally with an explosive with a more potent payload.
	Monster's Dance	20	Bronze	Have a guard incapacitate three civilians while he's poisoned (see overleaf).
	Bully	20	Bronze	Find and beat up Duccio. See page 69.
	The Conqueror	-	Platinum	Awarded once every other Trophy has been unlocked (PS3 only).

Spider Assassin

Begin your climb in the southwest corner of this astonishing building (📷 01), and the remarkable feat of reaching its spire in under 25 seconds is easier than you might think – though you may need to make a couple of practice attempts beforehand.

01

Show-Off

The tower directly south of Galata Tower presents an opportunity for straight flight to a zipline further to the south (📷 02). When you pass above the cord, press and hold the Empty Hand button to release the Parachute and have Ezio grab the zipline as he falls past it.

02

Mosh Pit

You must at least purchase one (and, realistically, both) Poison capacity upgrades before you attempt this; it is also vital that you have not purchased the Fast Poison upgrade. Travel to the Janissary camp in the far north of the Constantine district; it's just west of the Gul Mosque, and is visited during the Honor, Lost and Won Memory in Sequence 06. You cannot enter via the front entrance, as this will cause the Janissaries to attack. Instead, sneak in via a broken wall section from the nearby rooftops to the south (📷 03). Stand on the wooden roof. With a full supply of Poison

03

Darts, begin targeting the Janissaries below with darts, using the Camera Stick to shift between locked targets, and the Target Lock button to disengage once nearby victims have been dosed. This can be a little fiddly, but don't panic. Once you have poisoned those in the immediate vicinity, drop down and target those further south. As long as you are swift, it's possible to have ten under the effects of poison all at once.

An alternative venue to attempt to accomplish this feat is the main courtyard in Topkapi Palace, though the Janissaries here are often much quicker to identify and attack Ezio.

Monster's Dance

Though this feat can be accomplished with a little luck at any time you use poison in a confined space with plenty of civilians (such as the Grand Bazaar), a cynically inventive solution makes it easy to accomplish. Simply pick a guard close to plenty of pedestrians, then hit him with a Poison Dart. When he draws his sword, run over to him and use the Throw Money move to bait the trap; digitally simulated avarice in the surrounding citizenry will do the rest for you (📷 04).

04

Mouse Trap

This may take a few attempts to perfect, but the required technique soon becomes apparent after a couple of trial runs. Craft three Caltrop bombs (Impact Shell + British Gunpowder + Caltrop), then travel to the Tailor shop in the north of the Imperial district. Identify the scaffold (📷 05), then run through the nearby archway to reach the docks. Engage the ire of at least two full patrols, then lead them on a chase back to the scaffold. As you approach it, drop a Caltrop bomb directly in front of the wooden structure, then stand on the opposite side of the hazard to your opponents so that the maximum number are incapacitated as they sprint straight for you. With this accomplished, quickly run past the scaffold again and press the Empty Hand button to bring it crashing down on the individuals standing below.

Note that any scaffold will suffice: we simply reference this one as it's easy to find, and has a ready supply of guards in the vicinity.

05

8212002.TW90aGVyU2Fk
8212002.RmF0aGVyTWFk
2072002.Tm90aGluZ0IzVHJ1ZQ==
2072002.RXZlcnI0aGluZ0IzUGVybWI0dGVk
4022003.Qm9vZWRPZldhciN0h3JpZXM-

PRIMER

WALKTHROUGH

SIDE QUESTS

REFERENCE & ANALYSIS

MULTIPLAYER

EXTRAS

INDEX

MOVES OVERVIEW

GENERATING INCOME

WEAPONS

ARMOR

SHOPS

ENEMIES

TEMPLAR AWARENESS

ACHIEVEMENTS & TROPHIES

MISSION CHECKLIST

PRIMARY MEMORIES

SEQUENCE	MEMORY	REWARD (A)	PAGE
01	01	-	30
	02	-	30
	03	-	30
	04	-	32
	05	-	32
02	01	-	34
	02	150	34
	03	150	36
	04	250	36
	05	150	36
	06	100	38
	07	100	38
03	01	150	40
	02	150	42
	03	-	42
	04	250	44
	05	250	46
	06	400	48
	07	400	50
	08	-	50
	09	500	52
	10	700	52
04	01	1,200	54
	02	600	54
	03	900	56
	04	550	56
	05	700	58
	06	-	60
05	01	750	62
	02	1,500	62
	03	900	64
	04	1,550	64
	05	700	64
	06	1,200	66
	07	-	66
06	01	1,200	68
	02	950	68
	03	1,150	70
	04	1,000	70
	05	1,200	70
	06	1,350	72
	07	-	74
	08	1,600	74
07	01	950	76
	02	2,350	76
	03	900	77
	04	1,150	78
	05	1,800	78
	06	1,950	78
	07	-	78
08	01	4,500	80
	02	5,000	80
	03	-	80
09	01	-	81
	02	-	81
	03	-	81

SECONDARY MEMORIES

Secret Locations
(see page 102)

NAME	REWARD
Hagia Sophia's Secret	Ishak Pasha's Armor
The Impaler's Tomb	Vlad Tepes's Sword

Recruit Assassin Memories
(see page 92)

NAME	REWARD (A)
The Brawler	350
The Pupil	350
The Avenger	350
The Acrobat	350
The Beggars	350
The Pickpocket	350

Master Assassin Missions
(see page 96)

NAME	REWARD (A)
The Deacon, Part 1	700
The Deacon, Part 2	1,400
The Trickster, Part 1	700
The Trickster, Part 2	1,400
The Champion, Part 1	700
The Champion, Part 2	1,400
The Guardian, Part 1	700
The Guardian, Part 2	1,400
The Vizier, Part 1	700
The Vizier, Part 2	1,400
The Thespian, Part 1	700
The Thespian, Part 2	1,400

Faction HQ Missions (see page 98)

ICON	NAME	REWARD (A)
	Unfortunate Son	700
	Loose Lips	700

Book Quests
(see page 98)

NAME	REWARD (A)
The Polo Symbols: Hippodrome	400
The Polo Symbols: Galata	400
The Polo Symbols: Arsenal	400
The Polo Symbols: Forum of Ox	400
The Polo Symbols: Aqueduct	400
The Polo Symbols: Church I	400
The Polo Symbols: Church II	400

Piri Reis Missions
(see page 99)

NAME	REWARD (A)
Thunder	400
Smoke Screen	400
Cherry	400
Datura	400
Caltrops	400
Smoke Decoy	400
Sticky Situations	400
Tripwire	400

Challenges (see page 100)

ICON	FACTION	PAGE
	Thieves Guild	101
	Romanies Guild	100
	Mercenaries Guild	101
	Assassins Guild	100
	Bombs	101

Additional Memories (see page 109)

ICON	COLLECTIBLE	REWARD(S)
	106 Treasure Chests (Constantinople)	Akçe & crafting ingredients
	15 Treasure Chests (Secret Locations)	Akçe & crafting ingredients
	100 Animus Data Fragments	Unlocks Desmond's Journey episodes
	22 Viewpoints	Unfogs the map
	10 Ishak Pasha's Memoir Pages	Unlocks the Hagia Sophia Secret Location

Desmond's Journey
(see page 104)

NAME	REWARD
Part 1 to Part 5	Desmond Outfit

PRIMER

WALKTHROUGH

SIDE QUESTS

REFERENCE & ANALYSIS

MULTIPLAYER

EXTRAS

INDEX

MULTIPLAYER

With a wide range of new features, functions and destinations, the Assassin's Creed Revelations multiplayer suite may seem a little daunting to a first-time player. In this chapter, we provide a wealth of tips, tricks and tables that will help you to play at a competitive level from your very first foray into this engrossing play mode.

°SynchError***
7 anima\\eauStore.ddna\\6.8.8] fatal error: fate3 | reinitiate
ending Firmware ... Animus.2.03

BASICS

GAME PRINCIPLES

First things first: it is points, not kills, that are used to determine winners in Assassin's Creed Revelations multiplayer. While a high kill count is certainly an accomplishment, performing well in each match is a matter of *how* you perform your assassinations – not your final body count. With special bonuses acknowledging noteworthy feats, particularly those that involve stealth and subtlety, there is a definite onus on playing the mode in the way its creators intended.

While time spent inside the Animus completing the single-player adventure will certainly help to familiarize you with certain multiplayer concepts, it is important to recognize that this is a very different experience. The focus here is on free running, social stealth and assassinations, with a greatly simplified combat engine. Instead of open brawls, you will use a range of unlockable skills known as Abilities to hunt and kill targets, or evade aggressors.

Once a multiplayer session has been launched, your character will appear somewhere on the chosen map. You will notice that all citizens around you resemble one of the many playable characters, or "skins" (referred to as Persona in the game). In most Game Modes, some will look identical to you. All you know at first is that other human players are out there, hiding among the crowds, and you will be assigned a contract to kill one of them.

However, you will regularly find yourself cast in the dual role of hunter *and* prey. As you walk the streets in search of your contract, other Agents are likely to be tracking you. Naturally, stealth is of paramount importance. The new Approach Meter (situated in the upper right corner of the screen) starts at Discreet and can fluctuate between Incognito and Reckless in accordance with your actions. The former is always the most desirable state to operate in. A covert approach can be employed to evade the attention of your victims and potential executors, but you must always be ready to adapt your tactics and flee or hide if a rival assigned to kill you is closing in fast.

Another factor that you must take into account is that you may not be the only assassin hunting your prey. Multiple contracts can be awarded on the same target, so you will lose out if a rival beats you to the kill. This also means that you can be stalked by more than one competitor at once.

Finally, try to plan your assassination to get the best bonuses but always be ready for improvisation, and it is imperative that you keep moving at all times. Never linger in one place for too long, or think that you can lurk in wait for your target. Somebody, somewhere, is moving towards your location, and drawing closer by the second...

PRIMER

WALKTHROUGH

SIDE QUESTS

REFERENCE &
ANALYSIS

MULTIPLAYER

EXTRAS

INDEX

BASICS

SCORE &
PROGRESSION

ADVANCED TIPS

MAPS &
ANALYSIS

1 Player Data:

- The number shows your current scoring position. Victory is handed to the player with the most points at the end of the round.

- The number of red markers indicates how many Agents are stalking you.

- An Escape sequence begins when your pursuer reveals themselves.

2 Target Data:

- This portrait shows the skin (referred to as Persona in the game) of the Agent you have been contracted to find and kill. Beware of lookalikes and disguises. It will take a little while to become acquainted with all characters, but you'll soon gain the ability to recognize your target with a brief glance at his or her picture.

- The outline around the portrait becomes blue when your target is in your line of sight – but this may also mean that your victim can see you as well. The background of the portrait becomes blue when you are close to your target.

- The players hunting your target appear as blue markers below the picture. One arrow means that you are the only pursuer on this target.

- The Approach Meter shows your level of discretion and directly affects your kill bonus. The more careful the approach, the greater the bonus. Subtle, Low Profile actions (such as walking or hiding) gradually fill up the Approach Meter – from Discreet, to Silent and then Incognito. Conversely, performing High Profile actions (such as running) will cause your Approach Meter to empty to the Reckless level. A Chase sequence will ensue when your Approach Meter is fully depleted.

3 Compass:

- The primary function of this directional indicator is to show the approximate position of your contracted target. The width of the "fill" arc increases as you approach your target, becoming a full blue disc when you are in close proximity. It will turn bright blue whenever your target is in sight.

- Arrows may also appear on the outer edge of the Compass, indicating secondary targets in team missions (blue), and enemy pursuers (red).

- There is no Compass in Easy Deathmatch and Deathmatch modes.

4 Assassinate Button and Lock Button Icons:

- A contextual visual prompt over a character's head (**X**) indicates when a kill can be performed by pressing the Primary Weapon button.

- You can also lock on to a target by pressing the Target Lock button when the corresponding symbol appears over their head (🔒). The lock lasts while your target is in your line of sight, or until manually disabled. It will break if you lose sight of the target for more than a few seconds.

5 Abilities and Streaks:

- Icons in these slots show which Abilities and Streak bonuses are currently available to you.

- Abilities in Cooldown (that is, recharging after use) are replaced by a timer until available.

6 Session Information:

- This shows the countdown to the end of the round.

- You will also find information specific to your game mode here, such as team scores.

7 Players List:

- This shows the list of players in the current session, as well as their score. The list will disappear after a few seconds.

8 Session Events:

- This provides rolling news of Kills, Session Bonuses and other events as they occur.

CONTROLS

XBOX 360	PS3	BUTTON DEFINITION	COMMAND
L	L	L	Basic Movement
R	R	R	Camera Control
✛	⊞	Quick Inventory Buttons	Switch Targets in Team modes; select Abilities Set
A	✕	Legs Button	Fast Walk; Sprint/Jump (High Profile mode only)
B	◎	Empty Hand Button	Stun; Shove (High Profile mode only)
X	▢	Primary Attack Button	Assassinate
LT	L1	Target Lock Button	Lock Target
RT	R1	High Profile Button	High Profile Mode
LB	L2	Assassin Signal Button	Use Ability 1
RB	R2	Weapon Selector Button	Use Ability 2
R	R3	Center Camera Button	Center Camera
START	START	Pause Button	Pause Menu
BACK	SELECT	Map Button	Display extra information, such as the Players List, scores or Ability names

Control Notes:

- The Fast Walk command (hold Legs button) enables you to increase your movement speed by a barely perceptible degree, which can be invaluable for closing the gap on a victim, or pulling away from a would-be aggressor. This incurs no Approach Meter penalties.

- If you are forced to flee, the Empty Hand button can be held to bash through civilians in your path as you run.

- While walking through crowds, you will notice that the Assassinate button icon can appear above any civilian when you face them in close proximity. Killing innocents leads to the loss of your contract, so this is where the Lock function comes in useful. Press Lock when your suspected target is in your immediate sight, or hold Lock to aim at the target from a distance. A blue padlock (🔒) will then appear over your target's head (📷 01). The advantage of the Lock function is that the Assassinate icon only appears for this individual, meaning that you cannot accidentally strike an innocent. The Lock will break if you lose sight of a target for more than a few seconds.

- If an enemy makes a High Profile move while in plain sight, a Lock button icon will appear over their heads to enable you to focus your attention with ease.

01

CHASES AND ESCAPE

In all modes but Deathmatch, Easy Deathmatch and Steal the Artifact, a Chase sequence begins when a pursuer's Approach Meter is fully depleted. This is usually caused by performing High Profile actions while in the target's line of sight.

- **Pursuer:** Once you trigger a Chase, the Chase Timer appears on your HUD. You must now kill your target before they can hide from you. If you can keep your target in sight, they will be unable to hide. However, as soon as they turn a corner or disappear from view, the Chase Timer will begin to fill. If it fills up completely, they will have achieved an Escape – and you will have lost both the Chase sequence and the contract.

- Once a Chase begins, it's often a good idea to start free running and ascend to higher ground. Not only will your target have to work harder to hide, but you'll also increase the effective range of assassination through free running tackles and aerial kills. You could also try to use shortcuts whenever you have a good idea of where your target intends to run next (📷 02), or employ relevant Abilities at your disposal, such as Closure. You only have to regain sight of your target for a moment to refill the

Chase Timer completely. As exhilarating as a Chase can be, note that protracted pursuits will waste valuable match time.

- **Target:** When you are made aware that an assailant is closing in to assassinate you, an Escape Timer appears and the race begins. You must now attempt to leave your opponent's line of sight by turning corners, entering buildings or dropping out of view. Use Chase Breakers to gain distance (📷 03). If you succeed, the Escape Timer will turn yellow and begin to recede. When this occurs, you can slip into a hiding spot to turn the bar blue. The blue bar will decrease rapidly while you are hidden. If the assigned killer fails to catch you before the Escape Timer expires, you will have achieved an Escape and your hunter will lose the contract on your head. Successful Escapes earn extra points.

Even if a pursuer is hot on your heels, hope remains right up until they hit the Assassinate button. With a little luck, good reflexes or tactical sense (if you lure them to a hiding spot, for example), you can strike them first with your character's Stun move. This will incapacitate them for a few seconds, earning you a momentary reprieve – and extra points.

PRIMER

WALKTHROUGH

SIDE QUESTS

REFERENCE & ANALYSIS

MULTIPLAYER

EXTRAS

INDEX

BASICS

SCORE & PROGRESSION

ADVANCED TIPS

MAPS & ANALYSIS

HIDING SPOTS

Hay-filled carts and straw piles are the most obvious hiding spots featured in the multiplayer game, and completely remove you from view when you jump inside. All kills made from such places of concealment lead to generous bonuses (📷 04), but with the obvious drawback that you must remain stationary while another Agent may be closing in on your position. Furthermore, entering and leaving these hiding spots is clearly not the behavior of a civilian: such acts telegraph your intentions to anyone who happens to glance in your direction.

04

Social stealth is the most common method of finding a hiding spot, either by blending with a crowd of bystanders or by sitting on a bench. It is easy to make Low Profile transitions from one group to another, and you need only move briefly through a passing crowd when closing in on your target to earn a related kill bonus. Use the Fast Walk move to catch up with groups of citizens walking ahead of you.

A good hiding spot is the fastest way to end a Chase. Your judgment on whether to stay put or flee in such situations should be dictated by the time left on the Escape Timer, and the likelihood of whether your opponent can reach your hiding spot before it expires. If you successfully escape after a pursuit, it will not matter if your pursuer knows your location or even approaches you, as they will have lost the contract on your head.

CHASE BREAKERS

Each map features a number of Chase Breakers to enable competitors to briefly evade opponents in pursuit. There are three types to look for, readily identified by the white shimmer of their Animus matrix outline. Chase Breakers are triggered by any High Profile activity such as running, so you can pass them stealthily without incident. They also reset after a short period of time, so you must always make good use of the valuable seconds of grace they offer.

Lifts: Collide with the front of these devices to trigger them, and the counterweight will propel you instantly to roof level. Note that you can also drop onto a Lift from above – a tactic of great merit when a rival is almost directly behind you.

Closing Gates: Running through these passages will cause doors to swing shut or portcullis grates to fall. Time your entry carefully, and these Chase Breakers will slam shut in the face of your would-be assassin and force them to take another path.

Corner Helpers: As you bound over beams and balconies, these swinging handholds will not only break a vital element of the free running route behind you, but will often slip you immediately into the yellow "out-of-sight" status as you round the corner.

INTRODUCTORY SESSION 1 & 2

Players:	1	Duration:	∞
Objective:	Practice kills, stuns, and Escape sequences.		

Notes & Tips:

- These sessions are only intended as one-off tutorials. However, you can replay them as many times as you like to experiment with different approaches.

TRAINING GROUND

Players:	1-8	Duration:	∞
Objective:	Find and kill assigned targets in any way you see fit.		

Notes & Tips:

- This is a non-competitive mode.
- Use it to explore maps and practice your Abilities.

MANHUNT

Players:	4-8 players split into 2 teams	Duration:	2 rounds of 5 minutes
Objective:	Achieve the highest team score, hiding together as targets, and performing valuable kills as hunters.		

Notes & Tips:

- Both teams take a turn as hunters and the hunted.
- While hunted, blend with a crowd of civilians and use Morph to confuse your pursuers with a crowd of lookalikes. Fortify your position with a well-placed Tripwire Bomb, or employ a Smoke Bomb instead. Complete your defensive Abilities Set with the Blender and Enhanced Autobash Perks.
- Hiding with your team is the best way to rack up noteworthy points totals. If one of you is killed, there will always be someone on hand to score an easy Stun before fleeing.
- When on the offensive, coordinate with your allies to perform multiple kills.
- Firecrackers are the best way to identify your target in a crowd when you are in pursuit. Use Throwing Knives if your target decides to break cover and run. Add the Hot Pursuit and Sentry perks for a well-rounded offensive Abilities Set.

ASSASSINATE

Players:	4-8	Duration:	1 round of 10 minutes
Objective:	Identify, acquire and assassinate the target of your choice to achieve the highest score.		

Notes & Tips:

- As soon as you acquire a target, you vanish from his or her Compass but also lose sight of other Templars.
- It takes time to acquire your target, so be cautious.
- Identifying your pursuer with a Lock exposes them and empties their Approach Meter.

WANTED

Players:	4-8	Duration:	1 round of 10 minutes
Objective:	Achieve the highest score by killing assigned targets.		

Notes & Tips:

- You are both predator and prey, but you may only kill your contracted target.
- The higher your rank, the more pursuers will hunt you.
- Use your Compass to anticipate a target's route through an arena, and you may be able to catch him or her out as they round a corner.
- It's harder to hide in Wanted than in Deathmatch as your pursuer has a Compass. However, there are duplicates of your Persona wandering around, making it easier to blend and lure your pursuer into killing a civilian.
- When you blend with a group, try to pick one with at least one duplicate of your character.
- It can sometimes be more efficient to take the time to identify and escape a pursuer before tracking your own target. Staying alive enables you to complete Streaks and earn more points.

CORRUPTION

Players:	4-8	Duration:	3 rounds of 5 minutes each
Objective:	Achieve the highest score.		

Notes & Tips:

- When you start the session as Corrupted, kill your targets as fast as you can to prevent them from scoring.
- When Uncorrupted, hide and survive for as long as possible. You earn a greater bonus if pursuers are close to you — and the more Templars hunting you, the better the bonus will be.
- Defensive Abilities such as Decoy, Morph or Bodyguard can help you to survive longer when you are Uncorrupted.
- Avoid direct confrontations with Corrupted players at all costs: a contested kill will still corrupt you.

DEATHMATCH

Players:	4-8	Duration:	1 round of 10 minutes
Objective:		Achieve the highest score by killing assigned targets.	

Notes & Tips:

- You are both predator and prey, and can only kill your assigned target.
- You cannot trigger Chases, but your Approach Meter still allows you to earn Kill Bonuses.
- There is no Compass for any player in this mode.
- Deathmatch maps are very small, so it pays to get into static or moving cover as soon as you spawn. Your pursuer is never very far away.
- Each player's Persona is the only one of its kind in this mode, though you can use Abilities or Perks that create duplicates.
- The higher your rank, the more pursuers will hunt you.
- Disguise is a vital part of your Abilities Set in Deathmatch. The tiny maps make it easy to find and kill your target while the Ability is active, so you shouldn't have to watch your back for your pursuer. Just be sure to activate it when you are in a quiet spot.
- With no Compass, Deathmatch is all about line of sight and paying attention to your target's portrait outline. Find a static blend group near a corner of the map and you will only need to keep an eye on two directions. However, don't forget to scan the rooftops from time to time.
- Blender is a great Perk to have in Deathmatch, creating a civilian doppelganger every time you mingle with a crowd.

EASY DEATHMATCH

Players:	4-8	Duration:	1 round of 10 minutes
Objective:		Achieve the highest score by killing assigned targets.	

Notes & Tips:

- This is a simplified version of Deathmatch. The rules are broadly the same, though you cannot access your Abilities Sets.
- Each player's Persona is the only one of its kind in this mode. As Abilities and Perks are unavailable in Easy Deathmatch, this means that targets are very easy to identify.
- Easy Deathmatch is the best mode for new players to familiarize themselves with basic multiplayer concepts. Complexities such as the Compass and Abilities are disabled, the maps are tiny, and each competitor is assigned a unique character.
- With no Abilities or Perks at your disposal, blending with moving groups is the key to success on these small, congested maps.

ARTIFACT ASSAULT

Players:	4-8 players split into 2 teams	Duration:	1 round of 10 minutes
Objective:		The team with the highest number of captured artifacts wins.	

Notes & Tips:

- You will score by stealing the other team's artifact from their base and carrying it back to yours.
- You are a pursuer while in your territory, but become a target once in enemy territory. When you are carrying the artifact, enemies can kill you even in your own territory.
- When you defend your team's artifact, your Compass will blur each time you move too close to your home base, rendering it useless.
- Stealing the enemy artifact in a stealthy way will mean that you will not be immediately marked with an artifact icon above your head (🎒).
- It is vital that you learn the safest route back to base after stealing the artifact. Using Chase Breakers can be crucial to your success.
- Throwing Knives are particularly useful when defending, as they enable you to stop a fleeing enemy in his tracks and recover your artifact.
- Set a Tripwire Bomb at the nearest Chase Breaker to your base.
- Use the Disguise or Morph Abilities to blend in before making a dash for the enemy artifact. Drop a Firecracker or Smoke Bomb to facilitate your escape.
- While attacking, it's best not to use the Blender Perk – if you inadvertently brush against a crowd your opponents may spot one of the civilians transforming, revealing your position.
- Look out for Tripwire Bombs when you approach the enemy artifact, and while escaping the immediate vicinity.
- Use the Closure Ability to trigger all nearby Chase Breakers immediately after an enemy steals your artifact, making a swift escape more difficult.
- The Enhanced Autobash and Hot Pursuit Perks are particularly useful, especially if you adopt a defensive role, giving you the edge when chasing a fleeing enemy.

STEAL THE ARTIFACT

Players:	4-8	Duration:	1 round of 10 minutes
Objective:		Steal the Artifact and keep it for as long as you can to achieve the highest score.	

Notes & Tips:

- Once you steal the Artifact, you will remain a target until you are killed.
- When you run while holding the Artifact, an icon reveals your location to your pursuers (🎒).
- When you carry the Artifact, the more pursuers chase you, the greater the bonus. If you manage to survive two minutes as a carrier, you will receive an extra bonus.
- You will earn a bonus if you hide while carrying the Artifact. Hiding is much more profitable than running, especially if your pursuers are near you.
- The Templar who kills the carrier automatically becomes the new carrier.

PRIMER

WALKTHROUGH

SIDE QUESTS

REFERENCE &
ANALYSIS

MULTIPLAYER

EXTRAS

INDEX

BASICS

SCORE &
PROGRESSION

ADVANCED TIPS

MAPS &
ANALYSIS

ESCORT

Players:	4-8 players split into 2 teams	Duration:	2 rounds of 5 minutes each
Objective:	Achieve the highest score by killing VIPs, or by escorting them to checkpoints.		

Notes & Tips:

■ Coordinate your attacks on the two VIPs at the same time for maximum efficiency.

■ The Tripwire Bomb and ranged Abilities can help you eliminate a VIP without being killed.

■ Communication is vital in this play mode. When you escort a VIP, encourage your team to spread out and protect the VIP from all angles: rooftops, alleyways, hiding spots. If you have a teammate broadly in all directions, each participant can warn their allies when they spot an enemy entering their line of sight.

■ You do not have an Approach Meter when you defend, so do not waste time in preparing your approach.

CHEST CAPTURE

Players:	4-8 players split into 2 teams	Duration:	2 rounds of 5 minutes each
Objective:	Achieve the highest score by capturing the enemy team's chests, and by killing members of the opposing team before they reach yours.		

Notes & Tips:

■ It takes less time to capture a chest with your allies than it does when you're alone.

■ When you are defending chests, your Compass blurs each time you get too close to them. Create a perimeter just beyond this point.

■ The line of sight indication in your Target Data HUD is a great tool while protecting a chest. Keep the chest in view and you will immediately know that an enemy is poised to capture it whenever you see the outline around your target's portrait turn blue.

SIMULATION CATEGORIES

Simulation Categories are Game Modes or combinations of Game Modes linked thematically.

NAME	THEME/RULE	GAME TYPES	LIMITATIONS
Easy Deathmatch	Learn the basics	Easy Deathmatch	No abilities
Free For All	Solo play	Wanted, Assassinate, Deathmatch, Steal the Artifact, Corruption	-
Team Objectives	Team play	Manhunt, Chest Capture, Escort, Artifact Assault	-
Private	Custom games with friends	All	No XP or Abstergo Credits awarded

PLAYABLE CHARACTERS & CUSTOMIZATION

Though weapons and animations may differ between each avatar, there is no functional difference between them. Your choice of Persona, therefore, is very much a matter of personal preference – and, as you unlock further options, an opportunity to show off your experience with items that aren't immediately available. Level progression rewards you with custom packs that enable you to alter the in-game appearance of every character with different costumes and colors. Use the Characters section in the Data Hub to change or customize weapons (some unique to a character, and each having specific animations), appearance, clothes, colors and animations – including Taunts and Stun moves. Note that selecting your character's favorite weapons triggers special animations when used in matches.

THE COUNT

Name:	Vlad the Impaler
Availability:	Default

THE VANGUARD

Name:	Oksana Razin
Availability:	Default

THE GUARDIAN

Name:	Odai Dunqas
Availability:	Default

THE VIZIER

Name:	Damat Ali Pasha
Availability:	Default

THE DEACON

Name:	Cyril of Rhodes
Availability:	Default

THE THESPIAN

Name:	Lysistrata
Availability:	Default

THE TRICKSTER

Name:	Mirela Djuric
Availability:	Default

THE BOMBARDIER

Name:	Kadir
Availability:	Default

PRIMER

WALKTHROUGH

SIDE QUESTS

REFERENCE &
ANALYSIS

MULTIPLAYER

EXTRAS

INDEX

BASICS

SCORE &
PROGRESSION

ADVANCED TIPS

MAPS &
ANALYSIS

THE CHAMPION

Name:	Georgios Kostas
Availability:	Default

THE CRUSADER

Name:	Haras
Availability:	Unlocked only as part of a pre-order bonus, or if you have purchased a special edition of Assassin's Creed Revelations

THE SENTINEL

Name:	Vali cel Tradat
Availability:	Activate your Uplay Passport

THE RENEGADE

Name:	Shahkulu
Availability:	Complete Memory 03 of Sequence 07 in single-player mode (see page 77)

PRIMER

WALKTHROUGH

SIDE QUESTS

REFERENCE &
ANALYSIS

MULTIPLAYER

EXTRAS

INDEX

BASICS

SCORE &
PROGRESSION

ADVANCED TIPS

MAPS &
ANALYSIS

THE JESTER

Name:	Dulcamara
Availability:	Unlocked only as part of a pre-order bonus, or if you have purchased a special edition of Assassin's Creed Revelations. This character cannot be customized.

THE COURTESAN

Name:	Fabiola Cavazza
Availability:	Unlocked if you have reached level 50 in Assassin's Creed Brotherhood's multiplayer mode. This character cannot be customized.

THE DOCTOR

Name:	Seraffo
Availability:	Unlocked only as part of a pre-order bonus, or if you have purchased a special edition of Assassin's Creed Revelations. This character cannot be customized.

THE KNIGHT

Name:	Scevola Spina
Availability:	Unlocked on Uplay. This character cannot be customized.

SCORING SYSTEM

To repeat our opening advice, it is your score that matters – not kills. If you run up to a target in the street and brazenly execute them at the first opportunity, you might score a paltry 100 points. However, if you exercise a little restraint and incorporate just a few additional stalking techniques for bonuses, you could increase your points haul significantly. In essence, one good kill is worth several bad ones. With a time limit on the session, maximizing each kill score will enable you to make the most of a finite number of contracts.

Familiarize yourself with the following bonus tables, then think about how you can incorporate them into your playing strategies.

Kill and Approach Bonuses

Improve your stealth methods when approaching the target and kill them in interesting ways to earn multiple bonuses.

NAME	CONDITION	SCORE
Kill	Generic value for any basic kill	+100
Aerial Kill	Kill your target from above	+100
Contested Kill	Kill your target while he or she simultaneously stuns you	+100
Acrobatic Kill	Kill your target while climbing or crouching	+200
Grab Kill	Kill your target from below while he or she is on a rooftop	+450
Hidden Kill	Kill your target while hidden in a crowd, on a bench or in a haystack	+300
Ground Finish	Perform a finishing move on your target after he or she has been disabled by another Templar	+50
Execution	Use the Hidden Gun to kill a running target	+100
Reckless	Kill your target when your Approach Meter is on Reckless	+50
Discreet	Kill your target when your Approach Meter is on Discreet	+150
Silent	Kill your target when your Approach Meter is on Silent	+250
Incognito	Kill your target when your Approach Meter is maxed out	+350
Focus	Perform a kill after stalking your target for at least three seconds while the Assassinate button is displayed above his or her head	+150
Poison	Use Poison to kill your target	+200
Intercepted	Another Templar kills your poisoned target before the poison takes effect	+50
Mid-Air	Perform a kill with the Hidden Gun while your target is in the air	+100

Action & Session Bonuses

These are awarded for performing specific feats within a given session.

NAME	CONDITION	SCORE
First Blood	Perform the first kill of the session	+50
Revenge	Kill the Templar who killed you last before another Templar does	+50
Poacher	Kill a target while another pursuer is within 10m of where you stand	+50
Savior	Kill a target who is less than 10m away from his own target	+50
Honorable Death	Stun your pursuer when he or she kills you	+100
Stun	Stun your pursuer	+200
Escape	Escape from your pursuer	+100
Brutal Escape	Stun your pursuer to escape	+200
Hidden Escape	Hide to escape from your pursuer	+100
Out of Sight Escape	Break your pursuer's line of sight to escape	+150
Grounded	Kill your target while your target is stunned	+50
Multi-escape	Escape two or more pursuers at the same time	+100
Close Call	Escape a pursuer standing within 10m of where you are	+50
Lure	Another Templar kills or stuns a decoy, bodyguard or civilian lookalike	+100
Chain	Perform a kill followed by an escape or a stun within 10 seconds	+50
Variety	Earn 5 different bonuses in a session	+200
Greater Variety	Earn 10 different bonuses in a session	+400
Extreme Variety	Earn 15 different bonuses in a session	+600

The values in these tables may be adjusted in post-release updates.

PRIMER

WALKTHROUGH

SIDE QUESTS

REFERENCE & ANALYSIS

MULTIPLAYER

EXTRAS

INDEX

BASICS

SCORE & PROGRESSION

ADVANCED TIPS

MAPS & ANALYSIS

Team Bonuses

These apply to team-based games, and acknowledge cooperative behavior.

NAME	CONDITION	SCORE
Assist	An ally performs a kill or a stun on a target you had locked	+50
Assist Kill	Kill a target locked by a team mate	+50
Assist Stun	Stun a pursuer locked by a teammate	+50
Rescued	One of your allies kills your pursuer	+50
Rescuer	Stun a pursuer who is chasing one of your allies	+50
Knock Out	Your team stuns two pursuers within three seconds	+100
Revive	Help a stunned ally stand up	+50
Multi Kill	Your team kills two targets in less than ten seconds	+100
Diversion	Awarded when you kill a target who is being chased by an ally, or when an ally kills a target you are chasing	+50

Game Mode Bonuses

You will obtain these bonuses through actions or accomplishments relevant to a specific Game Mode.

NAME	CONDITION	SCORE
Hidden Alone	Earn this bonus every five seconds while hidden in a separate hiding spot, at least 20m away from your allies, during a Manhunt session	+10
Team Hidden	Earn this bonus every five seconds while hidden within 20m of your allies during a Manhunt session. The bonus increases with the number of allies nearby	+20 to +50
Team Capture	Given when a chest is captured by the team in Chest Capture	+50
Last Chest	Given when the third chest is captured by the team in Chest Capture	+50
Secured Chest	Given when you are in the capture zone as a chest is captured in Chest Capture	+50
Checkpoint	Given when a VIP reaches one or more checkpoints in Escort	+100 to +500
Possession	Given regularly when in possession of the artifact in Steal the Artifact	+25
Hidden Possession	Given regularly when in possession of the artifact while hidden in Steal the Artifact	+50
Proximity	Regularly awarded when at least one pursuer is within 20m in Corruption or Steal the Artifact	+20 to +80
Low/Medium/High Corruption	Periodically awarded as long the player remains Uncorrupted	+20 to +60
Sudden Death	Periodically awarded when only one Uncorrupted is still alive in Corruption	+120
Artifact Stolen	Steal the artifact in Artifact Assault or Steal the Artifact	+150
Artifact Score	Bring the other team's artifact to your base in Artifact Assault	+500
Support	Kill a target within 20m of an ally carrying the other team's artifact in Artifact Assault	+50
Recovery	Return a stolen artifact to your base by killing the carrier or picking it up when dropped in Artifact Assault	+50
Last Carrier	Be in possession of the artifact at the end of a Steal the Artifact session	+200
Best Streak	Beat the previous best score streak during a Steal the Artifact session	+200
Steal the Artifact	Carry the artifact for two minutes in a Steal the Artifact session	+400

The values in these tables may be adjusted in post-release updates.

LEVELS AND PROGRESSION

The points you earn from participating in multiplayer matches are converted into experience points (or "XP") that stay with your online profile and continue to accumulate with play. Whenever your total XP reaches a new threshold, your Templar trainee will "level up" and gradually advance from a raw recruit (Level 1) to a master assassin (Level 50 – and beyond with Prestige Mode). A Level increase usually grants a reward of one or more of the following:

- New Abilities, Perks, Kill Streaks or Loss Bonuses.
- A new custom Abilities Set.
- An Abilities Crafting point.
- Templar Profile elements (emblem, patron picture and title) and character customization parts (body parts and colors, weapons, stun and taunt animations). These are only cosmetic upgrades and have no effect on gameplay.
- Abstergo Dossiers and Videos, which offer information and revelations on the Templar Order's history and objectives.

Level progression improves your Agent's capabilities and increases your chance of success against other players online. You will find that opponents with greater experience have the advantage in terms of Abilities and score bonuses.

Rewards and items are not automatically awarded when you level up. To obtain newly unlocked features, you must purchase them from the Store using Abstergo Credits (△). You can earn credits in the following ways:

- Completing each session
- Finishing in the first three ranks of a session
- Being the best player of your team
- Leveling up
- Obtaining accolades

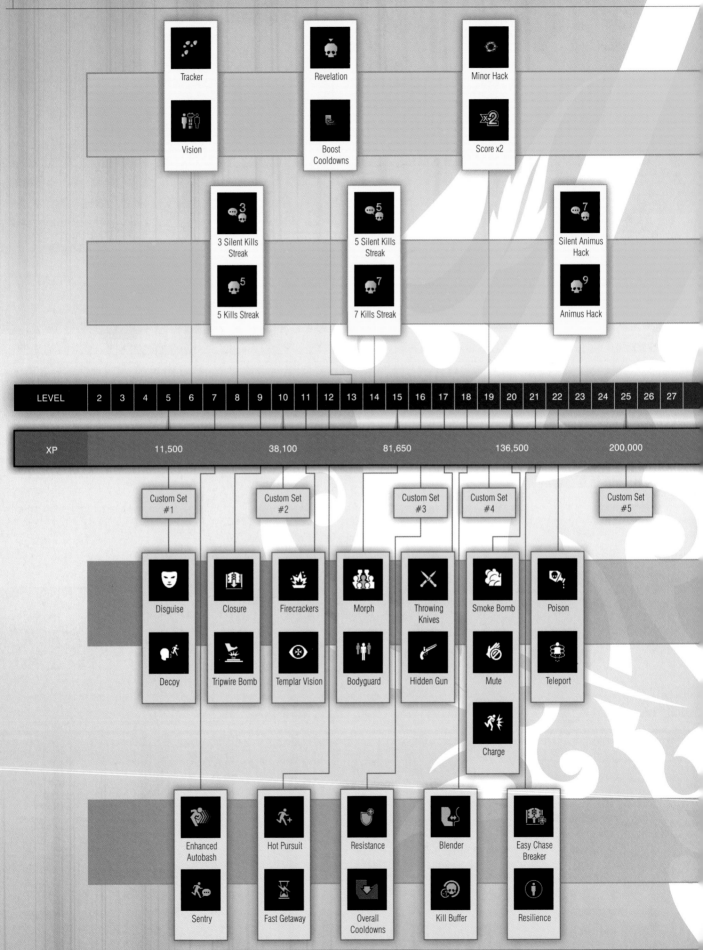

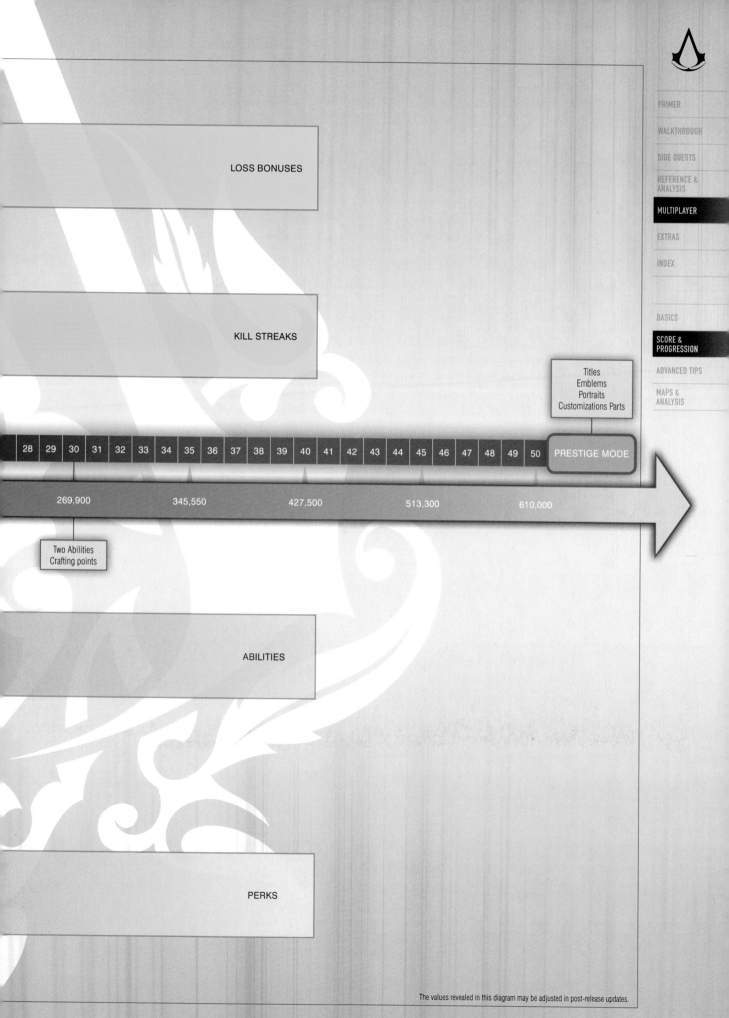

LOSS BONUSES

KILL STREAKS

Titles
Emblems
Portraits
Customizations Parts

| 28 | 29 | 30 | 31 | 32 | 33 | 34 | 35 | 36 | 37 | 38 | 39 | 40 | 41 | 42 | 43 | 44 | 45 | 46 | 47 | 48 | 49 | 50 | PRESTIGE MODE |

269,900   345,550   427,500   513,300   610,000

Two Abilities
Crafting points

ABILITIES

PERKS

The values revealed in this diagram may be adjusted in post-release updates.

PRIMER

WALKTHROUGH

SIDE QUESTS

REFERENCE & ANALYSIS

MULTIPLAYER

EXTRAS

INDEX

BASICS

SCORE & PROGRESSION

ADVANCED TIPS

MAPS & ANALYSIS

ABILITIES SETS

Abilities Sets grant your character additional skills, weapons or bonuses, all of which are detailed over the pages that follow. Each set is composed of:

- Two Abilities
- Two Perks (only one with Default Sets)
- One Streak
- One Loss Bonus

Initially you only have two Default Sets to play with. As you gain levels, you will unlock up to five Custom Sets, which you can freely define in accordance with your preferences or the challenges that lie ahead in a particular play mode.

		DEFAULT SET 1	DEFAULT SET 2
Abilities		Throwing Knives	Disguise
		Tripwire Bomb	Firecrackers
Perks		Sentry	Enhanced Autobash
		Unavailable	*Unavailable*
Streak & Bonus		5 Kills Streak	3 Silent Kills Streak
		Tracker	Vision

ABILITIES

Abilities can be used at any time, but are then unavailable for a Cooldown period as they recharge. As a rule, the Cooldown of an Ability begins when its effect ends.

The fifteen Abilities can be improved through Crafting, which enables you to improve up to two parameters of the chosen Ability. Once you unlock Custom Sets, you can choose which Abilities to equip.

ICON	NAME	UNLOCKED	EFFECT	NOTES
	Disguise	Level 5	Temporarily change your appearance to look like another Persona and surprise opponents.	■ Must be used when out of line of sight and is defeated by Lock. ■ Most effective when close to a lookalike of your true skin. ■ During an Escape, activate it right as you round a corner and turn around to surprise your pursuer. ■ There's a risk of being revealed when the effect expires.
	Decoy	Level 5	Change the appearance of anyone you target to mimic your own and cause them to run away, tricking your pursuers.	■ Good for misleading both pursuers and targets. ■ Very useful when you have spotted a pursuer approaching to send them away.
	Tripwire Bomb	Level 9	Explodes when a target or pursuer steps on it, preventing them from moving and performing any action during a short period.	■ You can drop the bomb at your feet or aim and throw it. ■ The bomb takes a few seconds to activate. ■ The Cooldown begins when the bomb is placed. ■ Place a bomb in a narrow corridor (between Closing Gates, for instance) and lure a pursuer for an easy stun opportunity.
	Closure	Level 9	Triggers all the Chase Breakers around you.	■ The Chase Breakers will all reopen after a few seconds. ■ They will also open upon your approach.
	Templar Vision	Level 11	Reveal the presence of other Templars in your line of sight.	■ Your targets are highlighted in blue; your pursuers are red. ■ This is useful to identify targets using Morph or Disguise. ■ Using this makes your Persona shine while active.
	Firecrackers	Level 11	Drop Firecrackers on the ground to blind opponents and scare citizens, potentially revealing the presence of your target.	■ Can be used to identify opponents; watch the movements of all affected individuals carefully. ■ Blinds both your target and any pursuers in the vicinity for a few seconds. ■ You can drop Firecrackers at your feet or aim and throw them. The latter can be a very efficient way to identify and/or stop a distant target.
	Bodyguard	Level 15	Creates a duplicate of your Persona who will protect you from pursuers.	■ A very effective way to confuse your pursuers. ■ Stay close to your duplicate for maximum efficiency and defensive stun opportunities.
	Morph	Level 15	Transforms characters from the crowd into your duplicates	■ This is very useful to hide from pursuers. ■ By default, you will morph four civilians. ■ Excellent for evasion and defense. ■ Offensive use: confuse an aware target preparing to Stun you. ■ Effective for delivering Poison.
	Throwing Knives	Level 17	Throw knives to slow down your pursuer or target.	■ Lock your target before throwing the knives. ■ Knives also prevent a victim from climbing. ■ Being hit by a knife will cause a target to fall while climbing. ■ A target that you have hit with Throwing Knives can still Stun you, so don't approach them recklessly.
	Hidden Gun	Level 17	Shoot down the targeted character after securing a Lock.	■ Only works on a contracted target. ■ No Incognito, Silent or Focus bonus for kill. ■ Good for rooftops and targets fleeing in the open.
	Smoke Bomb	Level 20	Throw a Smoke Bomb to confuse the crowd and Templar rivals.	■ You can drop the bomb at your feet or aim and throw it. ■ The Cooldown begins when the bomb explodes. ■ Practice the use of this weapon to master the activation delay. ■ Offensive use: score Silent and Focus bonus on target; prevent Chase. ■ Defensive use: paralyze one or more pursuers for a follow-up Stun.
	Mute	Level 20	Briefly prevents Templars around you from using critical moves.	■ While this is active, the Templars in your vicinity can no longer kill or stun you. This also locks their Abilities. ■ Useful to perform kills with the Focus bonus.
	Charge	Level 20	Rush straight ahead, scattering the crowd, to pounce on your target.	■ This will disperse nearby citizens, but also kill your target or stun your pursuer. ■ Good alternative to Templar Vision for locating and killing target in a group of identical skins. ■ Functions as a more effective Stun than the basic move due to its increased range.
	Teleport	Level 22	Instantly changes your location on the map.	■ You will teleport to a position approximately ahead of the direction you are facing. ■ This Ability takes a few seconds to activate.
	Poison	Level 22	Poison a target to slowly kill them.	■ You can only poison a target in close proximity. ■ The Cooldown begins as soon as the Poison is administered. ■ Has its own score bonus. ■ There is no kill animation, so you can escape flashpoints stealthily.

CRAFTING ABILITIES

PRIMER

WALKTHROUGH

SIDE QUESTS

REFERENCE & ANALYSIS

MULTIPLAYER

EXTRAS

INDEX

BASICS

SCORE & PROGRESSION

ADVANCED TIPS

MAPS & ANALYSIS

Crafting is the process by which you can customize every Ability by modifying and tweaking its parameters. This enables you to upgrade your Abilities in a way that best suits your strategy.

You can spend up to two points to enhance an Ability through Crafting. These points are obtained when you reach Level 30. Each Crafting operation also requires you to pay a fee with Abstergo Credits.

When you consult the following Crafting table, you will see that each Ability is defined by a set of parameters:

- **Range:** Covers the area of effect of the Ability, such as the radius of a Smoke Bomb or the targeting distance of a Charge, measured in meters of in-game distance.
- **Duration:** How long an Ability's effect will last.
- **Delay:** The time that an Ability takes to engage, in seconds.
- **Cooldown:** The number of seconds you must wait after activating an Ability before it can be used again. Ability upgrades, Perks and Streaks can all reduce Cooldown.
- **Execution Time:** The time it takes to perform the Ability.
- **Various Effects:** Some Abilities may alter the personal attributes of you or your target, or exert special effects on the arena.

ICON	ABILITY	PARAMETER	DEFAULT VALUE	UPGRADE #1	UPGRADE #2
	Tripwire Bomb	Range	2m	2.1m	2.2m
		Execution Time	5s	4.2s	3.5s
		Cooldown	90s	80s	75s
	Throwing Knives	Speed Decrease	20%	25%	30%
		Duration	2.8s	3.2s	3.5s
		Cooldown	50s	45s	40s
	Closure	Range	20m	25m	30m
		Duration	5s	5.8s	6.5s
		Cooldown	50s	45s	40s
	Smoke Bomb	Range	3.2m	3.4m	3.6m
		Duration	3s	3.5s	3.8s
		Cooldown	60s	55s	45s
	Teleport	Execution Time	2.5s	2s	1.5s
		Range	35m	40m	45m
		Cooldown	90s	80s	75s
	Poison	Delay	3.5s	5s	3.5s
		Bonus	200pts	250pts	300pts
		Cooldown	90s	80s	75s
	Bodyguard	Range	8m	10m	12m
		Duration	8s	10s	12s
		Cooldown	50s	45s	40s
	Morph	Range	3.2m	3.6m	4m
		Civilians Morphed	4	5	6
		Cooldown	60s	55s	45s
	Mute	Range	6m	6.5m	7m
		Duration	1.5s	1.8s	2.1s
		Cooldown	90s	80s	75s
	Charge	Angle	20°	25°	30°
		Duration	2s	2.5s	3s
		Cooldown	90s	80s	75s
	Templar Vision	Duration	3s	3.5s	4s
		Distance	25m	30m	40m
		Cooldown	75s	70s	60s
	Disguise	Duration	15s	18s	20s
		Cooldown	60s	55s	45s
		Effect	Standard	Improved	Elite
	Firecrackers	Range	5m	5.5m	6m
		Duration	4s	4.5s	5s
		Cooldown	75s	70s	60s
	Hidden Gun	Focus Time	2s	1.5s	1s
		Minimum Hit Chance	30%	45%	60%
		Cooldown	90s	80s	75s
	Decoy	Duration	10s	12s	15s
		Cooldown	50s	45s	40s
		Effect	Standard	Improved	Elite

The values in these tables may be adjusted in post-release updates.

STREAKS

Streaks are performance-based bonuses, earned through cumulative accomplishments or successive failures within each round.

A Kill Streak of successfully completed contracts will reward the player with extra points or a temporary new capacity. Players who consistently die or lose contracts will incur a Loss Bonus, which actually helps them to arrest their poor form by granting small advantages.

ICON	KILL STREAKS	DESCRIPTION	UNLOCKED
	3 Silent Kills Streak	Receive 250 points when you silently kill or stun three targets without being killed.	Level 8
	5 Kills Streak	Receive 250 points when you kill or stun five targets without being killed.	Level 8
	5 Silent Kills Streak	Receive 550 points when you silently kill or stun five targets without being killed.	Level 14
	7 Kills Streak	Receive 550 points when you silently kill or stun seven targets without being killed.	Level 14
	Silent Animus Hack	If you perform a seven Silent Kills Streak, this enables you to kill whomever you wish from a distance. You earn 100 points when you kill a non-target Templar.	Level 23
	Animus Hack	If you perform a nine Kills Streak, this enables you to kill whomever you want from a distance. You earn 100 points when you kill a non-target Templar.	Level 23

ICON	LOSS BONUSES	DESCRIPTION	UNLOCKED
	Vision	Reveals the location of out-of-sight targets until you perform a kill. Occurs after five deaths or stuns in a row.	Level 6
	Tracker	Reveals a target in your sight until you perform a kill. Occurs after five contract losses in a row.	Level 6
	Revelation	Reveals all pursuers in your sight until you perform a kill. Occurs after five deaths or stuns in a row.	Level 13
	Boost Cooldowns	Ability Cooldowns are reduced until you perform a kill. Occurs after five contract losses in a row.	Level 13
	Score x2	Doubles the points earned by your next successful assassination. Occurs after five deaths or stuns in a row.	Level 19
	Minor Hack	Enables you to kill your next target from a distance. Occurs after five contract losses in a row.	Level 19

PERKS

You can further customize your character by choosing two Perks, additional powers that remain active throughout the match. Perks are also unlocked through Level progression.

ICON	NAME	EFFECT	UNLOCKED
	Enhanced Auto-Bash	Increases the number of civilians you can barge aside before losing your footing while running.	Level 7
	Sentry	Increases the time a target will remain locked when you lose sight of him or her	Level 7
	Fast Getaway	Decreases the time required to escape a pursuer during a Chase.	Level 12
	Hot Pursuit	Increases your speed when chasing a target and slows down the depletion of your Approach Meter.	Level 12
	Resistance	Reduces your Stunned time.	Level 16
	Overall Cooldowns	Reduces all Ability Cooldown periods.	Level 16
	Blender	When you blend with a crowd, one of the civilians is automatically Morphed into your character's skin.	Level 18
	Kill Buffer	Decreases your Kill Streak by one instead of resetting it when you die.	Level 18
	Easy Chase Breaker	Automatically opens a recently closed Chase Breaker when you approach.	Level 21
	Resilience	Decreases the duration of Abilities used against you.	Level 21

The values in these tables may be adjusted in post-release updates.

PRIMER

WALKTHROUGH

SIDE QUESTS

REFERENCE & ANALYSIS

MULTIPLAYER

EXTRAS

INDEX

BASICS

SCORE & PROGRESSION

ADVANCED TIPS

MAPS & ANALYSIS

Style Accolades

ICON	NAME	CONDITION
	The Immortal	Stayed alive the longest.
	The Wanderer	Spent the most time walking.
	The Stalker	Earned the most Focus bonuses.
	The Wingman	Earned the most Assist bonuses.
	The Master	Earned the most Incognito bonuses.
	The Vicious	Had the most Ground Finishes.
	The Gargoyle	Spent the most time on rooftops.
	The Invisible	Had the greatest Approach bonuses.
	The Escape Artist	Made the most escapes.
	The Achiever	Finished first, second or third.
	The Drunkard	Was Stunned most often.
	The Stunner	Performed the most Stuns.

ACCOLADES

Accolades are rewards given at the end of each session that acknowledge excellence in a wide variety of categories; they reveal a great deal about your play style. By claiming several Accolades, you can earn additional Abstergo Credits. The first time you earn an Accolade, you unlock the corresponding Title.

Abilities Accolades

ICON	NAME	CONDITION
	The Hacker	Performed the most Animus Hacks.
	The Improviser	Used the greatest variety of Abilities.
	The Poisoner	Poisoned the most targets.
	The Undercover	Remained Morphed or Disguised longer than any other participant.
	The Victim	Spent the most time afflicted by Abilities.
	The Sniper	Had the most Hidden Gun kills.

Assassination Accolades

ICON	NAME	CONDITION
	The Professional	Had the best kills/deaths ratio.
	The Savage	Had the most contested kills.
	The Expert	Had the best single kill score.
	The Sacrificial Lamb	The first to die.
	The Survivor	Died the least.
	The Target	Died the most.
	The Champion	Had the highest score.
	The Slayer	Had the most kills.
	The Untouchable	Was never killed.

Modes Accolades

ICON	NAME	CONDITION
	The Savior	Revived the most allies.
	The Dependable	Played on the winning team.
	The Lone Wolf	Won a Free-For-All session.
	The Elusive	Was acquired in a lock less than any other participant.
	The Wise	Killed the least civilians.
	The Saint	Survived longest as Uncorrupted.
	The Thief	Stole the most Artifacts.
	The Machine	Had the longest Streak.
	The Watchdog	Killed the most targets near chests.
	The Robber	Captured the most chests.
	The Protector	Killed the most pursuers near VIPs.
	The Agitator	Killed the most VIPs.
	The Clumsy	Dropped the most Artifacts.
	The Glutton	Scored the most Artifacts.
	The Stalwart	Killed the most Artifact thieves.
	The Practiced	Made the most kills without being Stunned.
	The Lurker	Spent the most time blended with an ally.

CHALLENGES

Four types of Challenge are recorded in the Progression menu, unlocked by repeating the corresponding feat a certain number of times (specified in each table's Total column). Each Challenge has three milestones that reward you an XP bonus when completed. You also receive a new Title when reaching the third milestone.

Abilities Challenges

NAME	CONDITION	TOTAL	XP
The Deceiver	Stun a pursuer while Disguised.	x5	500
The Liar	Kill a target while Disguised.	x5	500
The Pyrotechnician	Use Firecrackers to kill a blended target.	x10	500
The Vanquisher	Use Firecrackers and Stun your pursuer.	x1	500
The Sly	Use a Tripwire Bomb to stop your pursuer.	x10	500
The Master Hunter	Use a Tripwire Bomb to stop and kill your target.	x1	500
The Knife Thrower	Use Knives to slow then kill a target.	x10	500
The Artful	Use Knives to knock down a climbing Templar.	x5	500
The Puppet Master	Make your pursuer kill a Decoy.	x10	500
The Manipulator	Earn a Lure bonus when your target Stuns a Decoy.	x5	500
The Trapper	Use Closure to block and kill your target.	x5	500
The Clever	Use Closure to block your pursuer.	x5	500
The Psychic	Use Templar Vision to find and kill your target.	x10	500
The Evanescent	Use Templar Vision to find and Stun a pursuer.	x5	500
The Observant	Use Morph to reveal and kill your target.	x3	500
The Chameleon	Perform a Stun from a Morphed crowd.	x5	500
The Boss	Make your pursuer kill your Bodyguard.	x5	500
The Sharpshooter	Use the Hidden Gun to kill a jumping or running target.	x5	500
The Huntsman	Kill three targets using the Hidden Gun in a session.	x3	500
The Magician	Use a Smoke Bomb to stop and Stun your pursuer.	x15	500
The Marauder	Stop two Templars with one Smoke Bomb.	x5	500
The Relentless	Mute and kill your target.	x10	500
The Quick-Witted	Mute and Stun your pursuer.	x10	500
The Brute	Use Charge to Stun your pursuer.	x10	500
The Aggressor	Charge a target in a crowd.	x10	500
The Sandman	Use Poison on a Stunned Templar.	x3	500
The Apothecary	Use Poison after Focusing on a target.	x1	500
The Evader	Use Teleport and earn an Escape bonus.	x3	500
The Unstoppable	Activate a Kill Streak.	x5	750

Style Challenges

NAME	CONDITION	TOTAL	XP
The Elite Templar	Score at least 6,000 points in a single session.	x1	500
The Artist	Perform a kill worth at least 700 points.	x5	500
The Versatile	Earn a Variety bonus.	x20	500
The Perfectionist	Earn a Greater Variety bonus.	x5	1,000
The Mass Murderer	Kill ten targets in a single session.	x3	750
The Usurper	Take the lead in the last ten seconds of a session.	x1	500
The Good Samaritan	Revive an ally.	x15	500
The Trespasser	Taunt a target you've just killed.	x3	500
The Provoker	Taunt a Templar you've just Stunned.	x3	500
The Vengeful	Earn a Ground Finish bonus.	x50	500
The Fighter	Perform four Stuns without dying.	x1	500
The Omnipotent	Perform a nine-kill Streak.	x1	750

The values in these tables may be adjusted in post-release updates.

PRIMER

WALKTHROUGH

SIDE QUESTS

REFERENCE &
ANALYSIS

MULTIPLAYER

EXTRAS

INDEX

BASICS

SCORE &
PROGRESSION

ADVANCED TIPS

MAPS &
ANALYSIS

Modes Challenges

NAME	CONDITION	TOTAL	XP
The Deathless	Stay alive for 60 seconds in Deathmatch.	x15	500
The Conqueror	Earn a seven-kill Streak in Deathmatch.	x3	1,000
The Competitor	Earn a Streak of five in Wanted.	x10	1,000
The Stealth Master	Earn five Incognito bonuses in Wanted.	x5	500
The Vulture	Kill an enemy who has just performed a kill in Assassinate.	x10	500
The Punisher	Stun, acquire and kill a pursuer in Assassinate.	x5	500
The Brawler	Perform two Stuns without dying in Steal the Artifact.	x3	1,000
The Audacious	Hide with three pursuers in close proximity in Steal the Artifact.	x10	500
The Finisher	Be in possession of the artifact at the end of a Steal the Artifact session.	x5	500
The Escapist	Survive Sudden Death while Uncorrupted in Corruption.	x1	750
The Pure	As Uncorrupted, perform three Stuns in one round of Corruption.	x1	750
The Vector	Kill an Uncorrupted during Sudden Death in Corruption.	x5	500
The Enduring	Earn the Multi-Kill bonus in Manhunt.	x10	500
The Medium	Kill a target near two Templars with the same Persona in Manhunt.	x5	350
The Master Thief	Capture a chest in Chest Capture.	x15	500
The Burglar	Capture a chest while hidden in Chest Capture.	x5	750
The Warden	Kill a pursuer near a VIP in Escort.	x10	500
The Swift	Stun an enemy and kill a VIP within five seconds in Escort.	x5	750
The Highwayman	Score with an Artifact in Artifact Assault.	x5	1,000
The Eradicator	Kill the target holding the Artifact in Artifact Assault.	x5	500
The Vigilant	Stun a pursuer near an ally.	x50	500
The Serial Killer	Play a session with every Persona.	x1	500

Assassination Challenges

NAME	CONDITION	TOTAL	XP
The Ambitious	Earn the First Blood bonus.	x5	500
The Unseen	Earn a Hidden Kill bonus.	x5	750
The Silent Master	Earn a Focus bonus.	x5	500
The Flying Templar	Earn an Aerial Kill bonus.	x25	500
The Killing Machine	Perform two Kills in less than seven seconds.	x1	500
The Wrestler	Stun your pursuer.	x50	500
The Sagacious	Stun your pursuer and kill your target within ten seconds.	x1	500
The Crafty	Perform two Stuns in less than seven seconds.	x5	500
The Gatekeeper	Use a Chase Breaker to Escape.	x10	750
The Runaway	Earn the Multiple Escape bonus.	x1	500
The Escapee	Escape your pursuer in a Chase.	x30	500

The values in these tables may be adjusted in post-release updates.

.TW90aGVyU2Fk
.RmF0aGVyTWFk
.Trf90aGluZ0lzVHJ1ZQ==
.RXZlcnl0aGluZ0lzUGVybWl0dGVk
.Qm9yZWRPZldhbGtpbmc3JoZXM=

GOLDEN RULES

■ Stay on the move. You have a target to track down and you are being hunted constantly. You should only remain still in very specific instances, such as when you are hiding from a pursuer.

■ Aim to complete your contracts with a good score bonus. Securing more kills than your rivals isn't helpful if they consistently accumulate twice the points.

■ Avoid surrendering points to other players by allowing yourself to be killed or Stunned. Be patient! Running towards a target will get you to them more quickly, but will also increase the likelihood you will be noticed (or, worse, Locked) by other Templars.

■ A player with higher XP and character resources will always have an advantage, so just keep playing. Your progression curve will flatten out, with higher Levels coming more slowly, but the advanced Abilities are worth striving for.

■ Improvise, don't strategize. Concentrate on finding your target as quickly as possible, but remain alert and be ready to switch tactics in an instant.

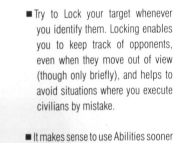

■ Try to Lock your target whenever you identify them. Locking enables you to keep track of opponents, even when they move out of view (though only briefly), and helps to avoid situations where you execute civilians by mistake.

■ It makes sense to use Abilities sooner rather than later. Even with default Cooldown periods, the assignment of contracts and tracking time with a full Abilities Set roughly equates to one Ability per kill.

TEMPLAR IDENTIFICATION TIPS

■ Use your Target Data HUD (see page 165) to switch between targets in applicable play modes, then go for the opponent who is closest, or in the most interesting location. Don't just settle for the first assigned target.

■ Blending isn't half as effective as standing next to a civilian with an identical Persona. Once a participant is close to an opponent, the Compass becomes a full disc and gives no further indication of which target to execute. This leaves the sticky problem of deciding who to strike, which should at the very least slow an opponent down.

■ Blending among moving crowds enables you to approach your target without being spotted.

■ Once you hear whispers, you know that your pursuer is drawing near. Conversely, once you hear your heartbeat, you know that your target is nearby. If you are finding it difficult to hear the whispers, try using headphones.

■ Moving at a higher elevation increases your chances of targeting your contract. If you are on a rooftop above them, the range of an air assassination while in pursuit greatly exceeds the proximity you would need to reach them at street level – and you won't take damage from falling. At the same time, rooftop activity marks you out to all other players as an Agent.

■ Some of the characters are harder to spot at a distance than others, particularly for new players. If there is one you find troublesome, simply choose that skin as your own to avoid this problem. There is a chance, of course, that your pursuers may have the same trouble identifying you.

■ Watch how AI-controlled civilians move and attempt to imitate them. Other players are just as busy as you, so a rough approximation will enable you to pass for an NPC on most occasions.

■ If your pursuer performs a high profile action while in your line of sight, a red triangle icon will appear above their head (▼), making them very easy to spot. When a player moves his camera to look behind, his character moves his head – use this to locate your rivals.

■ Take a moment to stop and look at which way the arc is moving on your Compass. By interpreting its width and direction, you may be able to intercept your target at the nearest intersection.

■ If your target is constantly running around on rooftops, you can either chase him up there for a Reckless kill, or save your time and earn a bonus by shooting him in the back with the Hidden Gun.

■ The moment you locate your target and assassinate them, even if striking from a hiding spot, you break your cover for the entire world to see. You are never more likely to be killed than at this moment, so you should often make a swift getaway after a kill rather than blending or hiding.

■ Use Poison or ranged weapons to avoid creating a disturbance, then make a discrete departure – the ensuing commotion may distract any opponents closing in on your approximate position.

PRIMER

WALKTHROUGH

SIDE QUESTS

REFERENCE &
ANALYSIS

MULTIPLAYER

EXTRAS

INDEX

BASICS

SCORE &
PROGRESSION

ADVANCED TIPS

MAPS &
ANALYSIS

HIGH PROFILE & CHASE TIPS

- When in close pursuit of a target, don't forget to regularly look around to identify opponents zeroing in on you.

- Press the Secondary Weapon button before reaching a Corner Helper to perform a Long Jump.

- You cannot be assassinated by normal moves while climbing or jumping. However ranged Abilities make short work of anyone scaling walls or free running.

- Chases favor the escapee, as they can use Chase Breakers and hiding spots to accelerate a time-out. For this reason, don't attempt to follow your target's exact footsteps: attempt to cut them off instead. Chases cost potential killing time, so a 50/50 gamble on whether they'll turn left or right will conclude the matter sooner rather than later. It's often better to ditch an adept opponent than enter a protracted pursuit.

- Always climb in steps, using beams and poles, and make distance on flat ground or free running surfaces. Scaling a wall leaves you open to ranged attacks.

- If you have your pursuer locked, press the Stun button rapidly as they close in for the kill and you have a greater chance of incapacitating them and ending their pursuit (📷 01). Worst-case scenario, you will get an Honorable Death bonus for your troubles.

01

SCORE & BONUS TIPS

- When your target is hiding in hay, jump in yourself. This will force him or her out, setting up an easy Hidden Kill bonus (📷 02).

- In any given round, try to mix up your kills. There are big points bonuses for variety.

02

- After you perform a kill, close proximity to other Templars will delay the assignment of another contract. Move to the outer edge of the map to reduce the waiting time.

- When another player kills your target, don't forget to finish them off for a Ground Kill bonus.

- Crafting (see page 181) is a good way to improve your favored Abilities, which will make it easier to score more points in each session.

- The better your approach is, the shorter the kill animation will be. This will help you to remain unnoticed and move on immediately to your next target.

ABILITIES SET TIPS

- As you level up, you will need to define tactical Custom Sets to get the best use of your Abilities, Perks and Streaks. The Custom Sets allow you to activate two Perks, whereas the Default Sets only feature one.

- Through advancement, you will acquire up to five Custom Sets for a range of reactive options, enabling you to choose various sets of complementary powers. You can switch Sets between rounds or after dying. We suggest that you give each Set a unique descriptive name to facilitate quick choices before respawns.

- If your opponents take to the rooftops, a focus on ranged Abilities may catch them out. If they act aggressively, defensive Abilities will humiliate them. If you suspect that the other participants are more experienced than you, choose a favorite Loss Bonus (such as Score x2) to remain competitive.

- To get you started on ideas for good combinations, here are some Abilities that complement each other:

  - **Templar Vision + Disguise:** Try this stealth combination to maximize your chances of a Stun.

  - **Tripwire Bomb + Disguise:** A defensive set that offers a good degree of protection, enabling you to attack while disguised.

  - **Morph + Smoke Bombs:** An efficient combo when you are performing well in a match. Good for both high-scoring kills and thwarting pursuit.

  - **Mute + Poison:** Accomplished players can achieve lucrative kills with these efficient tools.

- Remember that Abilities are not 100% reliable. The fog of a Smoke Bomb can be avoided during the explosion delay; the trap of a Tripwire Bomb can be defused by walking carefully around it; you can even escape the effect of Mute by staying out of your opponent's range for a second or two.

- Many Abilities have a counterpart that undermines them: for example, Throwing Knives can stop a Charge, and Firecrackers can reveal a Disguised or Morphed target.

TEAM TACTICS TIPS

- Whenever you are close to an ally who has just killed a target, run to the victim and perform a Ground Finish for an easy bonus. This can be achieved by all teammates and is a great way to maximize your score if you move in formation.

- If you see a teammate being Stunned while standing in close proximity, try to kill their target and then immediately revive your ally. You will not only save your cohort precious seconds, but also earn more points; remind him or her to perform a Ground Finish on the vanquished target.

- When you Lock a target, your partner sees them Locked too, which helps to coordinate your joint actions.

- Cooperative actions boost scores. Before rushing to complete a kill, check if you can't maximize the return by involving teammates. Plan your Profile Sets together for offense or support roles.

- If your partner is killed, their assassin is ripe for a Stun. Cover each other when close, as you will be drawing both of your hunters to the same location.

- Press the Secondary Attack button to revive a stunned ally and earn a bonus.

- Use your teammate to drive a target towards your location. Setting a trap with Disguise is effective, as many opponents will expect to recognize their pursuers.

- Adjust your solo and cooperative efforts to suit the situation. When trailing, work together on one target for quality kills and Team Bonuses. Once you take the lead, it can be advantageous to split up and take a target each.

- A Templar with an empty red icon above his head (▼) is chasing one of your allies. Kill or Stun him to save your teammate.

- Team cooperation is essential: pay attention to the location of your allies and their current status. In certain Game Modes, it makes sense to move as a pack to outnumber your opponents. You should also remember that a Chase Breaker that was closed by a teammate will automatically reopen for you.

12002.TW90aGVyU2Fk
12002.RmF0aGVyTWFk
72002.Tm90aGluZ0lzVHJ1ZQ==
72002.RXZlcni0aGluZ 20lzUGVybWl0dGVk
22003.Qm9vZWRPZ 2ldhcfN0b3.InZXMz

Legend (Chase Breakers)

 Lift   Corner Helper    Closing Gates

To help you to familiarize yourself with each arena, the maps that follow reveal the layout of the destinations you will visit, and include the positions of all Chase Breakers.

KNIGHTS HOSPITAL

In Deathmatch and Easy Deathmatch modes, the action centers around the small courtyard in front of the church. Use the haywains, bench and static blend groups to pounce on passing targets for Hidden Kill bonuses. The two Closing Gates nearby will aid your escape.

The long corridors below the archways that surround the central square area offer plenty of opportunities to escape a pursuer. Not only can you easily break their line of sight using the pillars and gateways, but you also have access to several closing doors.

The central square offers concentric routes for moving swiftly between inner and outer paths or from ground to rooftop, with many Lifts making transitions extremely fast. During Escapes, you can attempt to break line of sight in three dimensions.

The sprawling, open nature of Antioch makes it very difficult to hide in the open without employing Abilities such as Morph or Disguise. It's also tricky to escape during a Chase. Memorizing the locations of key Chase Breakers makes all the difference here.

The width of the streets makes it difficult to navigate efficiently at rooftop level.

This map features many haystacks that are handily located near closing gates. Running through these Chase Breakers and hiding immediately as you arrive on the other side can be very effective, offering you plenty of opportunities to Stun your pursuer. However, it should go without saying that experienced players will often anticipate this…

As this arena is situated on a hill, you will often find that your target is at a different elevation. Don't be impatient: if you climb a wall to take a shortcut, you will draw unnecessary attention to yourself.

The tight, narrow streets tend to force pursuers onto the rooftops in search of their quarry.

When you are being pursued, stick to the ground and use the twisting narrow streets to your advantage. There are also plenty of hiding spots and Chase Breakers to aid your escape.

SOUK

- You do not have access to any rooftops on this map, which keeps the action largely on the ground and among the crowds. Without the use of Abilities, it can be hard to shake off a pursuer on the exposed roads.

- Even without rooftops, you may learn to lose your pursuer by squeezing through the crowds. It is faster to weave between groups than to use the Shove move.

- The indoor souk area is a great place to escape. If you activate a Closing Gate your pursuer won't be able to follow you via an elevated path, forcing them to make a detour.

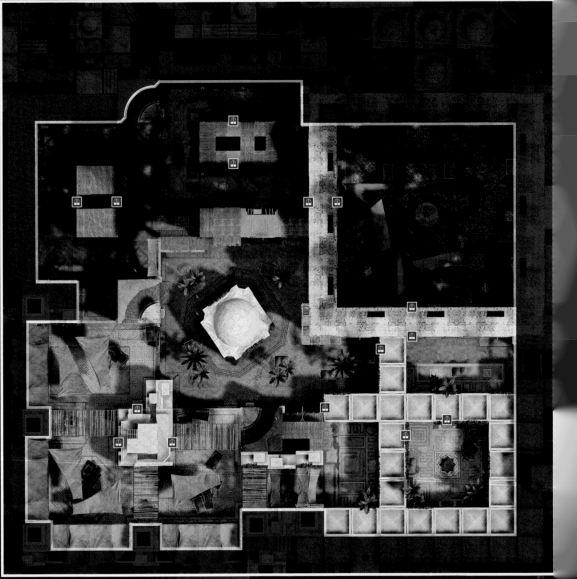

PRIMER

WALKTHROUGH

SIDE QUESTS

REFERENCE &
ANALYSIS

MULTIPLAYER

EXTRAS

INDEX

BASICS

SCORE &
PROGRESSION

ADVANCED TIPS

**MAPS &
ANALYSIS**

With its many tight turns, narrow alleyways and crossroads, this map makes it easy to shake off a pursuer. More than ever, be patient and try to remain silent at all times.

Aerial kills, Hidden Gun exchanges and even assassinations from ledges are a frequent feature of the upper routes, so watch the skyline.

Use the terraces and balconies to your advantage. While this might provide opportunities to air assassinate your target, being on high ground will sometimes help you to spot pursuers. A citizen halting for no reason below your position is most likely a rival Templar attempting to ascertain your exact location.

ROME

- The busy market square on the steps of the Pantheon offers plenty of blending spots and moving crowds for social stealth, but is open and exposed when your cover is broken.

- When attempting to escape a pursuer, leave the marketplace and look for the Closing Gates and Lifts at ground level. Aim to reach the hiding spots on the periphery of the map, using the buildings around the square to break line of sight.

- The rooftops offer a fast route across the entire map, but you'll be spotted very easily in transit.

MONT ST-MICHEL

The narrow streets in the lower section of the map favor the fleeing fugitive, with sufficient twists and turns to shake off even the most persistent pursuer.

This contrasts with the plaza in front of the church's main gate. Any high profile action here is likely to lead to immediate detection, though incoming pursuers are very easy to identify in such an open space. Use the stairways to the left of the gate to reach the underground corridors: this is a great location to shake off anyone on your tail.

PRIMER

WALKTHROUGH

SIDE QUESTS

REFERENCE & ANALYSIS

MULTIPLAYER

EXTRAS

INDEX

BASICS

SCORE & PROGRESSION

ADVANCED TIPS

MAPS & ANALYSIS

VENICE

- High buildings surround Piazza San Marco, granting an excellent vantage point for spotting your prey. Use the Lifts to reach these vantage points without attracting attention for too long.

- When looking to flee, the port area offers a chance of escaping a plaza encounter to make a quick leap into hiding.

- The main building that separates the plaza from the port has an elevated corridor connecting both areas. This is a great place to drop a Tripwire Bomb and lure pursuers. With only two possible points of entry, one of which will be protected by your bomb, you can hardly be taken by surprise.

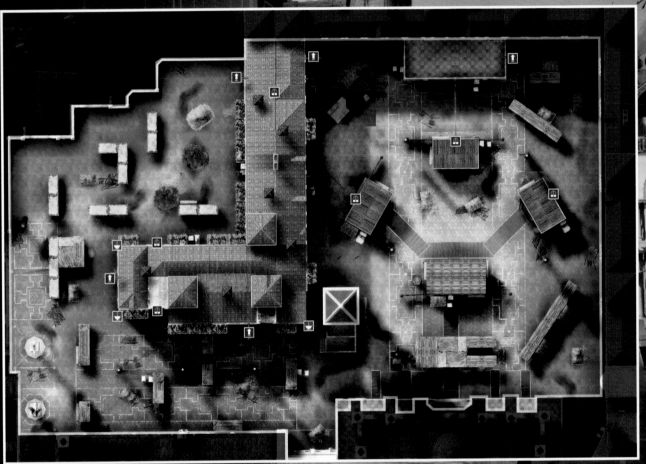

CASTEL GANDOLFO

- Though mostly based on terra firma, the many railings and balconies of this Papal summer residence make perfect spots for Focused assassinations and aerial kills on targets below and nearby.

- Though there are plenty of hiding spots in the frequent piles of soft red leaves, a pursuer will often have a good idea of where you're heading while tailing you down the Castel's linear corridors. Use the stained glass Chase Breakers to thwart them before turning the next corner to hide.

- Try to use hiding spots when they are closely packed and surrounded by groups of citizens. Nearby lookalikes will make it harder for other Agents to be certain as they attempt to intuit your location.

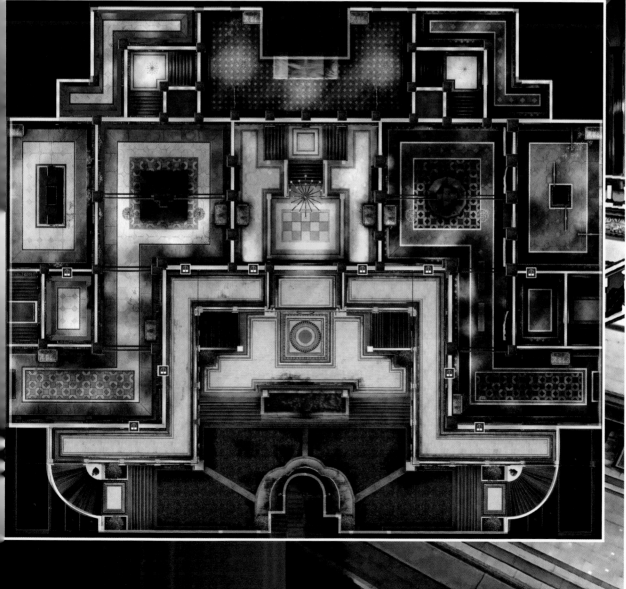

EXTRAS

After a short recap of all secrets and unlockable extras in Revelations, this chapter focuses on key narrative events in the Assassin's Creed series to date.

SECRETS

a.23082003.RmFjZXNJbiN0b25l
a.16082003.RXNjYXBl
a.23082003.V2hhdElzVGhpc1BsYWNl
a16052003.Q2hpY2Fnb 0dpcmxz
a.27082003.Tm90RmFyRW5vdWdo

UNLOCKABLES

If you happened to miss anything on your travels, use these checklists to identify any features and rewards that you have yet to unlock by completing optional memories and challenges.

Unlockables Overview

CATEGORY	UNLOCKABLE	UNLOCK CONDITION	NOTES	PAGE
Secret Locations	Hagia Sophia's Secret	Collect all 10 Memoir Pages.	Accessed through a secret door to the right of the main Hagia Sophia entrance.	102
	The Impaler's Tomb	Only available in specific Assassin's Creed Revelations editions, or as a preorder bonus.	Accessed through a secret entrance in the cemetery in the south of the Constantine district.	103
Outfits	Desmond	Complete all 5 parts of Desmond's Journey.	Outfits are accessed via the Inventory menu.	145
	Old Eagle	Activate a cheat (see "Cheats").		
	Armor of Brutus	Only available in specific Assassin's Creed Revelations editions, or as a preorder bonus.		
	Turkish Assassin Armor			
Maps	Ishak Pasha's Memoir Pages Map	Gather 25 Animus Data Fragments.	Once unlocked, purchase these maps from Book Shops.	109
	Animus Data Fragments Map	Gather 50 Animus Data Fragments.	The remaining 50 Animus Data Fragments automatically appear on the main map and mini-map.	109
Desmond's Journey	Part 1: Doubts	Gather 5 Animus Data Fragments.	Can be accessed via the giant portals on Animus Island.	104
	Part 2: Training	Gather 10 Animus Data Fragments.		105
	Part 3: Escape	Gather 15 Animus Data Fragments.		106
	Part 4: Metropolis	Gather 20 Animus Data Fragments.		107
	Part 5: Regret	Gather 30 Animus Data Fragments.		108
Multiplayer	Shahkulu (playable character)	Complete Memory 03 (The Renegade) in Sequence 07.	Multiplayer mode only.	77
	Vlad Tepes Customization Options	Complete The Impaler's Tomb (Secret Location).		103
Guild Rewards	Mercenary Faction Ability	Complete the second set of Challenges for each Guild.	Any Faction that you hire automatically use their new ability.	100
	Romani Faction Ability			
	Thief Faction Ability			
	Romanies Guild Crest	Complete the second set of Challenges for each Guild.	Unlocked at the Assassin's HQ, on a wall in the library.	
	Thieves Guild Crest			
	Mercenaries Guild Crest			
	Assassins Guild Crest			
	Bomb Faction Crest			
	Romani Stiletto	Complete the third set of Challenges for each Guild.	Unlocked at the Assassin's HQ; interact with the weapon racks.	
	Ottoman Mace			
	Broadsword			
	Altaïr's Sword			
	Increased Bomb carrying capacity		Allows you to carry an additional unit of each bomb type.	
Ultimate Equipment	Master Assassin's Armor Set	Train 7 Assassin Recruits to Level 11.	Accessed via the Inventory menu.	96
	Ishak Pasha's Armor Set	Complete Hagia Sophia's Secret (Secret Location).	Accessed via the Inventory menu.	102
	Yusuf's Turkish Kijil	Complete The Deacon, Part 1 (Master Assassin Mission).	Unlocked at the Assassin's HQ; interact with the weapon racks.	96
	Mehmet's Dagger	Complete The Champion, Part 1 (Master Assassin Mission).		96
	Almogavar Axe	Complete The Guardian, Part 1 (Master Assassin Mission).		97
	Vlad Tepes's Sword	Complete The Impaler's Tomb (Secret Location).		103
Secret Books	The Travels of Marco Polo	The Polo Symbols: Hippodrome	Unlocked in the Assassin's HQ library.	98
	One Thousand and One Nights	The Polo Symbols: Galata		
	The Book of Kings	The Polo Symbols: Arsenal		
	Nibelungenlied	The Polo Symbols: Forum of Ox		
	Illiad by Homer	The Polo Symbols: Aqueduct		
	The Canterbury Tales	The Polo Symbols: Church I		
	The Flute Girl	The Polo Symbols: Church II		
Uplay Rewards*	Assassin's Creed Revelations Theme	Purchase for 10 🟦 through Ubisoft's Uplay service.	Unlocks PS3 XMB or Xbox 360 Dashboard Theme.	–
	Solo Pack	Purchase for 20 🟦 through Ubisoft's Uplay service.	Unlocks Medicine Capacity Upgrade and 3 weapons from Assassin's Creed Brotherhood: Captain's Sword, Milanese Sword and Schiavona. Accessed via the Inventory menu.	
	Mediterranean Exclusive Missions	Purchase for 30 🟦 through Ubisoft's Uplay service.	Unlocks exclusive missions in the Mediterranean Defense metagame. Accessed via the Mediterranean Defense menu.	
	Multiplayer Pack	Purchase for 40 🟦 through Ubisoft's Uplay service.	Unlocks The Knight playable character, Templar Knight customization options, 3 Emblem symbols and an Emblem pattern. Multiplayer mode only.	

* 🟦 points are earned by reaching certain key milestones in the game if you have a Uplay account connected to your gamer profile. You obtain respectively 10, 20, 30 and 40 🟦 for completing Sequences 01, 03, 09 and reaching Level 20 in the Multiplayer mode.

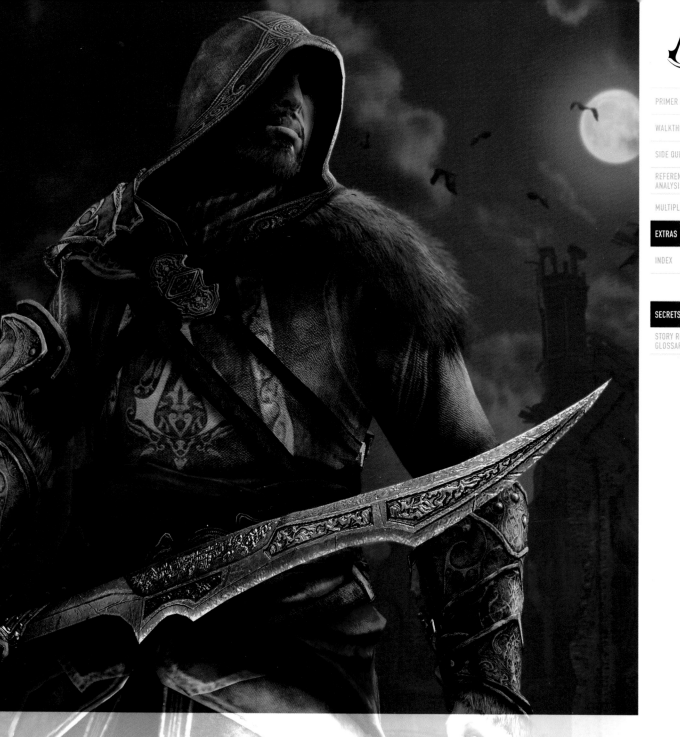

PRIMER

WALKTHROUGH

SIDE QUESTS

REFERENCE &
ANALYSIS

MULTIPLAYER

EXTRAS

INDEX

SECRETS

STORY RECAP &
GLOSSARY

CHEATS

Once unlocked by completing each Sequence with 100% Synch, these can be activated from the Options menu while replaying memories. Note that game progress is not saved while cheats are active.

CHEAT	UNLOCK CONDITION	EFFECT
Buns of Steal	Complete Sequence 02 with 100% Synch.	You are immune to injury.
Killing Spree	Complete Sequence 03 with 100% Synch.	During fights, you execute enemies instantly.
Ultimate Guild	Complete Sequence 04 with 100% Synch.	Raise all Assassins Recruits to the rank of Assassin.
Calling All Assassins	Complete Sequence 05 with 100% Synch.	There is no Cooldown timer for the Assassin Signal Meter, allowing you to use Assassin Signals repeatedly.
Permanent Secrecy	Complete Sequence 06 with 100% Synch.	Your actions do not raise the Templar Awareness Meter.
Infinite Ammunition	Complete Sequence 07 with 100% Synch.	You have limitless ammo for your ranged weapons.
The Old Eagle	Complete Sequence 08 with 100% Synch.	Unlocks the Old Eagle Outfit.

17.anima.23082003.RmFjZXNJblN0b25I
17.anima.16082003.RXNjYXBI
17.anima.23082003.V2hhdElzVGhpc1BsYWNI
17.anima.16052003.Q2hpY2Fnb0dpcmxxz

The Assassin's Creed series storyline tells of an ancient struggle between two opposing forces: the Templars, who seek to bring order to the world through absolute control, and the Assassins, who endeavor to preserve its freedoms. Both factions operate in secret, continually vying for possession of archaic artifacts and futuristic technologies to advance their cause throughout their centuries of conflict. By exploiting the capacity to relive moments in history via the recent Animus tech, the contemporary Assassins and Templars gain insights into events that affect the present – and so the two threads of the narrative weave together.

The first Assassin's Creed opened with the events of 2012, finding the dominant Templars on the brink of realizing their dream of a new world order. Each new chapter fills in another piece of the jigsaw puzzle, adding greater depth and new revelations to the common backstory.

We begin this section with a quick recap of the Assassin's Creed Revelations storyline. To refresh your memory on key events and plot strands in all four core episodes – and to perhaps further whet your appetite for installments to come – we follow this with a story glossary packed with known facts and lively speculation…

REVELATIONS: KEY EVENTS

The Revelations story continues directly from the conclusion of Assassin's Creed Brotherhood. Any triumph felt by the Assassins at claiming the Apple of Eden hidden beneath the Colosseum has been tempered by the tragic death of Lucy Stillman at the hands (though not, it is clear, at the behest) of a horrified Desmond. After stabbing her while under the control of forces unknown – though strongly suggested to be the First Civilization entity known as Juno – he collapses. Believing his condition to be a consequence of the Bleeding Effect, his Assassin friends place him in a special Animus program in an attempt to at least forestall fatal mental deterioration.

01

As his body is transported from Italy to a new (but, at this stage, unspecified) destination by Shaun, Rebecca and their commander William, Desmond regains consciousness (in a manner of speaking) on a strange island. He meets Subject 16 ( 01), now fully realized in a virtual body, who explains that Desmond is inside the original Animus test program – and that his mind has been fragmented, pushed to the brink of irreversible dementia, by the experience of reliving the lives of Ezio and Altaïr.

Sixteen informs Desmond that he can preserve his sanity by creating a Synch Nexus. This can be achieved by visiting key but hitherto unseen moments in the

stored memories of his ancestors, "finishing" their lives (or at least the parts of significance). This will enable the Animus software and his beleaguered synapses to somehow separate the two additional existences from his core identity – allowing him to awake from his coma.

02

Desmond resumes his exploration of Ezio's memories. We learn that, in his later years, the Master Assassin grew restless in the peace established by the end of Brotherhood's narrative. Puzzled by revelations he had witnessed but failed to entirely comprehend, particularly the inexplicable experience of being used as a communication conduit through which Minerva could address the mysterious "Desmond", Ezio travels east to investigate a secret library created by his predecessor, Altaïr. He arrives in Masyaf to find it under the control of Byzantine Templars, and narrowly escapes death when his identity is discovered. He finds that the library's impregnable entrance is locked ( 02), and that the Templars have long labored to gain access without shadow of success. To open it, he must find five unique keys to fit the openings on the imposing doorway.

To retrieve the keys, Ezio travels to Constantinople. On arrival he is drawn inexorably, perhaps by fate, into the intrigues of the imminent Ottoman royal succession following a chance encounter with the Sultan's grandson, Suleiman. Upon examination of each key, Ezio experiences lucid waking dreams that recount events from Altaïr's life with astonishing clarity. In time, nearing the end of his search, Ezio learns that Suleiman's uncle, Prince Ahmet ( 03) – groomed to succeed his father, yet an unpopular choice among citizenry and soldiery alike – is in league with Byzantine Templar agents. A flawed yet not entirely unsympathetic character, Ahmet wishes to possess the secrets of Masyaf's library – and the powers they may bring – to bring peace and unity to the empire he is poised to rule.

PRIMER

WALKTHROUGH

SIDE QUESTS

REFERENCE &
ANALYSIS

MULTIPLAYER

EXTRAS

INDEX

Despite Templar interference and the machinations of the covetous Ahmet, Ezio acquires the keys and returns to Masyaf. Inside the secret library he finds no books, no repository of incalculably valuable knowledge, but only Altaïr's skeletal remains, a sixth key resting in his hands (📷 04). As with those collected before, it communicates a powerful vision. In this, he finds that the secret chamber is not a library, as previously believed, but a strongroom. A dying Altaïr bids farewell to his son before entombing himself and his Apple of Eden to await Ezio's arrival. His final act is to "record" this last memory on the key, evidently a First Civilization artifact like the Pieces of Eden.

Ezio resolves to leave Altaïr's Apple of Eden where it lies, yet the device bursts into life. As he speaks to Desmond through the ages, he finally recognizes his role as a prophet: "I am only a conduit for a message that eludes my understanding".

Though Ezio cannot see Desmond, he reaches out to lay a hand on his shoulder... and Desmond is transported to a different place. In this otherworldly domain, Tinia (📷 05) – the third member of the First Civilization triumvirate after Minerva and Juno – tells Desmond how his people tried but failed to survive the great Catastrophe revealed at the close of Assassin's Creed II. The last act of the triumvirate was to transmit their accumulated knowledge to a single underground vault located in what is now known as the state of New York. Tinia informs Desmond that the answers to his questions lie inside this long-hidden place.

In the present day, the Assassins land and pass through Syracuse airport in Onondaga County, New York. Oblivious to Desmond's travails within the Animus, they are astonished when he begins to regain consciousness as they travel towards an unspecified destination (📷 06). After taking a moment to regard William, revealed to be his father, Desmond experiences a strange connection with the nearby Apple of Eden, which pulses in response.

"I know what we need to do," he says.

04

05

06

ASSASSIN'S CREED GLOSSARY

The Assassin's Creed series storyline is packed with recurring themes, characters, symbols and concepts set against a fascinating backdrop of alternative histories and conspiracy theories. In this brand new version of our glossary, we offer concise summaries of topics and individuals of note – with, of course, a little healthy speculation and possible interpretations of unresolved mysteries.

▌ TEMPLARS

The Templar Order ▶

In established histories, the Knights Templar order received papal recognition in 1129 and found fame through their military engagements in the Holy Land during the Third Crusade. However, the Templar organization – as represented in the Assassin's Creed canon – is certainly far, far older. Though the Knights Templar order was supposedly disbanded in 1312, this abrupt dissolution merely allowed the "true" Templars to vanish from public life and avoid further scrutiny, secretly infiltrating institutions of power and manipulating world events to suit their agenda.

The modern Templars conceal and bankroll their activities through Abstergo Industries, a multinational corporate conglomerate that – in contrast to centuries of subtle behind-the-scenes machinations – enables the organization to boldly conduct many of its less sensitive operations in plain sight. While this new public façade represents a subtle evolution, the order's principle goal remains unchanged: to achieve absolute power by acquiring and exploiting First Civilization technology to unify humanity. Though individual agents may be corrupt, and even willfully callous or cruel, it would be erroneous to characterize the Templar order as being necessarily "evil". They ostensibly strive to appoint themselves as humanity's custodians. "To achieve true peace," Ahmet argues in Revelations, "mankind must act and think as one body, with one master mind." Where leading Templar figures such as Al Mualim and Rodrigo Borgia once sought to exert control on a regional or continental level, their successors aspire to no less than global dominium.

Abstergo Industries ▶

Taking its name from the Latin verb meaning to "cleanse" or "wipe away", Abstergo is the modern identity of the Templar Order. This public front facilitates operations on a worldwide scale, with more sensitive enterprises (such as the development of the Animus and the acquisition of First Civilization artifacts) concealed in classified R&D programs. These are staffed by Templar loyalists and individuals either ignorant of their true role, or enjoined by intimidation or subversion to reveal no word of their activities.

Abstergo is active in countless fields, from telecoms to pharmacology, enabling the Templar order to exploit (if only indirectly) the finest scientific minds, bleeding-edge technology… and, of course, the political lobbying power and operating capital of a world-leading corporation. "The average American household contains three dozen Abstergo-owned products at any given moment," Desmond's mother once told him during his childhood.

Abstergo's most valuable invention is the Animus, a device that allows for the exploration of genetic memories. Human DNA, it transpires, records the experiences of every living person with astonishing accuracy, with each individual passing data on their life to their offspring at the moment of conception – a discovery unknown in mainstream science. The Templars have used the Animus to identify bloodlines that will lead them to the locations of First Civilization artifacts known as Pieces of Eden. These devices are defined by their astonishing capacity to generate illusions, and influence (indeed, control) human minds.

The Templars are racing to obtain an Apple of Eden with the express intention of installing it into a telecommunications satellite developed by an Abstergo subsidiary. From its position in orbit, they hope to use it to control Earth's population. The Eye-Abstergo satellite is set for launch on December 21st, 2012 – a portentous date.

PRIMER

WALKTHROUGH

SIDE QUESTS

REFERENCE & ANALYSIS

MULTIPLAYER

EXTRAS

INDEX

SECRETS

STORY RECAP & GLOSSARY

ASSASSINS

The Assassin Brotherhood ▶

For over 2,000 years, the Assassin Brotherhood has been fighting a war. Their weapons are intelligence, stealth and surprise. They will send a lone agent against a legion, and halt the march of ten thousand soldiers with the death of one. Assassins are sworn to preserve free will and to defend the liberty of every man, woman and child against abuses of power. The most famous line in their creed – "Nothing is true; everything is permitted" – is the Brotherhood's raison d'être, a defense of every individual's right to act of their own volition. The Templar philosophy of attempting to engineer peace and stability via the enforced surrender of self-determination is anathema to the Assassins, who regard it as little more than enslavement.

A clear example of the differences between the Templar and Assassin ideologies, in their purest forms, is witnessed during a conversation between Ezio and Ahmet in Revelations. When confronted after the murder of Yusuf and kidnap of Sofia, Ahmet proposes to use the power of a First Civilization artifact (though he would not precisely know it as such) to "destroy the superstitions that keep men divided":

Ahmet: "We both strive for the same end, Ezio. Only our methods differ. Do you not see that? Peace. Stability. A world where men live without fear. People desire the truth, yes, but even when they have it, they refuse to look. How do we fight this kind of ignorance?"

Ezio: "Liberty can be messy, Ahmet. But it is priceless."

Ahmet: "Of course. And when things fall apart, and the lights of civilization dim, Ezio Auditore can stand above the darkness and say proudly, 'I stayed true to my creed'."

When the Templars survived Altaïr's campaign and retreated to the shadows to regroup, the Assassins were also forced to adopt a more covert operation. By Ezio's time, they had become every bit as secretive as the Templars. The modern day organization exists under great pressure, and employs the cell structure of underground political resistance groups. Such strategies are essential to enable the Brotherhood to avoid the superior tracking and surveillance techniques that the resurgent Templars can employ through Abstergo.

Desmond Miles ▶

Desmond Miles was raised in a secret Assassin compound called The Farm. Unaffected by his parents' stories of the aeonian struggle against the Templar Order and the teachings of his tutors, he fled the commune at the age of sixteen. Rejecting his former life (indeed, describing The Farm's occupants derogatively as a "cult" and his parents as "conspiracy freaks" when quizzed about his upbringing), Desmond lived anonymously in New York until kidnapped by Templar agents in September 2012.

Held in captivity for several days, Desmond (labeled "Subject 17" by his abductors in the Abstergo laboratory) is compelled to use the Animus technology to experience episodes from the life of a direct ancestor, Altaïr Ibn-La'Ahad. After unwittingly leading the Templars to a specific memory featuring an Apple of Eden, Desmond escapes the secret facility with the aid of Lucy Stillman, an Assassin agent working within the Templar ranks.

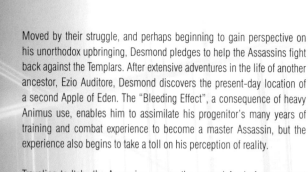

PRIMER

WALKTHROUGH

SIDE QUESTS

REFERENCE &
ANALYSIS

MULTIPLAYER

EXTRAS

INDEX

SECRETS

STORY RECAP &
GLOSSARY

Moved by their struggle, and perhaps beginning to gain perspective on his unorthodox upbringing, Desmond pledges to help the Assassins fight back against the Templars. After extensive adventures in the life of another ancestor, Ezio Auditore, Desmond discovers the present-day location of a second Apple of Eden. The "Bleeding Effect", a consequence of heavy Animus use, enables him to assimilate his progenitor's many years of training and combat experience to become a master Assassin, but the experience also begins to take a toll on his perception of reality.

Traveling to Italy, the Assassins recover the second Apple from a secret vault where Ezio had hidden it many centuries before. On touching the device, however, Desmond's body is commandeered by a strange force – almost certainly instigated by Juno, a First Civilization entity – that also freezes his companions, and forces him to kill Lucy. This leads to the events of Revelations, as recounted in the Story Recap on page 202.

In considering Desmond's overarching significance, it is necessary to make a distinction between affiliation and bloodline when using the term "Assassin". The Assassin Brotherhood has recruited many individuals, all of whom are valued for their contribution. In their respective times, the likes of Shaun Hastings and Yusuf Tazim earn the title of Assassin through their dedication and contributions to the faction's cause. But when Subject 16 declares the Assassins to be "children of two worlds" during Assassin's Creed II, he specifically references the rare bloodlines that run through Desmond Miles, Ezio, Altaïr, and others back to Adam and the genetic union with the First Civilization race. In this sense, Desmond and others of his bloodline are "true" Assassins who exhibit powers that ordinary humans could not hope to possess.

In Revelations, we discover that Desmond's genes contain an unusually high concentration of First Civilization DNA – a "gift" that his father William attributes to no more than one in ten million. What makes Desmond so unique is that he is the convergence of several important bloodlines. This, presumably, is the source of his (and his progenitors') physical acuity, powers such as Eagle Sense, and the capacity to more successfully interact with First Civilization technology. In a short but telling conversation between Rebecca and William, Miles senior is heard to comment that he does not have the "right genes to properly wield" the Apple of Eden retrieved from beneath the Colosseum in Rome. This might also explain why, when Juno addresses Desmond in Rome before the death of Lucy, his companions cannot hear her words – and, indeed, remain oblivious to her existence.

Lucy Stillman

Shaun Hastings

Rebecca Crane

Lucy Stillman ▶

Lucy Stillman was raised by the Assassin Brotherhood and trained by William Miles, Desmond's father. She became involved with Abstergo Industries when the company took an interest in her postgraduate research in cognitive neuroscience, which enabled her to gain a position on the Animus project – and, of course, to infiltrate one of the Templars' most secret programs. Regarded more as a hostage than a conventional employee during her time with the Animus division, she later helped Desmond escape the Abstergo laboratory. Lucy then assumed control of a small Assassin cell including Shaun Hastings and Rebecca Crane, tasked with monitoring and protecting Desmond during his return to the Animus to experience the life of Ezio Auditore.

When Desmond touches the Apple long hidden beneath the Colosseum at the end of Brotherhood, a force compels him to stab Lucy with his Hidden Blade as she and her fellow Assassins stand frozen. Juno's words at this time appear to make it explicitly clear that this occurs at her command: "There is one who would accompany you through the gate. She lies not within our sight. The cross darkens the horizon."

The final two sentences of this statement are open to a variety of interpretations, but the most plausible explanation is that Desmond's blossoming friendship – indeed, suggestions of growing intimacy – with Lucy might distract or deter him from the road the First Civilization would have him travel. "The cross darkens the horizon," feels like an oblique reference to secret Templar affiliation, which her Assassin upbringing renders unlikely, or perhaps a future betrayal. A line from Subject 16 (spoken during Brotherhood after the completion of ten "Rift" puzzles) could also insinuate a hidden allegiance, or simply that Desmond's burgeoning relationship with Lucy would never come to pass. "She is not who you think she is," cautions Sixteen. "Everything you hope to become, everything you hold dear. It's already gone."

Shaun Hastings ▶

The historian in Lucy's Assassin cell, Shaun was a university lecturer whose radical opinions saw him swiftly ejected from the ivory towers of academia. This same intellectual flexibility made him an ideal recruit for the Assassins, who needed somebody to reconcile accepted historical accounts with the secret wisdom of Templar influence on world events. With his remarkable knowledge of dates, people and culture, Shaun maintains the Database for Animus users and keeps Assassin agents informed with real-time research.

Rebecca Crane ▶

Rebecca's development of the Animus 2.0 (and successive updates) has enabled the Assassins to stay abreast with advances made by the Templars. She is often forced to work with stolen and salvaged components to keep her team's equipment functional – testament to her remarkable resourcefulness. This state of affairs led to the import of Subject 16's data cache into the Animus 2.0 after the installation of an Abstergo memory core appropriated from their laboratory by Lucy.

A geek and a technophile, Rebecca's interest in hacking and her knowledge of countersurveillance measures enabled Lucy's Assassin cell to remain hidden from Templar attention during their time in Italy.

William Miles ▶

William Miles is Desmond's father. He raised his son in a remote Assassin community called The Farm, located in the Black Hills of South Dakota, outside Rapid City. A senior member of the modern-day Brotherhood, William once oversaw the operations of a number of Assassin compounds throughout the Midwest during the 90s and early 2000s. This included an involvement with the

William Miles

Subject 16

PRIMER

WALKTHROUGH

SIDE QUESTS

REFERENCE &
ANALYSIS

MULTIPLAYER

EXTRAS

INDEX

SECRETS

STORY RECAP &
GLOSSARY

training of each community's children, including his son Desmond (and, later, Lucy Stillman), to prepare them for the conflict against the Templars.

William's devotion to the Assassin cause has left little time for his family. While his wife could understand the demands of his calling, young Desmond could not. His growing estrangement led the young Miles to run away from The Farm to live in New York City. There is no reason to believe that the Brotherhood – and, therefore, his father – knew of Desmond's whereabouts until his capture by the Abstergo Lineage Discovery and Acquisition Department.

Recently, William has taken responsibility for supervising Assassin cell structures operating throughout the world. After Desmond stabs Lucy, William arrives to assume direct control of their unit. He then flies with them to Syracuse, NY, presumably to reach a location discerned from information transmitted by the Apple of Eden found beneath the Colosseum prior to Lucy's death.

Subject 16 ▶

An Assassin captured by Abstergo Industries, Subject 16 – real name Clay Kaczmarek – preceded Desmond Miles as an unwilling Animus test subject.

The fate of Subject 16 is a stark warning of the dangers of prolonged exposure to the Animus. Having acquired the memories of many different ancestors, his own personality was corrupted by the Bleeding Effect. Working against his captors, Subject 16 hacked into the Animus and uploaded a "living" digital facsimile of his mind into the machine – later transferred

to the Brotherhood's Animus 2.0 after Lucy's theft of the Abstergo memory core. He then broke up his AI into many discrete fragments and scattered them throughout the Animus for Desmond – a man he knew the Templars were actively searching for – to discover (and, in doing so, automatically reassemble) at a later date.

Exhausted, paranoid, and suffering from the accumulation of too many overlapping identities, he committed suicide days later with the only implement available to him – a ball-point pen. His final act was to use his own blood to daub messages and symbols on the walls of the Abstergo laboratory in the hope that another Assassin blessed with Eagle Vision – presumably Desmond – might read them.

From Desmond's first experiences inside the Animus, Subject 16 has watched his successor, looking for opportunities to communicate with him. Indeed, many of the most tantalizing (yet often highly cryptic) clues have been provided by Sixteen. When the two meet in the Animus test program after the events of Brotherhood, Subject 16 takes it upon himself to guide his fellow Assassin in the steps necessary to negate the Bleeding Effect and regain consciousness in the real world.

Sixteen "distracts" the Animus software to allow Desmond to spend more time with Ezio, and later appears to sacrifice himself as the code that they exist in seeks to delete them. Whether this is his final contribution to the story, however, is far from certain.

Ezio Auditore da Firenze

Prince Suleiman

▌ REVELATIONS: KEY PROTAGONISTS

Ezio Auditore da Firenze ▶

A Master Assassin from the Renaissance era, Ezio spends much of his life embroiled in the age-old battle with the Templars. After accumulating the scattered pages of Altaïr's "Codex", Ezio travels to a First Civilization vault hidden beneath the Vatican. Entering the main chamber, Ezio encounters a holographic projection of a woman who introduces herself as Minerva. Ezio is dazzled by her words and the (to his mind, supernatural) visions that surround him, but cannot make sense of their import.

Ezio eventually hides an Apple of Eden he obtains during his struggles against the Templars in another vault beneath the Colosseum. By ensuring that clues to its location are only visible to an individual with Eagle Vision, Ezio knows that only one of his kind – which will turn out to be Desmond – can discover its location.

A period of relative peace follows, during which time Ezio grows restless. Curious to learn the genesis of the Brotherhood, he begins to research the history of the Assassins, which leads him to the discovery of a reference to Altaïr's "secret library".

After his quest to obtain the five keys required to open Altaïr's final resting place – each one a First Civilization device that communicates a scene from Altaïr's life – Ezio finally accepts his role as prophet, communicating one last message (Tinia's address) across the centuries to Desmond. With this, he finally relinquishes his role as an Assassin to, we can safely assume, begin a new life with Sofia Sartor – and, at long last, perpetuate his bloodline…

Prince Suleiman ▶

Young Prince Suleiman – the future Sultan, Suleiman the Magnificent – acquired a fondness for dressing in peasant garments and travelling incognito in search of unvarnished political opinions. It is during one of these outings that he meets Ezio. Impressed with his wisdom and broad knowledge of the world, and grateful for the assistance he later renders, Suleiman and the Assassin become friends.

Suleiman's father, Prince Selim, and his uncle, Prince Ahmet, are vying for the right to succeed their father. After surviving an assassination attempt

Sofia Sartor

Yusuf Tazim

PRIMER

WALKTHROUGH

SIDE QUESTS

REFERENCE & ANALYSIS

MULTIPLAYER

EXTRAS

INDEX

SECRETS

STORY RECAP & GLOSSARY

by the Byzantines, Suleiman feels he can no longer trust anyone inside the Sultan's immediate circle. With Ezio's help, he investigates the true purpose of the Byzantine's plotting. Their combined efforts lead to the discovery of Ahmet's involvement with the Templars and, ultimately, his death at the hands of Selim.

Sofia Sartor ▶

Sofia is the Venetian proprietor of an old bookshop in Constantinople. Unbeknownst to Sofia, this shop is built on the ruins of a trading post once owned by the Polo brothers, Niccolo and Maffeo, who took possession of Altaïr's collection of books, his Codex, and the five keys hundreds of years previously.

With her deep knowledge of scripts and ciphers, Sofia helps Ezio to decode the clues left behind by the Polo brothers in the margins of Altaïr's ancient books. This enables him to find the keys to the secret library in Masyaf. Despite Ezio's efforts to conceal his status as an Assassin, he cannot prevent Sofia from becoming

entangled in his conflict against Ahmet and the Templars, though he is quick to save her when she is taken hostage.

It is likely that Sofia, like Altaïr's wife Maria Thorpe, is also a forebear of Desmond.

Yusuf Tazim ▶

Leader of the Assassin Brotherhood in Constantinople, Yusuf wages a war against the Templars as they conspire to wrestle power back from the Ottoman dynasty that supplanted their Byzantine empire. He introduces Ezio to techniques and innovative technologies used by local Assassins, lending aid and assistance from his arrival in the region. This collaboration sadly leads to his untimely death, presumably at the hands of agents working for Prince Ahmet or his Templar allies.

Prince Ahmet

Tarik Barleti

Prince Ahmet ▶

Prince Ahmet is the Sultan's favored son, groomed from his early years to succeed him. After discovering a Masyaf Key and investigating its purpose, Ahmet becomes obsessed with obtaining the knowledge and power that may rest inside the mysterious library, which leads him into contact with the Templars – and, by extension, to betray his family by working with the Byzantines the Ottomans had fought to overthrow.

It could be argued that Ahmet is a Templar more by conviction than true allegiance – especially as he clearly laments the ideological divide that precludes friendship with Ezio and Suleiman, who he greatly admires. When confronted by Ezio, he reveals his affinity for the Templar philosophy: "I will open that library, and I will find the Grand Temple. And with the power that is hidden there, I will destroy the superstitions that keep men divided."

Suleiman's request that Ezio spare his uncle's life rather underlines the fact that he believes Ahmet to be misguided, but not beyond redemption. His father Selim shares a different view, however, and executes his disgraced brother without compunction.

Tarik Barleti ▶

Tarik is the leader of the Janissaries, the Sultan's elite household troops. He considers Ahmet a poor choice of Sultan, a man who would bring ruin to the empire in a time of crisis, and is brazenly forthright in sharing this opinion.

Ezio and Suleiman grow suspicious of Tarik, and appear to find confirmation that he is in league with Byzantine forces when he is seen to sell weapons to Manuel Palaiologos. This is but a ruse: Tarik is, in fact, secretly investigating the Byzantine's plans and Ahmet's fraternization with the Templars, seeking to better understand (and, later, destroy) these enemies of his Sultan. In a tragic and unfortunate twist, Ezio only discovers this fact after inflicting a mortal wound, believing him to be a traitor – though Tarik, in his "white room" valediction, is noble enough to attribute the cause of his death to his own hubris.

Manuel Palaiologos ▶

Manuel Palaiologos works with the Templars to satisfy his lust for power. He sees the Order as a means to an end – the reconquest of Constantinople in the name of his Templar uncle, Emperor Constantine XI.

Manuel Palaiologos

Altaïr Ibn-La'Ahad

PRIMER

WALKTHROUGH

SIDE QUESTS

REFERENCE & ANALYSIS

MULTIPLAYER

EXTRAS

INDEX

SECRETS

STORY RECAP & GLOSSARY

When Ahmet and Palaiologos join forces, with Ahmet adopting the role of leader, Manuel bides his time as he works to find the Masyaf Keys for the man who seems poised to inherit the Ottoman throne.

Needing weapons for the army the Byzantines require to challenge the Sultan, Manuel forms a misguided alliance with Tarik to purchase arms from the Janissary captain. This ultimately leads not to the glory he craves, but a meeting with Ezio's blade.

Altaïr Ibn-La'Ahad ▶

When Desmond is first subjected to the Animus in the events of Assassin's Creed, the memory he explores is that of Altaïr Ibn-La'Ahad ("The Son of None"). After inflicting a grievous blow to Templar power in his time by assassinating a sequence of high-ranking Order officials, Altaïr learns that he has been betrayed by the Brotherhood's leader, Al Mualim, and is forced to kill him.

When Altaïr picks up the mysterious Piece of Eden wielded by his former mentor,

the device triggers a holographic projection of Earth. Several locations are clearly marked around the globe, indicating that this Apple may have recorded the resting places of other Pieces of Eden or First Civilization vaults and temples.

As Desmond explores Ezio's life in Revelations, he experiences several of Altaïr's later memories. These show how Altaïr, after years fighting the Mongol threat, is once again betrayed by men of his own Brotherhood, and loses both a son and his love, Maria Thorpe.

At the age of 91, after entrusting the Polo brothers with his library, his Codex (to spread the Brotherhood's creed to Europe) and the keys to the Masyaf strongroom, Altaïr locks himself away to die, his Apple safely entombed with him. His secret sepulture remains undisturbed for the hundreds of years prior to Ezio's arrival. At this point, his successor accomplishes what Altaïr (having already passed on his genetic code) could not: to communicate the Apple of Eden's message (Tinia's address and the accompanying visions) to Desmond in the far future.

Animus ▶

A core concept of Assassin's Creed is the capacity of human genes to carry "genetic memories". Each time DNA is passed on, the sum of a progenitor's experiences, up to moments before conception*, is passed on to the resultant offspring. Every generation of humans, therefore, is a biological archive containing the sum of all previous generations – or, at least, the experiences of those who procreated, up until the births of their final children.

Genetic memories remain largely dormant, vestigial, untapped in modern homo sapiens. With the aid of the Animus, however, they can be isolated and decoded. The device requires a live human subject to operate, not only as the source of the DNA but as the necessary agent to interpret the memory. Advanced software extrapolates the available information to build a complete simulation, converting the ancestral memory into a full virtual representation. As the subject relives the memory, the Animus then captures and records a projection of their experience that is accessible to others as audiovisual media.

Intensive users of the Animus technology tend to experience dangerous side effects. The uncontrolled resurgence of memories outside of the Animus suggests that the technology can unlock a process that continues within the subject, causing hallucinations and leading to mental instability: the Bleeding Effect.

As explained in a conversation between William and Rebecca in Revelations, the Animus technology uses a scalable technique known as "avatar projection" to control how much a user looks or feels like any one of their ancestors. This was developed when Templar researchers discovered that subjects find it less traumatic to relive ancestral memories when they retain a clear sense of their own identity. Interestingly, in a moment that could be a mere detail or subtle foreshadowing, Rebecca goes on to comment that avatar projection may cause problems when differences are significant: "Like if a man tried to relive a woman's memories for instance. Very disorienting."

Animus 2.0

*For male parents, naturally. Further *in utero* transmission of data, though not confirmed, may occur between mother and child – as suggested by Desmond remaining with Maria Thorpe after she and Altaïr conceive their firstborn in a scene from Assassin's Creed II.

PRIMER

WALKTHROUGH

SIDE QUESTS

REFERENCE &
ANALYSIS

MULTIPLAYER

EXTRAS

INDEX

SECRETS

STORY RECAP &
GLOSSARY

Bleeding Effect ▶

The Bleeding Effect is the process whereby a subject interacting with the Animus "assimilates" the memories of his or her ancestors. This phenomenon has the initially advantageous consequence of endowing the recipient with a degree of their forebear's knowledge and training. This can confer an acrobat's practiced techniques of balance, acquired over a lifetime; an athlete's willpower in pacing and maximizing stamina; or simply years of practice in wielding a sword. In Desmond's case, in addition to heightened athleticism and combat prowess, it may also have been the catalyst for the manifestation of his Eagle Vision.

01

These benefits are not without an attendant cost, though, as the Bleeding Effect leads to potentially deadly complications. It is these side effects that cause Desmond to experience hallucinations and even full "memories" while disconnected from the Animus technology in Assassin's Creed II. At the end of Brotherhood's story, his mind becomes fragmented and confused by the accumulation of multiple overlapping identities (📷 01). This most unhealthy byproduct of the Bleeding Effect is why Subject 16 lost his grasp on reality, and ultimately took his own life to escape the madness that consumed him.

The living ghost of Subject 16 reveals that the worst symptoms of the Bleeding Effect can be negated by creating a Synch Nexus. This can be accomplished by "completing" the memories of the ancestors whose lives an Animus user has previously explored.

Eagle Vision & Eagle Sense ▶

Eagle Vision is a potential talent locked away in most humans, but innate to individuals with a sufficiently high concentration of First Civilization genes (the "children of two worlds", descendants of Adam – and presumably Eve). It grants the facility to discern and interpret signs and details that are invisible to others. Eagle Sense is an extension of that gift, sharpening all of the user's senses. This enables Ezio, more practiced in later life, to eavesdrop on conversations, and to infer the path that an individual has taken (or will take) with a glance (📷 02). Juno suggests that the true "sixth sense" possessed by her race, dormant in our species (who all share the capacity to some degree, but lack the means or understanding to exploit it), has even greater potential – but only if Desmond can unlock it. "Awaken the sixth!" she exhorts, forcefully, at the conclusion of Brotherhood.

02

One can assume that the First Civilization's advanced interaction with mankind through time is due to some form of precognitive ability. This might explain how Those Who Came Before foresaw future events in order to deliver the messages to Desmond, millennia later, in a most circuitous yet sophisticated manner. From this perspective, Minerva's words are especially revealing when she says that the First Civilization experiences time "differently". Likewise, Tinia gives further credence to this theory when he tells Desmond that the place where they meet is a "nexus of time".

Pieces of Eden ▶

Pieces of Eden are ancient artifacts that the First Civilization once created to control humans. Secret history holds that the Templars have possessed various Pieces of Eden through the centuries, using them to influence world events.

Al Mualim (Altaïr's former mentor) is responsible for much of what is known about the powers and physical characteristics of the artifact also referred to as an Apple of Eden – for instance, that it could conjure disguises and create multiple simulacra of the holder. Of far greater interest to the Templars is the effect that Al Mualim wrought on the stronghold of Masyaf while experimenting with its potential. It subjugated the minds of the entire town, turning civilians into obedient soldiers or causing them to see old friends as enemies. It seems certain that this power is the one the Templars intend to exploit with the Eye-Abstergo satellite.

We currently know of two Apples of Eden: the one once held by Altaïr, and another hidden beneath the Colosseum by Ezio (later retrieved by Desmond). In a secret email in the first Assassin's Creed, it was revealed that a Piece of Eden possessed by the Templars was destroyed in an explosion at Denver International Airport. This may have been Altaïr's Apple.

The conclusion of Assassin's Creed Brotherhood reveals an unexpected feature of the artifacts. Though they clearly extend certain powers to humans who wield them, with the degree of control exerted dependent on First Civilization genes, Pieces of Eden can also be employed to remotely manipulate the user – as Desmond experiences when he plunges his Hidden Blade into Lucy's abdomen.

Masyaf Keys ▶

The keys that Ezio acquires to open Altaïr's tomb are another First Civilization device – memory seals that were widely used by Those Who Came Before to archive their experiences. They enable the user to store memories for later playback. It has been suggested that the Templars developed the Animus by reverse-engineering hitherto unseen artifacts. The Masyaf Keys, if not a direct inspiration, are closely related to an equivalent First Civilization technology.

Codex ▶

The Codex is a collection of documents where Altaïr captured his thoughts, many of which concerned his discoveries regarding the Piece of Eden. After Altaïr entrusted the Codex to the Polo brothers, it went on an adventure of its own – plundered by Genghis Khan and inherited by his grandson, before Marco Polo acquired it for his contemporary, Dante Alighieri. The thirty pages of the Codex were then scattered

PRIMER

WALKTHROUGH

SIDE QUESTS

REFERENCE &
ANALYSIS

MULTIPLAYER

EXTRAS

INDEX

SECRETS

STORY RECAP &
GLOSSARY

Prophet & Prophecy ▶

For all of its revelations and blueprints, the true message of Altaïr's Codex is one of a prophecy. It tells of a prophet who will use Pieces of Eden to open a First Civilization vault. Rearranging the pages of the Codex into a map then shows the location of that vault.

The traditional role of a prophet is to deliver a message from the gods. This is ostensibly what Ezio does, capturing a speech from Minerva and passing it on to Desmond via genetic memory at the conclusion of Assassin's Creed II. That Ezio cannot comprehend her words is almost irrelevant – he's no more than a conduit*. Though facing Ezio, Minerva addresses Desmond directly in revealing the fate of her race, and the need for urgent action to save his own.

In Brotherhood, Ezio takes a more direct role, acquiring an Apple of Eden then hiding it away for Desmond to retrieve. The events of Revelations, where Altaïr once again directs Ezio across the centuries to deliver a message for Desmond (📷 04), further illustrate the astonishing capacity of Minerva, Juno and Tinia to manipulate human minds through time.

04

*Though it is interesting that the language barrier is not an issue – evidence, perchance, of another remarkable First Civilization technology.

by Ezio's great-grandfather to prevent them from falling into Templar hands. Years later, Ezio was able to collect and restore the parchments.

The hotchpotch nature of the work, consisting of blueprints, journals and revelations, is likely deliberate, an attempt to distract from the singular hidden message of the Codex. The pages can be arranged to form a map, drawn with invisible marks that reveal themselves to Eagle Vision (📷 03). This shows the location of the vault under the Vatican – the first step by which Altaïr directed the prophet Ezio to deliver a vital message to Desmond and, later, to journey to Masyaf.

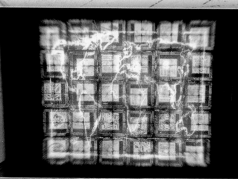

03

Vaults & Temples ▶

The First Civilization vaults and temples visited over the course of the Assassin's Creed story are sealed chambers where Those Who Came Before apparently worked, each laboring with a different method designed to save the world. Vaults were placed underground to avoid both the war that raged above (between humans and their masters) and the imminent Catastrophe – the coronal mass ejection that scorched the face of the earth.

After the cataclysm, the few survivors of the First Civilization decided to transmit the knowledge of all vaults into a single location: the very destination that Tinia instructs Desmond to visit at the close of Revelations (📷 05). Here, Tinia declares, Desmond will find answers to all of his questions, and possibly a way to prevent another Catastrophe from occurring.

Vaults and temples can be unlocked with specific codes, or the appropriate First Civilization technology, but there are further genetic or individual determinants involved in the security protocols. For example, when Ezio chooses to relinquish his Apple by placing it in the Vault beneath the Colosseum in Rome, he uses Eagle Vision to hide a password so that only a descendant such as Desmond can retrieve it in the future.

Of what is known, it seems the First Civilization had only ever intended for Assassins to use the vaults and temples – or, more specifically, pure and hybrid bearers of their DNA. This is why Ezio could enter the Vatican vault that remained resolutely sealed to Rodrigo Borgia in Assassin's Creed II.

How the Templars have apparently acquired so many artifacts throughout history is open to speculation, but it is certain that the Catastrophe and the war with humans did not allow for the orderly inventory and internment or destruction of all First Civilization technologies, as Juno confirms: "You possess the potential for understanding. But you broke our tools. Or turned them against one another. We have destroyed what we could. Sealed away what we could not. Most. Not all. And it does not take many to unwind the world."

05

218

Glyphs and Rifts ▶

After hiding an AI simulation of himself within the Animus, Subject 16 was able to conceal his software ghost and an assortment of messages and clues from his captors by creating symbols that would only reveal themselves to a brother Assassin's Eagle Vision (📷 06). In essence, Glyphs and Rifts are software hacks that enable the finder to access a hidden data cache. They are not part of the original memory, and so stand out as breaks in the program where Desmond disappears from the audiovisual feed viewed by those monitoring him.

06

The Truth ▶

"The Truth" is the name given by Subject 16 to a data file that he hid within the Animus software, discovered during the events of Assassin's Creed II. This code was broken into segments to conceal the message from unwelcome eyes, and was reassembled by Desmond during his first journey into Ezio's life. When decrypted, it was revealed to be a recording of an actual genetic memory of Adam and Eve, dating back to the time of the First Civilization and recovered during Abstergo's investigations (📷 07). It indicates that Subject 16 – and, by extension, Altaïr, Ezio and Desmond – must be directly descended from Adam's bloodline.

If this revelation were not enough, the "puzzles" Sixteen created to lock each fragment also exposed the startling degree to which the Templars have influenced world history and instigated many famous and terrible events. There are intimations that Pieces of Eden were exploited by Adolf Hitler in the development of Germany's war machine, and by President Lyndon B. Johnson in the Kennedy Conspiracy. The infamous Russian mystic Grigori Rasputin held Templar office while inveigling himself into the court of Tsar Nicholas II. With this knowledge, the Bleeding Effect clearly wasn't the only burden threatening Subject 16's grasp on reality.

07

▌MYTHOS

Adam and Eve ▶

Adam and Eve (📷 08) were born during the final years of the First Civilization. They appear in "The Truth", the data file that Subject 16 hid within the Animus prior to his death before the events of Assassin's Creed (but only discovered in the following episode). The video shows Adam and Eve rebelling against their godlike masters in Eden – a First Civilization stronghold where human slaves are at work – by daring to steal a Piece of Eden. This act of defiance may have been the first defense of free will committed by the incipient Assassin line; indeed, the brief fury in Juno's Brotherhood address intimates that it may even have contributed in part to the eventual extinction of the First Civilization.

The "Bloodlines" Glyph in Assassin's Creed II and Juno's soliloquies at the conclusion of Brotherhood (among other pieces of evidence) confirm that the First Civilization created "hybrid" humans – Adam and Eve – who possessed genetic material from their ruling race. Juno adds detail to Minerva's account of the First Civilization's downfall by confirming that the hybridization was a project of their society's twilight. At war with their slaves and unable to resist the Catastrophe, the First Civilization deliberately spliced their DNA into chosen humans as a way of preserving their genetic stock.

"After, when the world became undone," Juno intones, "we tried to pass it through the blood. Tried to join you to us. You see the blue shimmer. You hear the words. But you do not know."

Desmond is a distant son of Adam, half human and – though the manifestations are subtle – half god-race. If Subject 16's predictions are true, then a descendent of Eve possesses the other half of the First Civilization DNA sequence. If she and Desmond were to conceive children, might their offspring represent the rebirth of the First Civilization?

Could it be that certain First Civilization artifacts were sealed away not to protect them from human hands, but planted and, where necessary, strategically released to monitor and guide events in history? Dire warnings of a second Catastrophe

aside, it is possible that Minerva, Juno and Tinia are primarily motivated by a desire to guide the descendants of Adam and Eve to a particular destination. Altaïr and Ezio, as prophets, were subtly enjoined to sow seeds in time that now germinate to line Desmond's path – a track that appears to lead inexorably to Eve. Do the Capitoline Triad truly see him as Earth's savior from the impending Catastrophe, or the means to create scions in a new era?

08

First Civilization ▶

Also referred to as "Those Who Came Before", the First Civilization is held to be an advanced race that came to inhabit the Earth before mankind. Having remolded a primitive indigenous species into the slaves and workers that would later be known as humans, the First Civilization created certain devices (later described as Pieces of Eden) to control their workforce. Most humans, but not all, are believed to retain the dormant but still receptive neural configuration that rendered their ancestors vulnerable to enslavement by the technology.

To early mankind, the advanced nature of Those Who Came Before made them appear godlike, and they were long worshipped as divine saviors. Far from

PRIMER

WALKTHROUGH

SIDE QUESTS

REFERENCE &
ANALYSIS

MULTIPLAYER

EXTRAS

INDEX

SECRETS

STORY RECAP &
GLOSSARY

intangible, these beings walked among us and gave rise to the many different deities and pantheons of the cultures over which they ruled. Nevertheless, a war eventually broke out between the First Civilization and humans eager to win their freedom from eternal servitude. In their weakened state, Earth's overlords were unable to prevent the great Catastrophe that would deny them existence (📷 09).

So why are the First Civilization members so intent to help save their destroyers, here in the future? Are Minerva, Juno and Tinia ghosts in their machines, like Subject 16 within the Animus memory core? Or are they sophisticated recordings, intuitive echoes of a dead civilization? At the end of Revelations, Tinia claims to have no clear vision of what might happen in Desmond's time or his. For a race that can apparently employ human history as a preternaturally intricate Rube Goldberg machine, steering a single individual – Desmond – to a specific place and moment in time, this appears somewhat unlikely. We know of the genes carried by Desmond's line, and hints of an impending Catastrophe, but inferring the true motivation of beings of such incomprehensible sophistication is, at least for the moment, an impossibility.

Capitoline Triad ▶

The Capitoline Triad of Tinia, Juno and Minerva was a select sub-pantheon of supreme deities worshipped in Rome long before the Holy Roman Empire, prior even to the Republic. Ezio's encounter with Minerva confirmed that these deities were actually members of the First Civilization, their elevated status and accorded reverence potentially corresponding to some hierarchy of leadership among "Those who Came Before".

Even though Minerva's message is wildly incomprehensible to him, Ezio still describes the holographic "visions" he was shown as miraculous and magical when recounting them to his fellow Assassins. It is a perfect demonstration of how the First Civilization came to be regarded as gods by less sophisticated humans.

Minerva

Juno

Minerva ▶

Minerva is the holographic projection of a female entity who speaks to Ezio – or, more accurately, through Ezio – when he enters the Vault beneath the Vatican at the denouement of Assassin's Creed II. Though apparently long dead, Minerva was one of the last surviving members of the First Civilization after the Catastrophe annihilated her race many thousands of years ago. She warns of another imminent Catastrophe in Desmond's time, and claims that her kind had been developing a way to prevent it, with their labors hidden in secret vaults around the world.

Juno ▶

When Desmond penetrates the vault where Ezio hid an Apple at the end of Brotherhood, Juno reveals that the Catastrophe was so powerful that the few First Civilization members who survived it knew they were doomed to extinction. Researching ways to perpetuate their race, they attempted to interbreed with mankind, or at least splice their own genetic code into human DNA for safekeeping ("We tried to pass it through the blood. Tried to join you to us"). Subject 16's secret documents back up a hybridization project that began with Adam and Eve, and later perpetuated (at least partially) by the lineages that includes Altaïr, Ezio and Desmond.

Juno's point about looking into the future, but eyes "turning inward" to deal with a rebellious human threat, recalls Minerva's message that they should have been able to avoid the Catastrophe but were distracted. Pieces of Eden were locked away in vaults for safety, not safekeeping, to secure them from the hands of mankind

and yet Desmond is told to find such a device and activate it. It may be that the Pieces of Eden are not abandoned relics for the Assassin Brotherhood to protect or exploit, but tools wielded by the First Civilization across centuries to achieve their aims – be they benign or otherwise.

The perfunctory murder of Lucy (and Desmond's enforced surrender of free will in being the implement of the act) at Juno's apparent volition indicates that she, if not her peers, regards the First Civilization's former slave race without sentimentality. She may indeed act to serve a greater good – and yet it is hard to escape the conclusion that her methods could be drawn from a Templar manifesto…

Tinia ▶

The third in the deified First Civilization triumvirate, Tinia – also known as Jupiter and Zeus – informs Desmond that their long-sealed vaults were each dedicated to researching a single method by which the Catastrophe might be averted. Minerva, Juno and Tinia tested six methods in total, though none were completed before the coronal mass ejection scorched the planet.

Tinia reveals the existence of a single vault where he and his ilk stored all of the knowledge they gathered from their research, which lies a mere stone's throw from the location where Desmond awakes at the end of Assassin's Creed Revelations. Tinia makes it clear that this is where Desmond must go – but why?

source\S17.anima.16030002.V29vZFNtb2ll
source\S17.anima.08212002.TW90aGVyU2Fk
source\S17.anima.08212002.RmF0aGVyTWFk
source\S17.anima.22072002.Tm90aGluZz0lzVHJ1ZQ==
source\S17.anima.22072002.RXZicnl0aGGluZz0lzUGVybWl0dGVk

Tinia

PRIMER

WALKTHROUGH

SIDE QUESTS

REFERENCE &
ANALYSIS

MULTIPLAYER

EXTRAS

INDEX

SECRETS

**STORY RECAP &
GLOSSARY**

The Catastrophe ▶

The Catastrophe was a solar flare – or coronal mass ejection (📷 10) – that long ago scorched the world, flipping the polarity of Earth's magnetic field and exposing all life forms to deadly radiation. Small pockets of First Civilization survivors attempted to rebuild, but their numbers were too few; with a certain irony, their human creations proved more robust, and usurped their former masters. In time, vegetation and erosion dissipated any meaningful trace of the First Civilization's existence.

Instead of recording their nature and achievements, mankind deified Those Who Came Before and declared them of supernatural origin. The only evidence of the First Civilization now rests in their hidden subterranean vaults, and the remaining artifacts so highly prized by those who have grasped the truth.

10

Symbols ▶

From Subject 16's Glyph and Rift revelations to the icons found on Abstergo literature, the extent to which the conspiracies of Assassin's Creed have spanned the ages is reflected in the recurrence of powerful symbols.

Assassin's Creed Brotherhood's closing scenes reveal two symbols of particular interest. When Desmond asks about the location of the remaining vaults in Juno's temple, the Apple projects a Masonic Eye and a Phrygian Cap (📷 11). These could very well refer to the one document where the two symbols come together: the 1789 *Declaration of the Rights of Man and the Citizen*, a defining document of the French Revolution.

Interestingly, the Masonic Eye – a historically recurring signifier of the all-seeing eye of God – was also adopted in 1782 as part of the symbolism on the reverse side of the Great Seal of the United States. It appears on the American dollar bill. We learn from Tinia at the end of Revelations that the First Civilization transmitted their accumulated knowledge into a single vault located in the state of New York. Could the Apple have pointed the way to another of Desmond's ancestors from the 18th Century, either in France or the United States?

It could be that the First Civilization intends to save the Earth from a second imminent Catastrophe, and that Desmond will find the means to do so in Tinia's vault. But if Those Who Came Before were sufficiently close to having the technology at their disposal, why could they not prevent the first Catastrophe from occurring when they had the opportunity to do so?

There may be another explanation. When they warn of a second Catastrophe, perhaps the First Civilization entities do not mean a cataclysm against which they would be once again powerless. They could be referring to the launch of the Eye-Abstergo satellite, which might lead to the extermination of the Assassins – and, therefore, the DNA stock carried by Desmond and others. With the loss of its last genetic vestiges, the First Civilization would truly become extinct.

How exactly do Tinia, Juno and Minerva intend to revive their race? Children born of two hybrids (Desmond, and a descendent of Eve, each carrying half of the First Civilization DNA stock) could very well be the solution they aspire to. Subject 16's inane ramblings on Animus Island even suggest that it may be possible for a personality stored in the Animus technology to be transferred into a new physical vessel – a chilling prospect. But why, then, should Desmond save mankind from a Catastrophe, be it solar in origin or due to the actions of Templars, only to engineer the return of godlike entities who once ruled us as slaves?

11

source\S17.anima.22072002.Tm5XaGluZGVVH01ZO–

source\S17.anima.16082005.VonFUkVBUkVZTiUh

source\S17.anima.16082008.U29NdWNoTm9pc2U–

source\S17.anima.12062008.Q0FMTEhPTUUh

XZiTcni0aGlaZONDnk

source\S17.anima.04022011.SqV_IEFkZEdpbg–

source\S17.anima.17092011.VGhISk1a

source\S16.anima.08082012.SSBBbSBOb3QgQWxpdmU–

If you are looking for specific information, this alphabetical listing is just what you need. To avoid any potential spoilers, note that all entries that link to the Extras chapter are written in red.

PRIMER

WALKTHROUGH

SIDE QUESTS

REFERENCE & ANALYSIS

MULTIPLAYER

EXTRAS

INDEX

The Complete Official Guide to Assassin's Creed Revelations is a Piggyback Interactive Limited production.

PIGGYBACK

Managing Directors:	Louie Beatty, Vincent Pargney
Project Manager:	Matthias Loges
Creative Manager:	Carsten Ostermann
Localization Manager:	Simone Dorn
Editorial Director:	Mathieu Daujam
Author:	James Price
Map & Screenshot Editor:	Nicolas Decerf
Support:	Markus Bösebeck
Logistics:	Kristin Rüther
Art Directors:	Jeanette Killmann, Martin C. Schneider (Glorienschein)
Designers:	Cathrin Queins, David Loos, Christian Runkel, Christian Schmal

ENGLISH VERSION

Sub-Editing:	Maura Sutton, Daniela Bartels

FRENCH VERSION

Editors:	Mathieu Daujam, Claude-Olivier Eliçabe, Around the Word
Sub-Editing:	Thérèse Pargney

GERMAN VERSION

Editor:	Klaus-Dieter Hartwig
Sub-Editing:	Barbara Bode

ITALIAN VERSION

Editor:	Synthesis International srl
Localisation Managers:	Emanuele Scichilone, Marco Auletta

SPANISH VERSION

Editor:	Synthesis Iberia SL
Localisation Manager:	Gus Díaz

PRODUCTION

Preprint:	Uli Banse, Katharina Börner, Nicole Hannowsky, Ilse Hüttner, Anke Mattke, Stefan Polaschke, Petra Reidath, Arwed Scibba, Torsten Wedemeier (AlsterWerk)

The Complete Official Guide to Assassin's Creed Revelations is co-published in North America by Piggyback Interactive Limited and Prima Games, a division of Random House, Inc.

PRIMA GAMES

President:	Debra Kempker
Publishing Director:	Julie Asbury
Senior Sales & Marketing Director:	Mark Hughes

SPECIAL THANKS TO:

Frank Adler, Beatriz Esteban Agustí, Thomas Altemeier, Julie Asbury, Antoine Bailly, Marion Daujam, Oscar del Moral, Oliver Dorn, Simone Fuller, Paul Giacomotto, Tobias Giesener, John Holder, Martin Holder, Patrick Jöst, Rishi Kartaram, Anskje Kirschner, Angela Kosik, Aaron Lockhart, Stephanie Sanchez, Wolfgang Schallert, Marcel Sommer

SINCERE THANKS TO ALL OF THE CONTACT TEAM AT UBISOFT. YOUR DEDICATION AND SUPPORT HAS BEEN INSPIRATIONAL. CHAPEAU!

Adam Steeves, Alain Corre, Alexandre Amancio, Ambre Lizurey, Brent Ashe, Carl Caldareri, Julien Delalande, Clémence Deleuze, Cyrille Imbert, Darby McDevitt, Etienne Allonier, Falko Poiker, François de Billy, Gabriel Parent, Guillaume Carmona, Maria Loreto, Martin Schelling, Matthew Zagurak, Nicolas Raffenaud, Raphael Lacoste, Yves Guillemot

ASSASSIN'S CREED REVELATIONS TEAM

Adam Steeves, Adrian Bursumac, Adrian Buzatoaia, Adrian Coman, Adrian Dinu, Adrian Ghetu Bejan, Adrian Haidu, Adrian Iacob, Adrian Iliescu, Adrian Scheiber, Adrian Simpetru, Adrian Tila, Adrian Valentin Simion, Adrian-Stefan Tureac, Alain Abbyad, Alain Chenier, Albert Ionut Nicola, Aldo Sampaio, Alex Gingras, Alex Radu, Alexandra Botiz, Alexandra Ionescu, Alexandre Amancio, Alexandre Bazzotti, Alexandre Beaumont, Alexandre Begnoche, Alexandre Breault, Alexandre Morin, Alexandre René, Alexandre Troufanov, Alexandre Voyer, Alexandru - Valentin Petrisor, Alexandru Agapie, Alexandru Alexe, Alexandru Bogdan Eremia, Alexandru Bonlu, Alexandru Dogeanu, Alexandru Gogonea, Alexandru Hansa, Alexandru Ionut Ionita, Alexandru Marius Calin, Alexandru Marius Mihulin, Alexandru Mirescu, Alexandru Podeanu, Alexandru Simion, Alexandru Tebeica, Alexandru-Cristian Balae, Alexandru-Daniel Duicu, Alexandru-Florin Negraru, Alexis Palangié, Alin Oprea, Alina Dumitrache, Alin-Cristian Rosoiu, Ambre Lizurey, Amélie Bouchard, Amélie Chabanne, Amélie Sorel, Ana Madalina Craciun, Andrea Fyrett, Andréane Meunier, Andreea-Claudia Girlovan, Andrei Begu, Andrei Bogdan Sandru, Andrei Brancusi, Andrei Bulgaru, Andrei Catalin Ionescu, Andrei Ene, Andrei Georgescu, Andrei Ionescu, Andrei Liviu Ionescu, Andrei Lupu, Andrei Miltode, Andrei Niculae, Andrei Stanciu, Andrei Strambei, Andrei Trandafir, Andrei-Bogdan Fuiorea, Audrey St-Pierre, Aurel-Cristian Stanica, Avlamy Ramassamy, Aymar Azalzia, Bénédicte Jouzel, Benoit Tilizien, Berenger Deswaziére, Bernard Fluet, Bernard Roberge, Bill Cheung, Bjorn Swenson, Bogdan Adrian Pantazi, Bogdan Andrei Arghir, Bogdan Dumitru, Bogdan Ivan, Bogdan Lamba, Bogdan Liviu Costea, Bogdan Preda, Bogdan-Antonio Mustata, Bogdan-Constantin Seceleanu, Bogdan-Nicolae Tonu, Brent Ashe, Bruce Low, Bruno Aitken, Bruno Bouchard, Bruno Leblanc, Bruno Senécal, Bruno St-André, Carl Caldareri, Caroline Bergeron-Lyonnais, Catalin Andrusca, Catalin Borangic, Catalin Daniel Balan, Catalin Pecingine, Catalin-Patrick Ivan, Catherine Auger, Chae Dickie-Clark, Chris Hendry, Chris Pinto, Christian Cimon, Christine Blondeau, Christine Ruby, Christophe Martin, Claudiu Demian Constantin, Claudiu Marian Stoianol, Claudiu Tulus, Codrut Cosmescu, Constantin Fotea, Constantin Veteanu, Constantin Vilceanu, Corey May, Cosmin Burescu, Cosmin I. Popa, Cosmin Spinu, Cosmin-Claudiu Vilcu, Cristi Arama, Cristi Fedatov, Cristian Craciun, Cristian Draghici, Cristian Nidelea, Cristian Tanase, Cristian Tornescu, Cristian-Robert Simion, Cristin Ghihanis, Cristina-Ioana Craciun, Damien Kieken, Dan Cristian Cristofan, Dan Dragomir, Dan Zaharia, Dan-Alexandru Ciobanu, Daniel Badea, Daniel Desjardins, Daniel Dragan, Daniel Luca, Daniel Mendez, Daniel Mihail Ilie, Daniel Sunel, Daniel Tremblay, Dan-Laurentiu Hosman, Darby McDevitt, David Beddoes, David Bilodeau, David Bolle, David Harvey, David Lacoste, David Leduc St-Arnaud, David L'Heureux, David Paquette, David Rancourt, David Thibault, Diana Alecsandra Tufan, Diana Ioana Boicea, Diana-Elena Chivu, Dominic Spada, Dominique Grandmont, Elaine Duffy, Eliade-Ioan Teodorovici, Eliot Canepa, Éric Binet, Etienne Allonier, Eugene Cordwell Jarvis, Eugène Mishibinijima, Falko Poiker, Florin Catalin Gafton, Florin Cristea, Florin Popescu, Florin Sanda, Ford Dye, Francis Denoncourt, Francis Favreau, Francis Lefort, Francis Vaillancourt, François Cournoyer, François de Billy, François Gemer, François Poirier, François Tétreault, Frédéric Beaudin, Frédéric Tardif, Frederik Audet, Gabriel Comsa, Gabriel Graziani, Gabriel Parent, Gabriel Sebe, Gary Jason Ng Thow Hing, George Alexandru Cotofana, George Enescu, George Stercu, George Tanase, George-Eduard Tarcavu, Gheorghe Sorescu, Gilbert Arcand, Gilles Beloeil, Giovanni Masin, Gregory Belacel, Gregory Fromenteau, Guillaume Boisvert, Guillaume Cassel, Guillaume Corbeil, Guillaume Payant-Tougas, Guillaume Ruest, Guylaine Rhéaume, Hadrien Grandry, Hani, Barakat, Hau-Nghiep Phan, Hong Jun Fang, Hugues Chiasson, Ilie Muntean, Ioan Manea, Ion-Dumitru Vornicescu, Ionel Dan Stefan, Ion-Lucian Cora, Ionut Caravan, Ionut Octavian Dima, Ionut Tanasele, Ionut Uceanu, Ionut-Catalin Negrescu, Ionut-Daniel Sandu, Irina Stoica, Isabelle Gagnon, Iulian Baraghin, Iulian Hogea, Iulian Tudose, Jacinthe Massey, Jacob Lee Golescu, Jacques Alce-Gabriel, Jaime Cifuentes Olivares, Jason Tremblay, Jean Guesdon, Jean-Dominic Audet, Jean-François Dupuis, Jean-François Morin, Jean-Marc Goulet, Jean-Michel Dignard, Jean-Philippe Dagenais, Jean-Philippe Sabary, Jeff Simpson, Jeffrey Yohalem, Jérémi Valiquette, Jessie Martel, Johanna Wloskiewicz, Jonathan Moreau, Jonathan Pilon, Jonathan Villani, Juan Esteban Diaz, Julie Boudreault, Julie Ferguson, Julien Desaulniers, Julien Lemaire, Julien Prince, Justine Gareau, Kama Dunsmore, Karim Sylvestre, Karl Gendron, Kathleen Morrison, Kyu-Chul Youn, Laurence Letalien, Laurent Bertrand, Liana Popescu, Lisa Charman-Gaillard, Liviu Ganea, Louis Rousseau, Lucian Olaru, Lucian Puscasu, Magdalena Dadela, Malika Sahla, Marc Allaire, Marc-André Belleau, Marc-André Ostiguy, Marc-Antoine Sénécal, Marc-Olivier Riel, Margaret Tsai, Margherita Seconnino, Maria Loreto, Marian Blanaru, Marian Iacob, Marian Magiaru, Marian Vlasceanu, Marie-Eve Robidoux, Marie-Lou Landry, Marie-Pier Drouin, Mariève Charette, Marius Grigore, Marius Pasarica, Marius Silvian Rosianu, Martin Deschambault, Martin Hultberg, Martin Maheux-Lessard, Martin Pelissier, Martin Samuel, Martin Schelling, Marvin Joseph, Masao Kobayashi, Mathieu Blouin, Mathieu Casgrain, Mathieu Desmarais, Mathieu Faber, Mathieu Girard, Mathieu Hector, Mathieu Laurin, Matthew Zagurak, Matthieu Garaud, Max Bricault, Maxime Dubois-Bergeron, Maxime Faucher, Maxime Lebel, Maxime Mercier, Maxime Mulumba, Médéric Chassé, Mélanie Pouliot, Mélanie Tremblay, Melissa Allard, Michael Donnell, Michael Kuntze, Michel Beaulac, Michel Bouchard, Michel Leduc St-Arnaud, Michel Thibault, Michelle Wu, Mihai Alexandru Nuta, Mihai Dobre, Mihai Dobre, Mihai Laurentiu Ghimpu, Mihai Mreana, Mihai Nita, Mihai Sorin Cazangiu, Mihai Vlad Iordan, Mihail Bichir, Ming Yin, Mircea Nutu, Mireille Lalancette, Moroiu Andrei Daniel, Mustapha Mahrach, Nicholas Grimwood, Nicholas Routhier, Nicolae Norea, Nicolae-Alexandru Rosca, Nicolas Guérin, Nicolas Leclerc, Nicolas Painchaud, Nicolas Raffenaud, Nikolas Schmidt, Norbert Gil-Sobraques, Oana Loredana Voicu, Octavian Andrei Vasiliu, Octavian Constantin, Octavian Martinica, Oliver Merlov, Olivier Ged, Olivier Guilbault, Olivier Saillant, Olivier-Félix Dupuis, Omar Bouali, Ovidiu Traian Vasilescu, Pascal Barriault, Pascal Bélanger, Pascal Gauthier, Pascal Lavallières, Pascal Mathieu, Pascal Savignac, Pascal Theriault, Pascal Van Dorpe, Patrice Blanchet, Patrice Blanchet, Patrice St-Pierre-Plamondon, Patrick Bonin, Patrick Fagan, Patrick Lambert, Patrick Limoges, Patrick Melanson, Patrick Plourde, Patrick Sévigny, Paul W. Rodgers, Peter Chan, Peter Pavlou, Philippe Bourbeau, Philippe Deshaies, Philippe Lalande, Philippe Ringuette-Angrignon, Pierre Sackhouse, Pierre-Louis Samson, Pierre-Luc Grenon, Pierre-Luc Lachance, Priscilla Nguyen, Radu Constantin, Radu Ilica, Radu Ionut Lungescu, Radu Muscalu, Radu Nedea, Radu-Emanuel Constantin, Rangner Ferraz Guimarães, Raphael Lacoste, Razvan Andrei Safta, Razvan Badea, Razvan Cristian Girleanu, Razvan Marasescu, Richard Farrese, Richard Gagnon, Richard Neron, Robert Neculau, Robert Peralta, Roshan Cyr, Ryan Deschamps, Samuel Watson, Sandra Pourmarin, Sasha Boutin, Sébastien Toader, Sébastien Bergeron, Sébastien Genest, Sébastien Larrue, Sébastien Lévesque, Sébastien Olscamp, Sébastien Puel, Sébastien Sauvé, Serge Daigle, Sergiu Androne, Sergiu Androne, Sergiu Cosmin Gavan, Simon Lacoste, Simon St-Gelais, Sorin Ionita, Sorin Stefan Balasa, Sorin-Alexandru Tuta, Stefan Aluneanu, Stefan Daniel Burdulea, Stefan Paraschiv, Stefan Rosu, Stefania Simion, Stéphane Arbour, Stéphane Blais, Stéphane Gobeil, Steve Labrecque, Steve Laroche, Steven Dumont, Steven Parenteau, Sylvie Beauchamp, Sylvie Tremblay, Teddy Cristian Nicolae, Thierry Beaumont, Thierry Carle, Thomas Deslugues, Tiberiu Bogdan Bunea, Tristan Bernier, Tudor Susanu, Tudose Ciprian Iulian, Unai Gómez Onrubia, Vale Nelu, Valentin Cosmin Istrate, Valentin Georgescu, Valère Delorme-Gauthier, Valérie Hénaire, Victor Jereghi, Victor Pop, Vincent Beauregard, Vincent Legault, Vincent Ouellet, Vincent Presseau, Vincenzo Beretta, Virginie Cinq-Mars, Vlad Apostol, Vlad Ionescu, Vlad Toma, Vladimir Eskandari, Vladimir Pavel Popescu, Wafaa Benhammou, Wayne Murray, Yan Thouin, Yanick Maher, Yann Le Guyader, Yannick Blanchot, Yi Qing Wang, Youssef El Aakouchi, Yves Breton, Zainea Andrei, Zakaria Ahmed Bellarah, Zhensheng Xie

CONTENTS

INDEX

If you would rather play with a minimum
of assistance, the guide's comprehensive
Index can be used to jump to your topic
of interest whenever you need a hint or
specific piece of information.

VERTICAL TAB

The vertical tab on the right-hand margin of each double-
page spread is a navigational tool designed to help you
find your way around the guide. The top section lists the
individual chapters, while the lower section highlights
the part of the chapter you are currently reading.

UPDATE NOTICE

We have taken every step to ensure that the contents of this
guide are correct at the time of going to press. However,
future updates to Assassin's Creed Revelations may contain
adjustments, gameplay balancing and even feature additions
that we cannot anticipate at the time of writing.

a.23082003.RmFjZXNJblN0b25l
a.16082003.RXNjYXBl
a.23082003.V2hhdElzVGhpc1BsYWNl
a.16052003.Q2hpY2Fnb0dpcmxxz
a.27082003.Tm90RmFyRW5vdWdh

We are very proud to present the final opus of Ezio's trilogy: Assassin's Creed Revelations.

We only managed to accomplish this ambitious project thanks to the amazing, combined effort of several Ubisoft studios around the world. We are very pleased with the final result and we sincerely hope you will enjoy playing this game as much as we enjoyed producing it. We truly believe that both gameplay and plot of this new adventure will keep you entertained into the early hours and stimulate a range of powerful emotions. We know how much you appreciate the stories, the world and the experience of Assassin's Creed games, so you will see that we have further developed the three pillars of our brand: navigation, social stealth and combat. We hope you appreciate these developments and that they spice up your gaming experience.

This is Ezio Auditore's last adventure. He embarks on a personal journey, searching for meaning to his life as a master assassin. This quest has him relive the key moments of Altaïr's life… and finally provides him with answers. The thrilling and surprising conclusion of Ezio's saga will hopefully address some of your own questions.

In the spirit of building on past Assassin's Creed adventures, it was only natural to partner with Piggyback on this guide. Working closely together, we have made sure this book is totally comprehensive; from the main storyline to all side quests and background analysis, from all secrets to specifics on the most difficult challenges. Every detail has been compiled here in order to enhance your gaming experience; all information has been carefully presented so that you advance through the game at your own pace.

Thank you for being part of the Assassin's Creed universe. We will keep working hard to make sure you enjoy our games.

Martin Schelling
Producer